Paul Stafford is a property law barrister with a particular expertise in manorial law and mineral rights. The work is mostly advisory in nature, sometimes litigious, and usually of significant complexity. He receives enquiries and instructions from clients across the globe. He has submitted evidence to Parliament, lectured and published articles on the subject. This is his first book.

A Brief Guide to Modern Manorial Law

A Brief Guide to Modern Manorial Law

Paul Stafford
M.A. (Oxon.), D.Phil. (Oxon.)
Barrister of Gray's Inn and of Lincoln's Inn

Law Brief Publishing

Published 2025 by Law Brief Publishing, an imprint of Law Brief Publishing Ltd
30 The Parks
Minehead
Somerset
TA24 8BT

www.lawbriefpublishing.com

Paperback: 978-1-913715-43-4

This book is dedicated,

with permission and grateful

thanks, to

The Institute

PREFACE

Manorial law, as a discrete branch of property law and one which to the 21st century mind may seem antiquarian and of academic interest only, once commanded an importance which kept it at or close to the centre of disputes litigated in the highest courts of the land. Although the institution of the manor was in continual decline from 1290, when it was no longer possible for new manors to be created, it is a remarkable fact that the 19th century was a golden age for property lawyers skilled in manorial law and the conveyancing that went with it. The fees earned by conveyancers, attorneys and barristers must have contributed significantly to the costs of building the magnificent Hall and Library of Lincoln's Inn in the 1840s. The great property law reforms in the legislation of 1922-1925 abolished copyhold tenure and thereby ended the need for the manorial customary courts that had administered it, but the legislation did not abolish manorial courts[1] or seignorial (i.e. lordship) titles or manors themselves, while it extinguished only some but not all of the manorial rights or dues that were incident to title. In a well-known lecture given in 1931, the barrister and prolific property law textbook writer and editor Cyprian Williams [2] looked back on the reform legislation of 1922-1925 and said:

---

1 This was only done by the Administration of Justice Act 1977: see s 23 and Sch 4, Part 1. These provisions ended the jurisdiction of ancient courts, including courts baron and customary courts, to determine legal proceedings 'but any such court may continue to sit and transact such other business, if any, as was customary for it immediately before the coming into force of this section': see s 23(1). Excepted from abolition were the Estray Court for the Lordship of Denbigh and the court leet for the Manor of Laxton.

2 His father, Joshua Williams QC (1813-1881), had been a leading property law practitioner, author, and teacher of generations of mid-Victorian law students.

> As it seems to me, neither the paramount lordship of the crown, nor the seigneury of any mesne lord has been abolished.... [Although] manorial incidents will before long be extinguished and escheat for the cause of want of heirs has been abolished, the fundamental principles of the law of ownership of land remain the same as before the legislation of 1925. Land is still the object of feudal tenure; the King remains the lord paramount of all the land within the realm; every parcel of land is still held of some lord.... And the greatest interest which any subject can have in land is still an estate in fee simple and no more.[3]

Williams' conclusion that in important respects feudalism continued to underlie English property law was re-stated and developed in 2008 by Edward Nugee QC in an important article in the *Law Quarterly Review*.[4] 'The theme of this article,' he wrote, 'is that the feudal system is alive and well, that there are many more cases of superior and inferior freehold estates in England and Wales than is generally recognised, [and] that the Land Registration Act 2002 does not deal adequately with manorial rights.' Included among those rights identified as not adequately dealt with were mineral rights and sporting rights. Nugee also drew attention to the issue of whether a seignory title should be registered as land under the 2002 Act. Although the definition of land in the Act did not specifically exclude a manor, he thought it likely that it would be held to be limited to corporeal land; and, if so, a seignory without land could not be registered even though a seignory was a superior estate in freehold in the same land where the inferior estate[5] was required by the Act to be registered.[6] The Act's alteration of the previous law by no longer allowing seignories to be registered was even more of an anomaly where the lord

---

3 T. Cyprian Williams, "The Fundamental Principles of the Present Law of Ownership of Land" (1931) 75 *Solicitors' Journal* 843 at 847-848.

4 "The Feudal System and the Land Registration Acts" (2008) 124 *LQR* 586-607.

5 In other words, what had been the corporeal land of the manor.

6 See s.2.

or lady of the manor as owner of the seignory was and remains entitled to ownership of any manorial waste.[7]

Until the 1922-1925 legislation, lords and ladies of the manor and manorial courts had generated an impressive variety and quantity of documents which amounted to a *de facto* system of land registration. There were various classes of documents all designed to establish proof of ownership of land and rights relating to it: strict settlements with details of family landholdings; inclosure agreements, acts and awards with details of boundaries, allotments, exchanges, exceptions and reservations; and the records of manorial courts baron or customary courts with details of transfers of freehold, customary and copyhold land together with the exceptions and reservations affecting them. The framers of the Law of Property Act 1922 did not at first appreciate the importance of preserving this documentation; and when they did, they could legislate only for the preservation of the records of manorial courts but not for the preservation of private documents of title. The consequence is that historic documentation affecting land ownership today may be incomplete, but where it exists its importance and availability often goes unrecognised and unexplored. It is normal for evidence on manorial law issues in property cases to consist mostly of historic documentation and the inferences to be drawn from that documentation. It is important that practitioners and judges are aware of not only this but also that the analysis of such documentation is no straightforward exercise because the

---

[7] The word 'seignory' is of medieval French origin and in English is commonly known as 'lordship'. The term 'seignorial rights' may be considered equivalent to 'lordship rights', whereas the term 'manorial rights' may not mean the same thing if used in connection with rights deriving from ownership of land. As far as possible, this book uses the terms 'lordship' or 'lordship rights', although both terms may appear in judgments and practitioner texts. For what can happen when there is confusion between seignorial rights and manorial rights see *Townley v Gibson* (1788) 2 Term Rep 701; 100 ER 377, discussed at pp.17-18 and 151.

documentation must be understood in its historical context. The past is another country.

What I have set out to do in this book is to share such knowledge as I have acquired from nearly twenty years' experience dealing with advisory and litigation work on manorial law. Until I began writing I did not realise the extent to which manorial law today is primarily the product of the 19th century judiciary and those practitioners who appeared before them who wrote extensively on the subject. Until the creation of the Incorporated Council of Law Reporting for England and Wales in 1865, the reporting of judicial decisions was unsystematic and the quality of reports variable; but that should not dull the modern lawyer to the weight and authority of statements of the law about manors given by Lord Kenyon CJ, Lord Lyndhurst and Baron Parke (later Lord Wensleydale). From 1865 until the early 20th century, which produced a great deal of learning from the bench and practitioner textbook writers on manorial law, case reports are much better edited: there are clear headnotes, arguments from counsel, notes of judicial interventions, and judgments by (often senior appellate) judges well-versed in manorial law which are usually succinct and much shorter than they now are. Careful reading of the textbooks and law reports from this period is likely to be necessary when researching or arguing cases today.

The subjects addressed in the chapters which follow reflect those which I have found repeatedly arise in practice: devolution of title, registration, wastes and commons, the effect of inclosure acts and awards, the enfranchisement of copyhold, and mines and minerals. Case law on manorial mineral reservations gets a chapter to itself, not just for its own importance but because the Court of Appeal's recent decision in *Wynne-Finch v Natural Resources Body for Wales* arguably raises more questions than it answers in terms of its approach to the construction of inclosure acts and its understanding of the operation of the Copyhold Acts.[8] The similarity between the contents of the book and the issues identified by Nugee in 2008 is no coincidence. The vestiges of feudalism, the rights

---

8 [2022] 3 All ER 162.

acquired and reserved over centuries by landowners who were lords or ladies of the manor, and the manorial law impact of the Land Registration Act 2002 all raise problems which occur in practice and may need adjudication in the courts. The likelihood of this increases where the growing interest in renewable energy and underground minerals means that manorial law questions, involving ownership and use of common land and construction of minerals reservations, move centre stage. Where this happens, it does so in the context of major commercial transactions where the stakes are high. There is now an active market for lordship titles where the validity of what is on offer is likely to require careful checking by prospective purchasers, and the market is creating circumstances where surface landowners who find themselves confronted by unexpected claims from title holders may need to start by challenging the validity of their title with investigation of its devolution.[9] Acquisition of lordship titles is apparently becoming a business model for those wanting to exploit the commercial potential such titles may have in relation to mineral ownership, unoccupied land as manorial waste, and the holding of markets and fairs.

The introductory chapter covering the historical and legal development of the manor, and based on work by historians, legal historians and historical geographers, is intended to provide context for the subsequent chapters and in particular the case law decisions with which they deal. There is a chapter on evidence which identifies the principal primary sources of documents, and their location, as well as the published secondary sources which parties to disputes on manorial issues can investigate. Proportionality should of course direct investigation, and archival research is likely to be more expensive than online research or analysis of secondary sources; but an unwillingness to seek out and address publicly available evidence may be seen by a court as unhelpful at best and perhaps negligent at worst. The final chapter provides extracts

---

9 See my article "Title Challenge", *Property Law Journal* (24 Jan 2011), pp.18-21.

of and a commentary on statutes and historic practitioner textbooks relevant to manors.

Notwithstanding its length, this book is called *A Brief Guide* because it is selective. Coastal manors, Welsh manors and sporting rights are all important subjects which, for reasons of time and space, the book only lightly touches on, and there is nothing on markets and fairs.[10] For reasons of time and space the focus has had to be narrower, and with an emphasis on practicality based on case law and statute. For a longer and comprehensive account of manorial law the leading work is unquestionably Christopher Jessel's *The Law of the Manor*, whose third edition was published in 2024. Authors of law books on the same subject commonly have different perspectives and emphasis, and when both are consulted that difference may be constructive for those readers who have to advise clients and argue cases.

Writing a book is a journey. This book has taken five years to write during intervals from work and with progress delayed by illness, lock-down, caring and bereavement. The invitation to write it was given to me by Tim Kevan and Garry Wright of Law Brief Publishing, and their encouragement, patience and support have been essential to its completion. There have also been many others who have helped along the journey, wittingly or unwittingly, and in ways great and small. I should like first to thank David Ainger, whose gift to me on his retirement of his annotated copy of *Scriven on Copyhold* enabled me to see how the Victorian age understood the law of the manor and excited a deeper interest in the subject. My thanks are then due to all who gave their time, knowledge and experience of real property, manorial and minerals law to read and comment on draft chapters of the book: Gregory Hill (like David Ainger, former Conveyancing Counsel of the Court), who allowed me to draw on his magisterial knowledge of property law for the chapters on registration and wastes and commons; James Maxwell of the Rural Estates Department at Farrer & Co and Upper Tribunal Judge Mark West for the two chapters on minerals; and retired Judge

---

[10] See Pease, Chitty and Cousins, *Law of Markets and Fairs* (7th edn, 2020).

Edward Cousins, formerly Principal Judge of the Land Registration Division of the Property Chamber and now of Radcliffe Chambers, for the chapter on legislation. I should also thank all those solicitors who have instructed and worked with me on manorial cases, and in particular Ben Hatton, James Maxwell (again), Hugh Bruce-Watt, Rupert Mead, Robert Keylock, Lauren Forrester, Andrea Bruce, Richard Jones, Emma Newton, Vivienne Williams, Suzanne Middleton Lindsley, Alun Rhys Jones, Rebecca Rees, Adam McGiveron, Andrew Mellor and Michael Baxendale, who long ago sent me my first manorial case. At Ten Old Square I have been warmly encouraged and supported by my former colleague, Eason Rajah KC, Jeremy Callman and Helen Bunce, and I have been efficiently assisted by all members of the Clerks' Room whenever information has been needed from the Library of Lincoln's Inn, whose staff have been unfailingly kind and helpful. I must make special mention here of the late Catherine McArdle. Finally, my wife Louisa has sustained me day and night with endless cups of tea and coffee in the garret where this book was written, and my relief at its completion will be exceeded only by hers. Without her love and forbearance it would not have been possible.

The responsibility for mistakes in the text is entirely my own. Please would readers who identify mistakes write and tell me what they are with a view to correction in any future edition.

I have attempted to state the law as at 31 January 2025.

Paul Stafford

Ten Old Square
Lincon's Inn
London WC2A 3SU

CONTENTS

TABLE OF CASES

TABLE OF LEGISLATION

TABLE OF STATUTORY INSTRUMENTS

CHAPTER ONE

THE MANOR AND ITS DEVELOPMENT

Introduction

The English manor existed as a working institution from Anglo-Saxon times until the end of 1925. Its zenith ran from the Norman Conquest of 1066 until 1289, when the statute of *Quia Emptores* initiated a process of gradual decline drawn out over many centuries and not yet concluded. The manor occupied a central place in the property law of England, and from 1536 in the property law of Wales, which did not end until the great legislative reforms contained in the property acts of 1922 to 1925. The ending was not synonymous with extinction, and the presence of the manor in legal analysis of property issues remains today. Legal education and procedural reform have worked to reduce awareness of that presence because legal history is not widely taught, and because manorial cases often raise registration points which are usually assigned to First-tier Tribunal judges or their deputies rather than, as in the past, to Chancery judges. Although reported case law on manorial disputes is now thin, manors remain of continuing importance for questions about land ownership, commons and mineral rights. These questions matter to landowners, developers, local authorities and, increasingly, to those concerned with the commercial exploitation of minerals and renewable energy.

Before 1289: Origins to *Quia Emptores*

The primary legal concept underlying the manor was the doctrine of tenure – i.e. how land is held of A, with superior title, by B who has inferior title. At the heart of the doctrine was the legal fiction that all land was ultimately held of the Crown. Escheat and *bona vacantia* are expressions of the fiction today; but in the two centuries after the

Norman Conquest the fiction was much closer to reality. In 1066 Duke William of Normandy seized the English Crown and quickly rewarded his supporters with lands taken from the English nobility. This involved the imposition of a feudal structure on Anglo-Saxon landholdings. While landholdings varied in size, they operated on a basis of open field farming where land around settlements was divided into strips for cultivation. Sheep and cattle grazed on common lands, while uncultivated outlying lands, known as waste, were gradually diminished by the process of assart which involved reclaiming waste for use as arable or pasture.

Anglo-Saxon England had operated a manorial system, but one which still reflected tribal loyalties and was less rigid in its institutions and obligations compared with the more thorough-going Norman feudalism which took its place. Norman feudalism was a social, political and economic system that made the peasantry dependent on land and its lord at a time when royal power was weak and security depended on the protection which only the strong could provide. Its structure is often likened to a pyramid with its foundation resting on personal ties of service. At its apex stood the king as lord paramount; at its base were serfs, who differed from slaves only in that their lives were regulated by custom of the land to which they were attached, and the extent of whose freedom was measured by the nature of the customs which the owner of the land allowed. Between king and serf was a hierarchy of lesser and greater lords each owing obligations, of a military, spiritual or labouring kind, to their immediately superior lord. In return for performance of those obligations, the lord granted land; and the obligations attached to land grants determined whether tenure was free or unfree. The characteristic of free tenure was that its obligations were known and not of a servile nature. The characteristic of unfree tenure was that its obligations were not only servile but unknown from day to day. An unfree tenant held land at the will of his lord, and might not quit that land or be free of his obligations without the lord's consent.

Except for allodial land (which is primarily the ancient possessions of the Crown, the foreshore and the seabed below low water mark extending to the seaward territorial limits) [1] all land in England was held in manors; and every manor had its lord and those dependent on him. The manor was both a territorial unit and a collection of rights over manorial land and resources, and the lordship of a manor included ownership of both. It is dangerous to generalise about medieval manors because they varied greatly both in size and nature, and variation itself could be influenced by region and district. There was no uniform pattern of independent, adjoining landed estates because some manors could be inter-dependent and lands could be inter-mixed. Most manors were agriculturally self-sufficient, but their characteristics depended on location, ownership, and the circumstances in which the manor was created. They also evolved over time in response to famine, plague and war. Not all manors had manor houses because their owner could be an absentee lord; and for those that did, the capital messuage, as the house was described in manorial or title documents, could be a functional building if used by an absentee lord's staff or, alternatively, it could be more substantial with stables, barns and other outbuildings used for farming purposes.

Most manors had demesne land, which can be thought of as a home farm reserved for the lord. Again, the size of demesnes varied greatly. Demesne land could be arable, pasture, meadow or woodland, and would be worked by the lord's tenants in return for their own holdings of land (or 'tenements'). Free tenants, who would pay money rents, had defined, infrequent and comparatively modest tasks. Unfree tenants, or villeins, worked more regularly for the lord and even harder at busy times of the agricultural year. Even here, there was no inevitability that all manors had unfree tenants. Some had very few or none.[2]

The number of manors expanded significantly after 1066 in response to population growth, the development of a cash economy, and the implications of inheritance: landowners created new manors from

---

1 *R (Parkes) v Dorset County Council* [2024] 1 WLR 4337 at [185] (Holgate J).

2 Mark Bailey, *The English Manor c. 1200-1500* (Manchester, 2002), p.7.

existing ones to provide for their children. This took place in the context of an active land transfer market. Land could be sold either by substitution, where the purchaser held directly of the vendor's superior lord, or by sub-infeudation, where the purchaser held of the vendor and owed service to him. Sub-infeudation created difficulty for the Crown and its chief lords if neither the vendor nor the new owners of land had the resources to provide them with the services and payments due for tenurial incidents that the vendor had previously provided. To resolve the problem, the Statute of *Quia Emptores* was passed in 1289, prohibiting sub-infeudation and permitting only substitution in order to preserve the rights and revenues of lords intact. But the unintended consequence was to prevent the creation of new manors after 1289, and the nexus of tenure based on personal service which had characterised the early medieval manor was slowly dissolved.[3]

1289 to 1660: Villeinage to copyhold and the end of fiscal feudalism

The period from 1289 to the early 17th century saw a variety of social, economic and legal changes which together reduced the number of manors and contributed to their decline as a self-sufficient agricultural unit and instrument of socio-economic control. First, plague from the mid-fourteenth century onwards led to rural depopulation and, for lords, made cash a more valuable commodity than services. Lords needed rents, and although rents could and usually did exist alongside those feudal incidents which provided income to the lord, the commutation from services to rents destroyed the earlier foundation for distinguishing between free and unfree tenure. Second, the need for more business-like management of land led to more systematic keeping of manorial records, particularly in relation to the granting of land. It is important here to be aware of the distinction between meanings of 'free' in different contexts. People could be free or unfree depending on their

---

3 For a more extensive discussion of *Quia Emptores*, see chapter 8. There is a broad historical overview in Sir Maurice Powicke, *The Thirteenth Century* (Oxford, 1953), pp.379-80.

position in the social hierarchy. But land too could be free or unfree according to the tenure on which it was held. From the 14th century onwards, as free men paid for and took grants of what had been unfree land, and unfree men took grants of free land, the distinction between free tenure and villein tenure became irrelevant and disappeared.

Records were made on the rolls of manorial courts, set up by lords to deal with criminal, civil and administrative matters relating to the manor; and tenants were provided with a copy of that part of the roll dealing with their admittance to or surrender of a particular piece of land. With a more active land market and a desire shared by both lord and by tenant for certainty about the terms on which land was held, the practice developed of conveying land with unfree tenures using the words 'at the will of the lord and in accordance with the custom of the manor'. The first part of this phrase denoted two things: that the lord owned the freehold, and that there was a period of time for which the land could be held by the grantee – i.e. the quantity of his interest, or estate. The estate represented the extent of the grantee's possession of the land, and it was terminable at the will of the lord.[4] The second part of the phrase, 'according to the custom of the manor', denoted the tenure in terms of the custom of the manor. This identified what the grantee could do with the land. However, the will of the lord and the custom of the manor could be in conflict. If a lord had charged an entry fine to a tenant of unfree land who had fulfilled his services, and where the custom of the manor was that land should be held for years or for lives or by inheritance, the lord could not simply evict the tenant at will. The manorial records and court rolls formed precedents and evidence in the royal courts: first in the Chancery and then, from the mid-16th century, in the royal courts of common law. Both came to accept that manorial landholding and custom were the proper subject of their own jurisdiction.[5] In the 1560s the royal courts provided tenants with personal remedies in damages for trespass; and then, in the 1570s, a

---

4 C.M. Gray, *Copyhold, Equity and the Common Law* (Harvard, 1963), pp.8-9.

5 Gray, pp.34-51, 58-66.

proprietary remedy for ejectment, where tenants could recover possession of land.[6] Lords could no longer forfeit their tenants' lands at will.[7]

What emerged in the place of villein tenure was copyhold tenure, so called because the tenant's right to hold his land was evidenced by a copy he was given of the relevant page from the manorial court roll recording his tenancy. Though still unfree, by the early 17th century copyhold tenure was established as having a status whose rights could be maintained in the courts against infringements by lords. Copyholders could assert these rights both in the customary court of the manor, where the lord or his steward presided, and, if they got no satisfaction there, in the royal courts.

By contrast, the position of free tenure had in some respects become more onerous as the Crown's need for money focused on maximising income from feudal incidents from those who held of it *in capite* and by knight service: the aristocracy and gentry. Free tenants had from 1066 held of their lord only for life, with the consequence that on death there were payments by way of relief to be made to the lord before the new tenant could take up the holding. During the 13th century, legislation had limited the amount of relief to be paid, although this did not bind the Crown whose right of primer seisin entitled it on the death of a tenant to take possession of the land for its own profit and retain possession until relief was paid. For those who were tenants in chivalry, there were also the incidents of wardship and marriage. The right of wardship entitled the lord on the death of a tenant to take possession of the land and its profits until the heir was 21.[8] The right of marriage entitled the lord to select a husband for a female ward. Exploitation of these powers was disliked or resented by those on the receiving end, and medieval lawyers developed the concepts of the will and the use to avoid

---

6 A.W and C. Barsby, *Manorial Law* (1996), p.38.

7 Eric Kerridge, *Agrarian Problems in the Sixteenth Century and After* (1969; republished by Routledge in 2006), p.71.

8 If male. The age was 14 or 16 if female: see Barsby, p.16.

them. Land could not be devised by will to pass to heirs but, because of *Quia Emptores*, it could be alienated by a grant to feoffees (usually friends, neighbours or lawyers) on trust to re-grant it after the tenant's death to such beneficiaries as he should name in his will. From around 1400 the Chancery protected the rights of such beneficiaries, which did not exist at common law.[9]

The will and the use together denied the Crown of a lucrative source of income. Henry VIII sought to address this through the Statute of Uses of 1536, the Statute of Wills of 1540 and the establishment of the Court of Wards the same year. These measures together were the principal features of what legal historians have called 'fiscal feudalism'. The 1536 Statute provided that where A was seised of property to the 'use, trust or confidence' of B, then B was to be regarded as seised of the property for all purposes in law and for such estates as he had or would have had in use. The use was therefore executed, and the consequence was that the beneficial owner of land would die seised of it so that his will would be ineffective and the land would be subject to feudal incidents.[10] The statute applied not only to tenants in chivalry but to tenants in knight-service and even tenants in socage.[11]

Creative thinking by lawyers to get round the Statute of Uses spilled over into the law of wills, which were the subject of the 1540 statute. Before it, landowners had been unable to dispose of their freehold by will to someone other than an heir or descendant; this meant that if there was no heir or descendant then the land escheated to the lord who, because of the gradual disappearance of mesne lords since 1289, was normally the Crown. The Crown's right of escheat was lucrative and, to prevent estate planning from diminishing its value, the Statute of Wills

9 David M. Walker, 'Statute of Uses 1535' in *The Oxford Companion to Law* (Oxford, 1980), p.1185.

10 J.H. Baker, *An Introduction to English Legal History* (5th edition, Oxford, 2019), pp.275-276.

11 Tudor lawyers quickly found ways of avoiding the statute – e.g by the long lease (see the 4th edition of J.H. Baker (2002), pp.256-57, n.46); or by the formula 'A to use of B to use of C' (Walker, loc. cit., p.1185).

effected a compromise by giving landowners, for the first time, the power to dispose of the freehold to someone other than an heir or descendant. However, the statute required tenants by knight-service to leave at least one third of their land to descend, and this one third remained potentially subject to escheat. At the same time the Crown established the Court of Wards and Liveries to supervise the Crown's rights to wardships and other feudal incidents, thereby increasing collection of royal revenue. The Court was active for over a century but so disliked that Parliament closed it in 1646. Its existence, and fiscal feudalism with it, ended after the Restoration with the Tenures Abolition Act of 1660.[12] The tenures affected by the Act were those in chief and by knight-service, which henceforth were held in socage. This meant that military service and other incidents owed to the Crown were abolished. Whereas the presumption at common law before the Act had been of a tenure in chief by knight-service, the presumption after it was of tenure in chief by socage.[13] That transformation meant that the aristocracy and gentry joined those who had previously held in socage and were liable to the Crown only for small amounts or for none.

The Tudor legislation enabling fiscal feudalism coincided with the events of the English Reformation and the expropriation by the Crown of lands belonging to monasteries and religious orders. The transfer of land ownership on so large a scale disrupted the constitution and operation of the manors on those lands, and the attempts by Mary through the Crown Lands Act of 1556 to return them to those from whom they had been taken complicated the position still further. After Mary's death and Elizabeth's accession in 1558, land transfers made pursuant to the 1556 Act were largely or wholly undone by the Religious Houses Act of 1559. Elizabeth's reign was notable for a steady flow of decisions by the courts dealing with manorial law which, in the early 17th century, became the subject of Sir Edward Coke's *Compleat Copyholder.*

---

[12] 12 Car 2 c 24

[13] Baker (4th edition), p.257, n.48.

1600 to 1925 and beyond: Enclosure, enfranchisement and reform

From the late 16th to the mid-19th century, and beginning in the central Midlands counties,[14] the predominant feature of manorial development was enclosure.[15] Enclosure involved turning communal lands into private holdings, often in such a way as to create farms and turn them into contiguous units. Open fields of cultivated land gradually disappeared, and commons and wastes were reduced in extent. The process began because landowners wanted to keep more sheep, but it continued because of more general improvements in livestock breeding and the introduction of new crops and crop rotations. Enclosure, it was widely believed, increased agricultural productivity and profit. The new holdings required hedgerows, walls, ditches, ponds and drainage.[16] It has been estimated that well over 20% of the land area of Britain had been enclosed by 1750, a further 21% between 1750 and 1830, and a further 3% by 1914.[17]

Enclosure or 'approvement' (as it was originally known) had started in medieval times, and the Crown soon recognised that protection must be given to the interests of those freeholder tenants who depended on common lands. The protection was needed to stop acquisitive lords encroaching on common land for themselves. Legislation was enacted obliging lords to leave enough waste to meet the requirements of their freehold commoners. This was done through the Statute of Merton of 1235, which applied to commons appendant (i.e. to commons where rights of common attached to a corporeal hereditament by operation of law), and the Statute of Westminster II of 1285, which applied to commons appurtenant (i.e. to commons where such rights were

---

14 W.G. Hoskins, *Local History in England* (3rd edn, 1984), pp.70-74.

15 The historic spelling was 'inclosure', and I have followed the historic spelling when referring to Inclosure Acts.

16 Kerridge, p.111.

17 J.V. Beckett, 'Agriculture' in the *Oxford Companion to British History*, edited by John Cannon (Oxford, 1997), p.12; and the same author's 'Enclosures', p.348.

attached to a corporeal hereditament by grant or prescription.)[18] For those who were not freeholders but customary tenants, the availability of redress against arbitrary enclosure was in equity through Chancery; and so if lords could not enclose through unity of possession when a tenancy determined, the safest way of achieving enclosure was by way of agreement.[19] The scope and nature of agreements varied according to the extent of land and the number of parties involved. Thus a lord might enclose demesne open field lands and a part of the waste proportionate to the demesne's rights of common while giving up the demesne's rights over the rest of the common and preserving the rights of common of other tenants. Such an agreement might involve formal exchanges of land between lord and tenants.[20] A broader agreement, which became typical in the 18th and early 19th centuries, could involve mutual extinction of common rights and the enclosure of common fields and wastes as well as land exchange. This type of agreement was usually arrived at after one or more of the wealthier promoters – who could be, but did not have to be, a lord – had commissioned surveyors as independent experts to report and recommend how the enclosure should proceed with lands allotted for maximising improvement and to mutual advantage. Where such lands were held on different tenures or estates, the commissioners could recommend what tenures and estates should apply following exchange and allotment. Where agreement was achieved, it would usually be drafted by counsel.[21]

---

18 Kerridge, p.94.

19 Kerridge, pp.94-99.

20 Kerridge, p.99, citing the decision of Lord Verulam LC in the 1619 case of *Cartwright v Drope* (Tothill 110). The decision in the selected documents in Kerridge's book at p.185 is extracted from J. Ritchie, *Reports of Cases decided by Francis Bacon in the High Court of Chancery 1617-1621* (1932), pp.183-87.

21 Kerridge, pp. 103, 117. New tenures of copyhold could not be created by agreement because copyhold was a creature of custom and therefore of fact. However, Parliament was sovereign and, where an Inclosure Act provided for exchange and allotment of lands (as most did), Parliament could alter the status of land from freehold to copyhold within the Act if

The formalities of enclosure were of various kinds. It was always possible to proceed by way of private agreement, but the practice quickly developed of recording the agreement in authoritative form. Where exchange and allotment involved demesne and other manorial lands only, confirmation of the agreement could take place within the manorial court.[22] Later, recourse was had to the royal courts and in particular to Chancery to give the agreement its blessing. The more extensive the lands, the more parties were likely to be involved; and the difficulty of obtaining agreement, which had to be unanimous, and delays in court, made the process a long one. By the mid-18th century, the preferred route was by Private Act of Parliament. This was a process more expensive than court proceedings but provided greater security for those involved and was easier to complete because it required not unanimity but only the consent of the majority of landowners affected.[23] In some cases, parliamentary acts were no more than confirmatory of existing landholdings themselves resulting from earlier agreements.[24]

Parliamentary enclosure began in Leicestershire and Northamptonshire in the 1750s and spread gradually outwards to Cornwall and north-west Wales by the mid-19th century.[25] Counties in the upland areas of England and Wales included extensive wastes and commons, which avoided enclosure until the mid-19th century.[26] Overall, enclosure

its promoters required. See *Watkins on Copyholds* (4th edition, 1825), by Thomas Coventry, vol 1, pp.51-52.

22 Kerridge, at pp.112-13, cites examples of such agreements from the court rolls of Whaddon manor in 1548 and Bremhill manor in 1578.

23 Kerridge, pp.112, 117.

24 *Doe v Davidson* (1813) 2 M & S 175; 105 ER 348.

25 Kain, Chapman and Oliver, *The Enclosure Maps of England and Wales, 1595-1918* (Cambridge, 2004), pp.16-17.

26 Hoskins, op cit, p.74.

affected at least 7.62 million acres in England,[27] of which just over half was pasture and waste and 41.3% was open fields. Lords of the manor, tithe-owners (clergy and non-clergy, as well as lords of the manor themselves) and other landowners were the distinct interests involved in an enclosure, and they entrusted their representation to commissioners charged with making the decisions about partition, exchange, allotment and compensation which were the principal features of the enclosure award.[28] The power to appoint commissioners held by lords of the manor and other wealthy landowners offered opportunities for corruption and disregard for the poorest who had no say in the process but were most at risk from its outcome.

The cost and complexity of private Inclosure Act procedure was a source of frequent complaint to government, and in 1801 Parliament approved the Inclosure Consolidation Act.[29] Its long title was 'an Act for consolidating in one Act certain provisions usually inserted in Acts of Inclosure, and for facilitating the mode of proving the several facts usually required in the passing of such Acts.' Provisions generally included in a private Inclosure Act would now apply to all enclosures, subject to express provision to the contrary. Acts therefore became shorter and the enclosure process less expensive. The 1801 Act, however, focused on the enclosure of commons and wastes rather than common fields, and not until 1834 did a further act address the exchange and consolidation of holdings in common fields, meadows or pastures.[30] An act facilitating the enclosure of open and arable fields had to wait until 1836.[31] Under the 1836 Inclosure Act, two-thirds in number and value of the possessors of any rights in common fields could

---

27 Kain, Chapman and Oliver, p.26. The breakdown is 7.62 million acres for England and 525,880 acres for Wales.

28 Kain, Chapman and Oliver, p.30.

29 41 Geo III c. 109. This paragraph draws on T.E. Scrutton, *Commons and the Common Fields: The History and Policy of the Laws relating to Commons and Enclosures in England* (Cambridge, 1887), pp.155-57.

30 4 & 5 Will. IV c.30.

31 6 &7 Will. IV c. 115.

nominate commissioners, enclose the common fields and exchange them. The Act did not apply to waste lands or manorial rights, and no common fields could be enclosed under it within ten miles of London. An act of 1840 made the awards of the 1836 Act commissioners final and extended the 1836 Act to Lammas lands[32] – i.e. to commons where commoners could graze their stock after harvest from Lammas Day on 12 August until the following 6 April.[33] The 1836 and 1840 Acts enabled what has been called 'blanket authorization for enclosure by agreement',[34] provided the requirements as to land type and supporters were complied with; but the time had come when promoters of enclosure would no longer be able to nominate commissioners.

From the 1830s onwards successive governments legislated increasingly across a range of matters affecting the ownership of manorial land as well as land generally. Although its focus was not specifically on manorial lords, the Tithe Commutation Act of 1836 involved the creation of official commissioners to oversee the survey and valuation of land whose owners were required to pay a parish rentcharge.[35] The Enfranchisement of Copyholds Act 1841 was the first of a series of copyhold acts passed in 1843, 1844, 1852, 1858 and 1887, concluding with a consolidating act of 1894.[36] The 1841 Act saw the establishment of the Copyhold Commissioners, who were responsible for

---

32 3 & 4 Vic. c.31.

33 8 & 9 Vic. c. 118. Lammas lands differed from common lands, which were uncultivated wastes to which no severalty rights attached. Lammas lands were commonable lands – i.e. lands held in severalty during a portion of the year but then, after the severalty crop had been removed, were commonable: see G.W. Cooke, *The Acts for facilitating the Inclosure of Commons in England and Wales* (1864), p.42.

34 John Chapman, *A Guide to Parliamentary Enclosures in Wales* (Cardiff, 1992), p.3.

35 See National Archives catalogue: *How to look for records of...Tithes*: https://www.nationalarchives.gov.uk/help-with-your-research/research-guides/tithes/

36 57 & 58 Vic.c.46

administering applications for enfranchisement under the Act them and whose main function was to keep a record of deeds of voluntary enfranchisements. The 1852 Act allowed landlords and tenants to require and compel the extinguishment of copyholds, and the commissioners' functions expanded with powers to make awards for compulsory enfranchisements.

Drawing on the commissioner models of previous acts, the General Inclosure Act 1845 appointed commissioners who were to examine each enclosure application and, if they accepted it, draw up a scheme containing a provisional order for enactment by Parliament.[37] Orders were to be submitted for approval by Parliament in annual tranches, and between 1845 and 1867 nearly 900 enclosures were dealt with in this way. Inclosure Commissioners were government officials with judicial powers and discretions, and their establishment was an important step towards government intervention and regulation of the enclosure process. They administered the various Inclosure, Conveyancing and Commons Acts, concerning the enclosure of waste and commonable land, exchange of land, and partitions and divisions of intermixed land. As well as making awards and orders, the commissioners arbitrated disputed claims, settled compensation and regulated the use of commons. The Inclosure Act 1851 authorised the appointment of commissioners to perform the functions of all three commissions under the joint title of the Copyhold, Inclosure and Tithe Commission. By the Settled Land Act 1882, this combined Commission was merged into a body of Land Commissioners for England under the Home Office. In 1889, the Land Commissioners' functions concerning land tenure administration, land use and land improvement, passed to the newly established Board of Agriculture.

The impact of 19th century legislation on the manorial system was steadily to erode its importance within the broader framework of land ownership. The reduction in extent of copyhold tenure owed more to the need of lords to simplify and have cheaper conveyancing and to

37 8 & 9 Vic. c. 118.

obtain commercial rents from copyhold land. It had little or nothing to do with any principled wish to liberate copyhold tenants from the remaining shackles of medieval serfdom. *Scriven's Law of Copyholds and Manors*, which first appeared in 1823 and established itself as the leading practitioners' textbook on the subject, was published in its seventh and last edition in 1896. Copyhold tenure was abolished on 1 January 1926, when copyholders became freeholders and there were many instances where the implications of their enfranchisement needed to be worked out. This relied on the availability of manorial documentation. Parliament recognised this in 1924 by introducing a new section into the Law of Property Act 1922, providing by section 144A(1) that 'All manorial documents shall be under the charge and superintendence of the Master of the Rolls.'[38] Abolition of copyhold tenure brought to a virtual end the role of manorial courts, which had declined steadily in numbers and jurisdiction. However, lordship titles, minerals, commons and wastes all remained in the new legal landscape shaped by the reforms of the 1922-1925 property legislation. The failure of that legislation[39] to require compulsory registration of manorial rights, titles or interests, created a degree of uncertainty about their existence or application in circumstances where the relevant documentation was increasingly hard to find. The Land Registration Act 2002 has addressed that uncertainty but left many issues unresolved.

---

38 The new section was added by the Law of Property (Amendment) Act 1924 which was hurriedly passed after the decision in *Beaumont v Jeffery* [1925] Ch 1 where Lawrence J held that the sale of manorial documents was lawful.

39 And specifically of the Land Registration Act 1925.

CHAPTER TWO

MANORS AND THE LAW

This chapter looks more closely at the law's treatment of manors as they have evolved from medieval times to the present. The evolution matters because the present is affected by the past. Cases today involving manors, even where manorial points seem at the margins, will probably raise issues from the manor's earlier development which need to be understood so that adequate legal advice can be given. Just as all cases are fact specific, so all manors were different and unique, with owners and geography crucial in determining their structure and development. Royal, ecclesiastical, private, upland, lowland, coastal are just some of the features to be borne in mind when considering the evidence about any particular manor. Alongside these features it must always be remembered that a 'manor' consists of three elements: lordship, land and rights. These may be combined, or they may exist separately. Whenever the word 'manor' is used in an old document or in a book, it is necessary to ask which one or more of these three elements is being referred to. Historically, the rights of a lord or lady of the manor could either be seignorial rights – i.e. rights that were incidental to the lordship title – or rights that were incidental to the lord or lady's ownership of the soil. The draftsman's failure to distinguish between these two categories of rights in an Inclosure Act of 1777 was fatal to the lady of the manor's ability to retain the ownership of mines and minerals upon an inclosure of commons and wastes. The mines and minerals were referred to in a clause of the Act which reserved only seignorial rights, and such rights could only be of an incorporeal nature. However, mines and minerals were corporeal as part of the soil and therefore 'resolvable into the ownership of the soil'. There was nothing in the Act to reserve them out of the freehold grants to the allottees even though, with appropriate drafting, this could have been done.[1]

The constituent parts of a manor

According to the seventh and last edition of *Scriven on Copyhold*:[2]

> A manor usually consists of and comprises the following particulars, that is to say: (1) the manor house (or mansion house), with the demesne lands occupied therewith; (2) the freehold tenements holden of the manor; (3) the copyhold tenements holden (and which remain also parcel of) the manor; (4) the waste lands of the manor, with the soil thereof, and the mines and minerals therein or thereunder; and (5) the services, which are to be rendered by the tenants of the manor, together with the Court Baron ...; and not infrequently an advowson is appendant to the manor; and the seashore may be parcel of the waste lands of the manor...

The word 'usually' is a qualification and indicates that what follows is a generalisation. The five particulars reflect a model adopted by the courts before, during and after the time that Scriven was in print. Although the model has been criticised,[3] it remains of value as an analytical tool so long as it is remembered that not all manors had the five particulars and that Scriven was careful to distinguish between manors and lordships.

1 *Townley v Gibson* (1788) 2 Term Rep 701 at 705-706; 100 ER 377 at 379 per Lord Kenyon CJ.

2 Edited by Archibald Brown (1896), p.4.

3 *Gadsden & Cousins on Commons and Greens* (3rd edition, 2020), pp.5-7

The lordship, rights incidental and manorial rights

The lordship, or seignory, is the title held by the lord or lady of the manor. It cannot be sub-divided. As an incorporeal hereditament, it was and remains intangible, capable of being inherited, bought and sold. Despite being an incorporeal hereditament, it may nevertheless carry important inchoate corporeal rights. The owner of a lordship title has a right to ownership of manorial waste, which in practical terms means any open and uncultivated land which is unregistered or unoccupied within the boundary of the historic manor.[4] The lordship also carries with it a right to the provision of copies of manorial documents as defined under section 144A(6) of the Law of Property Act 1922.[5] Originals of manorial documents are usually found today at either the National Archives or local record offices or museums. Section 144A(5) of the 1922 Act provides: 'in particular the lord of the manor shall remain entitled to require [copies of manorial documents] to be produced to him, or in accordance with his directions, free of any cost.'

The lordship can and today usually does exist in gross, without attachment to land. As Scriven put it, 'Manors which have originally been well created may in course of time have ceased to have any demesne lands annexed to them; and where that has happened, the manor becomes a seignory or manor in gross.'[6] The point at which a lordship becomes a lordship in gross is therefore the date when the owner of the lordship ceases to own any demesne land.

The terminology of manorial ownership can be confusing. The expression 'seignorial rights' is equivalent to 'rights incidental to lordship' or, as time passed, 'manorial incidents'; but, depending on the context in which the words appear, these may differ from the more

---

4 See *Burton v Walker* [2014] 1 P.& C.R. 9; [2013] 3 E.G.L.R. 129, CA.

5 Section 144A(6) of the LPA 1922 is set out at p.240.

6 *Scriven on Copyhold*, p.3.

widely used 'manorial rights'.[7] This last can give rise to misunderstanding because it fails to distinguish between rights that are incidental to ownership of manorial land and rights which are incidental to lordship title itself. Thus a lord's right to minerals was originally incidental to his ownership of manorial land and not to his ownership of lordship title. If land was sold out of the manor, the lord's pre-sale entitlement to minerals beneath the land was transferred as part of the freehold unless there was an effective minerals reservations clause excluding minerals from the sale. Conversely, as noted above, the lord's right to waste was incidental to his lordship title, and if an owner of lordship title can identify unclaimed waste as land within the historic boundaries of the manor at the time he acquired the lordship, then he may be able to establish title to the land and with it the ownership of any minerals beneath. However, if mineral rights were successfully reserved by a lord, they were severed from the land and at that point became incidental to the title.

Rights incidental to lordship were described in the Law of Property Act 1922 with a different term: 'manorial incidents'. Section 128(2) listed those attaching to copyhold tenure as

> (a) quit rents and chief rents and other similar rents or payments,
>
> (b) fines, reliefs, heriots, and dues (including fees payable to stewards),
>
> (c) forfeitures, other than forfeitures for the conveyance or attempted conveyance of an estate of freehold in the land, and for alienation without licence whether by way of sale, lease, mortgage or otherwise,
>
> (d) rights as to timber...

[7] For the meaning of the term 'manorial rights' in the LRA 2002, see Law Commission 271, *Land registration for the 21st century: A Conveyancing Revolution* (2001), paras 8.40 and 8.41.

These were all to be extinguished as from 1 January 1941 at the latest but until then would remain pending agreement between the lord and the enfranchised copyhold tenant as to the amount of compensation to be paid to the lord for extinguishment. Where agreement had not been reached by 31 December 1935, either the lord or the tenant could apply to the Minister of Agriculture and Fisheries to determine the amount of compensation. This was to be done in accordance with the detailed compensation provisions set out in the Copyhold Act 1894 as modified by the LPA 1922.[8] The documents containing compensation arrangements as they affected specific manors are held at the National Archives.[9]

The term 'manorial rights' was formerly more expansive and less exact then seignorial rights or manorial incidents. As well as in judgments,[10] it was frequently found towards the end of private Inclosure Acts as the title of a broadly drawn saving clause reserving to the lord all those things that were not to pass from him to the new owners of those lands which had been his wastes and commons but were now allotted to them under the Act. It comprised not only franchises,[11] which were grants

---

8 See LPA 1922, sections 138-142.

9 For the relevant National Archives classes of documents, see below chapter 7, p.251

10 See, for example, Ashurst J in *Townley v Gibson* (1788) 2 Term Rep 701 at 706; 100 ER 377 at 380; and Lord Keeper Henley in *Wake v Conyers* (1759) 30 ER 165 at 167; 2 Cox 359 at 363.

11 These included rights to goods and chattels of felons; waifs (stolen goods that had been hidden); estrays (beasts, not being wild, found wandering unlawfully in the manor); wreck; treasure trove; fairs, markets and tolls; free warren (jurisdiction over forest and vesting in the lord of such wild animals as were deemed beasts and fowls of warren); free chase or park (similar, in the nature of smaller forests, but not subject to forest laws); and free fishery. For an extensive treatment of franchises see *Scriven*, pp.264-288.

expressly or impliedly received from the Crown, but jurisdictions and their profits, royalties, incorporeal rights and other fruits of tenure.[12]

However, the reforms of the 1922-1925 legislation, which abolished copyhold and extinguished a wide range of manorial incidents, have led to a narrower definition of the term 'manorial rights' propounded by the Law Commission and accepted by HM Land Registry. The relevant Land Registry Practice Guide explains:[13]

> In their report Land Registration for the 21st century – A Conveyancing Revolution (Law Com 271), the Law Commission took the view that 'Manorial rights' has a precise meaning. Such rights are narrower than the appurtenances deemed to be included in the conveyance of a Manor by virtue of the Law of Property Act 1925 section 62(3) (or the Conveyancing Act 1881 section 6(3)). The rights in question were listed in some detail in paragraphs 5 and 6 of Schedule 12 to the Law of Property Act 1922. Although this list of rights relates to the effect of enfranchisement under the Law of Property Act 1922 it may nevertheless be taken to be "a comprehensive statement of these rights" (see Law Com 271 at para 8.41). They are:
>
> > (5) An enfranchisement by virtue of this Act of any land (including any mines and minerals hereinafter mentioned) shall not affect any right of the lord or tenant in or to any mines, minerals, limestone, lime, clay, stone, gravel, pits, or quarries, whether in or under the enfranchised land or not, or any right of entry, right of way and search, or other easement or privilege of the lord or tenant in, on, through, over, or under any land,

[12] These included, amongst others, the rights listed above set out at LPA 1922, s.128(2)(a) to (d).

[13] HMLR PG 66: 'Overriding interests that lost automatic protection in 2013' at para 3.6.3.

> or any powers which in respect of property in the soil might but for the enfranchisement have been exercised for the purpose of enabling the lord or tenant, their or his agents, workmen, or assigns, more effectually to search for, win, and work any mines, minerals, pits or quarries, or to remove and carry away any minerals, limestone, lime, stones, clay, gravel, or other substances had or gotten therefrom, or the rights, franchises, royalties, or privileges of the lord in respect of any fairs, markets, rights of chase or warren, piscaries, or other rights of hunting, shooting, fishing, fowling, or otherwise taking game, fish, or fowl.
>
> Provided that the owner of the enfranchised land shall, notwithstanding any reservation of mines or minerals in this Act (but without prejudice to the rights to any mines or minerals, or the right to work or carry away the same), have full power to disturb or remove the soil so far as is necessary or convenient for the purpose of making roads or drains or erecting buildings or obtaining water on the land.

The rights under paragraph 6 may be those of the lord or others to enforce any liability subsisting at the commencement of this Act 'for the construction maintenance cleansing or repair of any dykes, ditches, canals, sea or river walls, piles, bridges, levels, ways and other works required for the protection or general benefit of any land within a manor or for abating nuisances therein'.[14]

However, in another Practice Guide, the Land Registry warn that a lordship title may not have the benefit of the Schedule 12 manorial rights:[15]

---

[14] The full text of para 6 is set out below at chapter 8, p.287.

[15] HMLR PG 22 'Manors', para 4.1.

A lord of the manor may exercise certain rights usually known as 'manorial incidents'. Such rights could no longer be created after 1925. The main manorial rights can be summarised as:

- the lord's sporting rights
- the lord's or tenant's rights to mines or minerals
- the lord's right to hold fairs and markets
- the lord's or tenant's liability for the construction, maintenance and repair of dykes, ditches, canals and other works

These are just examples and it does not necessarily follow that such rights are legally exercisable. Registered lordship titles usually make no reference to any manorial incidents in the register. It may be that the benefit of the rights was not included in an earlier sale of the lordship title.

Those intending to purchase lordship titles and those dealing with owners of lordship titles need to keep these points firmly in mind. The scope of manorial rights conveyed with a lordship title can only be determined from the title document itself and the devolution of title from previous owners. The lordship will, however, carry entitlement to the free provision of copies of manorial documents from public archives,[16] and a claim to any land which is manorial waste at the time of the current owner's acquisition of the lordship.

Custom

Although modern cases will only rarely give rise to issues of manorial custom, the term needs to be understood because it so frequently occurs in the reports of manorial decisions. Sir Edward Coke wrote in the early

[16] Pursuant to LPA 1922, s 144A.

17th century that 'customs are defined to be a law or right not written, which being established by long use and the consent of our ancestors, has been and is daily practised.'[17] In the Court of Appeal in 1897, the logical and evidential issues which the legal understanding of custom raises were summarised by Vaughan Williams LJ in *Mercer v Denne*: [18]

> Most cases with regard to validity of custom are difficult of decision. The fact is that reason recoils from the proposition that legal memory goes back to an arbitrary date at the beginning of the reign of Richard I., A.D. 1189, and, if one finds proof of uninterrupted modern usage, there is a natural inclination to presume the previous existence of the custom right back to 1189, even though the facts may be such as to force upon reason the conclusion that the modern usage could not in fact have been adopted for more than a few generations. Judges, therefore, presume everything possible which would give a custom a legal origin, and find in favour of a manifestly modern custom as being an extension which falls within the reason of so much of the modern usage as may well have existed throughout legal memory.

A modern view expressed in a leading textbook, in a passage approved by the Court of Appeal, explained custom in this way: 'a custom really amounts to a special local law, a local variation of the common law. The common law recognises such variations only if they are ancient, certain, reasonable and continuous. To be 'ancient' a custom must date back to the year 1189, the beginning of legal memory; but ancient origin may be presumed if there has been long enjoyment and there is no proof of a later origin.'[19] By the end of the 19th entry it seems to have become

---

[17] *The Compleat Copyholder*, section XXXIII.

[18] [1905] 2 Ch 538 at 577 (not a manorial case).

[19] Megarry & Wade, *The Law of Real Property*, 6th edn (2000), para 18-078, approved by Carnwath LJ in *Oxfordshire CC v Oxford City Council* [2006] Ch 43 at [31] (overturned, though not on this point, by the HL at [2006[] 2 AC 674).

settled law that 'a regular usage of 20 years unexplained and uncontradicted is sufficient to warrant a jury in finding the existence of an immemorial custom... and from such modern usage, unless the contrary appear, the jury ought to presume the immemorial existence of the right'.[20]

Devolution of lordship title

Devolution of lordship title is an important question whenever lordships are bought and sold. In *Corpus Christi College (Oxford) v. Gloucester County Council*, Lord Denning MR observed that

> Nowadays there are few, if any, manors left intact. The lords of the manor have sold off the house and lands to strangers. Nothing remains in the lordship except the title of lord of the manor and the right to hold the manorial documents. This bare title and right is sometimes put on the market and sold for a nominal figure of £200 or £300.[21]

Within several years of this observation, made in 1982, lordship titles began to come on the market both at auction and by private sale fetching sums that were well beyond nominal. Titles offered for sale without land or without rights attached are titles in gross and may be registered or unregistered. A registered title will previously have been examined by the Land Registry on its owner's application for first registration, and the decision to register title will have been made by the Land Registry at the end of its process of examining the title's devolution and validity. That process will not be infallible, and even a registered title is subject to challenge so that a prospective purchaser may wish to make enquiries of their own. Where an unregistered title is concerned, the risks of purchasing a title where the manor has become

---

20 *Brocklebank v Thompson* [1903] 2 Ch 344 at 350 per Joyce J (cited with approval by Carnwath LJ in *Oxford CC v Oxford City Council* at [2006] Ch 43 at [31].

21 [1983] 1 QB 360 at 365G

extinct or which the vendor has no right to sell are significantly greater. Since 13 October 2003 an unregistered title has no longer been capable of registration, and so a purchaser will not need to worry about persuading the Land Registry that he has good title. However, the validity of the title will still depend on its devolution to the vendor, and any worthwhile investigation of title will have to begin with that. That investigation will probably need to cover descent by will or by settlement as well as by exchange and purchase. A further complication arises because most manors today are reputed manors as opposed to real manors and, before 1882, different conveyancing rules governed their transfer.[22]

Reputed manors

An operating manor had to have at least two tenants holding freeholds of the manor subject to escheats in favour of the lord.[23] That had been the invariable position when manors were first created after 1066. It was a position which reflected the custom of the time, but it could only be maintained so long as sales of land by lords to others proceeded by way of sub-infeudation rather than substitution. *Quia Emptores* ended that process after 1289, when substitution alone was possible so that purchasers of land from lords held it no longer of the lord but of the crown. The consequence was that the number of freeholders holding according to original custom declined, and while the decline was gradual and took place over centuries it was also irreversible. To an extent the decline was concealed because sales of manorial land could be subject to conditions binding the purchaser and successors in title to payments or other obligations to the lord, so that a connection between lord and freeholder remained even though the freeholder was not holding of the

22 In *Crown Estates Commissioners v Roberts* [2008] EWHC 1302 (Ch); [2008] 4 All E.R. 828; [2008] 2 P. & C.R. 15; [2008] 2 E.G.L.R. 165, Lewison J noted at [137] that 'most manors today are reputed manors'.

23 *Glover v Lane Clerk* (1789) 3 TR 445; 100 ER 669

lord subject to escheat.[24] The implications and consequences of a manor becoming a reputed manor are discussed below.[25]

Manorial land

Manorial land was as varied as the landscape itself. In addition to the arable and grazing land (that textbooks and judicial descriptions of manors often focus on), there were upland pastures, hillsides, woods and forests, mines and quarries, meadows, marshes, rivers, ponds and, for coastal manors, cliffs, foreshore and fundus. Land owned and used by the lord himself was known as demesne land,[26] and lords might and usually did allow their tenants on to demesne land for various purposes such as grazing cattle or taking hay, wood or stone. These activities became customs of the manor. Land occupied by tenants of the manor was either leasehold or copyhold. The distinction between leasehold and copyhold was not always obvious because all manorial tenants before 1290 held under tenures imposing widely varying obligations, which again became customary to a particular manor. The distinction between

24 Per Lord Kenyon CJ at 447; 669: 'For many of the places that are called manors would not be found to be such in point of law, if the matter were strictly examined. To constitute a manor it is necessary not only that there should be two freeholders within the manor but two freeholders holding of the manor, subject to escheats' Lord Kenyon was making the point that by 1789 there were many to whom the distinction between manors 'in point of law' – i.e. true manors – and those with less than two freeholders subject to escheats – i.e. reputed manors – was not obvious.

25 See below the sections on manorial courts (pp.30-33) and conveyancing of manors (pp.58-60).

26 'Upon these authorities [Coke, Bracton, Fleta, Blackstone], we think we are fully warranted in saying, that, though the word "demesne" may in some cases be applied to any fee-simple lands a man holds, yet it is more correct and usual to apply it to the lands of a manor, which the lord of that manor either actually has, or potentially may have, *in propriis minibus* [i.e. in his own hands]' *A-G v Parsons* (1832) 2 C&J 279 at 308; 149 ER 120 at 132 per Lord Lyndhurst CB.

free and unfree tenures was based on the level and nature of personal service the lord required, with richer (free) tenants paying money rents and poorer (unfree) tenants providing extensive agricultural services on demesne lands. The latter, known as villeins, are more accurately described as serfs in the years after the Norman Conquest; but later, in response to changing economic conditions, the courts supervised the transformation from villein tenure to copyhold tenure.[27] This process was established by around 1500.

The agricultural revolution from 1600 onwards brought about changes in manorial area and tenures. Demesne land continued to be sold off as freehold to third parties, and once land had gone out of the manor it could not come back in if the lord bought it back again.[28] It was his freehold land but outside the manor. Equally, land acquired by the lord from third parties could not come into the manor for the first time. Lords found it increasingly profitable to grant leases, whether of land that had always been demesne or of land which had become demesne when copyhold tenure came to an end. When land was sold as freehold, lords could and often did include provisions in the deed of sale reserving to themselves particular rights in relation to the land such as ownership and working of and access to mines and minerals. Sale as well as exchange of land could occur within a process of statutory enclosure where a lord and neighbouring landowners would be parties to an award granting allotments of freehold and copyhold to each other.[29]

27 See *Garland v Jekyll* (1824) 2 Bing 273 at 293; 130 ER 311at 318 per Best CJ.

28 *Delacherois v Delacherois* (1864) 11 HLC 62 at 102-103 per Lord St Leonards. There is a tentative exception to this in *R v Duchess of Buccleuch* (1704) 6 Mod 150 at 151, 87 ER 909: 'Lands once severed from a manor, can never after become parcel of it in reality, but it may in reputation; as if lands, part of a manor, be aliened away absolutely, and re-purchased, and an unity of possession for a considerable time after.'

29 In the 18th century copyhold could be and was created through a parliamentary enclosure award pursuant to statute: see the Middlewood Moor Act of 1762 and the Award and Plan of 1763 enclosing common

Manorial land in the 19th century continued to decline in area as a result not just of freehold sales but of voluntary and then statutory enfranchisement of copyhold lands under a series of Copyhold Acts between 1841 and 1894. The 1894 Act permitted compulsory enfranchisement at the request of the lord or the tenant. [30] The abolition of copyhold tenure in 1926 did not abolish manors in the sense of lordships or of all manorial rights. Thus manorial land and its identification remain important today not just because of the right to waste which attaches to lordship but because relations between landowners and what they can do on their respective lands may be subject to earlier agreements by their predecessors in title involving a lord of the manor.

Manorial courts

In *Crown Estate Commissioners v Roberts*, [31] the purchaser of the lordship of a coastal manor was in dispute with the Crown over his claim to a series of rights based on the prerogative powers of the Lords Marcher in Wales.[32] In his judgment, Lewison J said:

> One of the essential ingredients of a manor was its court. The principal court was the court baron, which amongst other things settled property disputes between the tenants of the manor. It also dealt with succession to copyhold land by recording

---

land that was part of the ecclesiastical manor of Lanchester, held by the Bishop of Durham. This could not have been done by private agreement because copyhold was a creature of fact and, as Coke put it, 'custom is the very soul and life of copyhold estates': *The Compleat Copyholder*, section XIX.

30 Section 1.

31 [2008] EWHC 1302 (Ch).

32 The lordship in question was the ecclesiastical manor of St David's in Pembrokeshire. The rights claimed were (i) Wreck de mer; (ii) A several fishery (i.e. an exclusive right to fish in the sea); (iii) Treasure trove; (iv) Sporting rights; and (v) Estray.

> changes of copyholder. The free tenants of the manor were the jury. The suitors were also drawn from among the free tenants. Since no one can be both suitor and juror, it followed that the court could not be held once the number of free tenants fell below two. As Blackstone put it (2 Bl. Comm 91): "This court is an inseparable ingredient of every manor; and if the number of suitors should so fail, as not to leave sufficient to make a jury or homage, that is two tenants at the least, the manor itself is lost."
>
> In the modern law a manor that has been lost in this fashion is known as a reputed manor.[33]

Since at least the early 17th century, the royal courts have taken the view that a manorial court baron is essential to the working of a manor and that without it, however much or little land remains in the lord's ownership, the manor is dissolved. However, dissolution in this context does not mean what it says and can be misleading because the term applies only to the cessation of the working manor. A manor was dissolved by the loss of its court baron, which occurred when the number of free tenants holding tenements of the manor subject to escheats fell below two.[34] What remained was a 'reputed manor' – in other words, a manor by reputation only.[35] Yet a reputed manor was not simply the ghost or shadow of the manor now dissolved. Depending on the circumstances, it could be far more. The lord of a reputed manor could have demesne lands, used by himself, or copyhold lands where surrenders could be made or admittances taken of copyhold titles in a customary court where the lord's steward was judge, and the lord could be entitled to any prescriptive or customary rights that had not been

---

33 At [9]-[10].

34 *Glover v Lane Clerk* (1789) 3 TR 445; 100 ER 669.

35 A reputed manor may also be referred to in the reports as a *quondam* [i.e. 'sometime'] manor: see, for example, *Soane v Ireland* (1808) 10 East 259; 103 ER 773.

severed from the lordship or the lord's own lands.[36] As Sir Edward Coke put it in *The Compleat Copyholder*, 'this in the eye of the world is a manor, though in the judgment of the law it cometh far short of one.'[37]

Thus alongside the court baron was a customary court. Scriven describes the first as a 'common law Court Baron' and the second as a 'Customary Court Baron'.[38] Where a manor had only copyhold tenants and a customary court baron, it was no more than a reputed manor. The distinction is important because, as noted above, the conveyancing rules governing the transfer of real manors and reputed manors were different until 1882, and this may affect devolution of title. However, the similarity between the names of the two courts is confusing, and if records are found referring simply to a 'court baron' they need to be examined to see which type of court baron it is. If the subject matter refers to free tenants and disputes between them, or with penalties imposed that could only be imposed on freeholders, it will be a common law court baron; if it relates only to matters concerning copyhold tenants, and with penalties imposed that could only be imposed on copyholders, then it will be a customary court baron. It is possible that both the court baron and the customary court met at the same time, and that the record of proceedings is of both.

A court that was not a manorial court but was held with them was a court leet. Active after the Conquest, and obtained by lords by franchise from the Crown, its jurisdiction included criminal matters within the boundaries of the manor, weights and measures, the regulation of common fields, and the view of frankpledge. As a royal court, it was a court of record but its profits went to the lord. The rising importance of Justices of the Peace from the 16th century reduced the importance

---

36 *Soane v Ireland* (1808) 10 East 259 per Lord Ellenborough CJ at 262; 103 ER 773 at 773-74; *Smith v Smith* (1816) 2 Price 101 at 111 per Wood B and Richards B; 146 ER 34 at 38: *Scriven on Copyholds* (7th edn, 1896), pp.9-10.

37 Coke, *The Compleat Copyholder* (1635) section XXXI.

38 *Scriven on Copyholds*, p.4.

and numbers of courts leet, but certain aspects of their jurisdiction survived into the 20th century.[39] From 1977 those that remained, with one exception, pursuant to s 23(1) of the Administration of Justice Act 1977, ceased to have any jurisdiction to hear and determine legal proceedings.[40]

Freehold and socage

The relative advantages and disadvantages of freehold and copyhold tenure evolved during the 16th century to the point where Sir Edward Coke, writing early in the 17th century, could say:

> How many freeholders are there at this day charged with base services? As many (I doubt not) as there are copyholders. No marvel then that many able men turn copyholders, and many peasants turn freeholders: no marvel, I say, that men of all sorts and conditions, promiscuously, turn both freeholders and copyholders, [since] there is such small respect had unto the quality of the land in the reservation of our services. Yet observe, I pray, though time hath so enfranchised these copyholders,[41] that they have in a manner shaken off all villein service; yet they retain a badge of their former bondage, for they remain still subject to their lord's will; therefore at this day they are termed tenants at will. But with freeholders otherwise it is, for they are not in that subjection to their lords.[42]

39 *Scriven on Copyholds*, pp.434-448; Jessel, p.323.

40 The exception was the court leet of the manor of Laxton which, at the time of the 1977 Act, continued to operate the open fields system.

41 Coke's use here of the word 'enfranchised' does not have the same meaning as it later had in the sense of copyhold land becoming freehold land. Coke's word is better understood more generally in the sense of being given legal recognition and protection.

42 *The Compleat Copyholder*, section VII.

At the time Coke wrote, free tenures still extended to military service and this may have been a reason why 'able men' were turning copyholders. However, the most common species of freehold after the abolition of military service by the Tenures Abolition Act 1660 was tenure by free socage. The term derived from *per servitium socae* ('by service of the plough') and although not of a military nature, the tenure resembled knight-service which was converted to it by the Act. Socage was held of a superior lord by fealty, was subject to relief and to escheat to the lord, and the only services incident to it after the Act were fealty, suit of court, quit rent, relief and (sometimes) heriots. [43] Although socage tenure was freehold, the nature of ownership which it conferred was different in certain important respects from that of the fee simple absolute in possession and the concept of freehold as it is understood today. Socage tenure was part of a manor and therefore subject to constraints derived from the custom of the manor, but these constraints diminished over time either by commutation of services through payment to the lord, or by sales of land out of the manor (usually on payment to the lord for his consent), or by the exchange and allotments of land pursuant to Inclosure Acts. Such developments reduced the number of free tenants of the manor and led to the decline and eventual disappearance of the court baron.

Copyhold

Whenever there is need to know about the pre-1926 circumstances of holdings or transactions involving a particular plot of land, an understanding of copyhold is of importance. First, if a registered title states that the land or part of it was formerly copyhold, there may be a question of whether the land remains subject to rights reserved in favour of the lord. That will involve looking at the date and circumstances of enfranchisement, whether the land was enfranchised pursuant to private agreement or statute, and whether there were any private or statutory reservations of rights in favour of the lord. Those rights may include

[43] *Scriven on Copyhold*, p.260.

ones relating to mines and minerals. Second, if copyhold land was granted subject to reverter, the circumstances of the grant may need to be examined if the question of reverter arises. Third, owners of land that was formerly copyhold may have rights of common over nearby lands. Manorial documents relevant to these matters must be evaluated within a contextual understanding of copyhold because the meaning and implications of language about copyhold are not immediately obvious.

In *Corpus Christi College Oxford v Gloucestershire County Council*, Lord Denning described a manor and the place of copyhold within it.[44]

> In mediaeval times the manor was the nucleus of English rural life. It was an administrative unit of an extensive area of land. The whole of it was owned originally by the lord of the manor. He lived in the big house called the manor house. Attached to it were many acres of grassland and woodlands called the park. These were the "demesne lands" which were for the personal use of the lord of the manor. Dotted all round were the enclosed homes and land occupied by the "tenants of the manor." They held them by copyhold tenure. Their titles were entered in the court rolls of the manor. They were nearly equivalent to freehold, but the tenants were described as "tenants of the manor."

Although these words make no reference to the evolution of copyhold from villeinage and villein tenure, the description of copyhold title as 'nearly equivalent to freehold' was, in many manors by the 19th century, justified.[45] In the 1877 edition of his textbook *Principles of the Law of*

44 [1983] QB 360 at 365B-C. This passage, although possibly *obiter*, was followed and relied on by Lewison J in *Crown Estate Commissioners v Roberts* [2008] EWHC 1302 (Ch) at [11].

45 'The copyholder now has a permanent interest in his estate as long as he performs his services, and the lord has certain rights and dues; and as long as the copyholder performs his services and pays the dues, he has the same permanent interest in his estate as if it were freehold.' See *Garland v Jekyll* (1824) 2 Bing 272 at 293-294; 130 ER 311 at 318-319 per Best CJ.

Real Property, Joshua Williams described the incidents of contemporaneous copyhold tenure as follows:

> The tenure of an estate in fee simple in copyholds involves, like the tenure of freeholds, an oath of fealty from the tenant, together with suit to the customary court of the manor. Escheat to the lord on failure of heirs is also an incident of copyhold tenure. And before the abolition of forfeiture for treason and felony the lord of a copyholder had the advantage over the lord of a freeholder in this respect, that, whilst freehold lands were forfeited to the crown by treason of the tenant, the copyholds of a traitor escheated to the lord of the manor of which they were held. Rents also of small amount are not infrequent incidents of the tenure of copyhold estates. And reliefs may, by special custom, be payable by the heir. The other incidents of copyhold tenure depend on the arbitrary customs of each particular manor....[46]

Copyhold, at least in its later development, can also be thought of as a privileged form of leasehold. The freehold ownership of copyhold land remained in the lord,[47] but the different types of copyhold tenure gave the tenant something distinct from and better than a lease. The Law of Property Act 1922, which abolished copyhold when it entered force on 1 January 1926, defined copyhold land as including

- Land commonly known as customary land or customary freehold land where the freehold is in the lord and not in the customary tenant, and

- Land of copyhold tenure held for life or lives or for years, whether or not determinable with life, where the tenant has by

[46] Joshua Williams, *Principles of the Law of Real Property* (1877 edn (reprinted in 2006 in Elibron Classics series)), p.233.

[47] *Scriven on Copyhold*, p.43.

custom a perpetual right of renewal, subject or not to the fulfilment of any conditions,

- Land held in free tenure for life or lives or for years whether or not determinable with life (but subject to custom) where the tenant has by custom a perpetual right of renewal, subject or not to the fulfilment of any conditions.[48]

The Act then defined 'tenant' as including

> all persons holding by copy of court roll or as customary tenants or holding land subject to any manorial right or incident, and whether the land is held to them and their heirs or to two or more in succession or for life or lives or years, and whether the land is held of a manor or not.[49]

Copyhold retained until its abolition those feudal characteristics which had originated in villein tenure, where a man held land at the will of his lord. This was or was little better than serfdom because the tenancy was entirely dependent on the lord's caprice. But by the 1480s, in cases where a tenant had been evicted by his lord, judges in the royal courts had developed a change in tenurial doctrine. The change, protective of the tenant, was that a man still held at the will of his lord but in accordance with the custom of the manor. As the doctrine further developed, so did protection because it was the judges who decided whether a custom was reasonable and ruled that 'the lord will not break a custom which is reasonable'.[50] From this development two main types of copyhold tenure emerged: copyhold for lives and copyhold of

48 LPA 1922, s 189.

49 LPA 1922, s 189, and Copyhold Act 1894 s 94. The expression 'manor' includes a reputed manor.

50 See Littleton, *The New Tenures* (1481), sections 73-77, quoted in *Baker and Milsom: Sources of English Legal History,* Second edition by Sir John Baker QC (Oxford, 2010), pp.218-219.

inheritance. The courts regarded these as customs, and a manor could have one or the other or both.[51]

With a copyhold for lives (usually three), a lord could create successive interests by granting to A and his assigns for A's life, and then to B and C for their lives. When A died, B might nominate D as a new third life, so that the copyhold was perpetually renewable. Or, after the third life, the land might go back to the lord. With a copyhold of inheritance, the land on A's death would pass to his heir; but A could also exchange the land with another copyholder within the manor, X, or sell it to Y. Where land changed hands in this way, it would be surrendered to the lord to the use of X or Y.[52] Surrender to the lord would be made at his customary court, either to the lord or, more usually, his steward; and it would be followed by the admittance of whoever was the new copyhold tenant. The process of surrender and admittance for all kinds of copyhold would be recorded on the court roll, and the new tenant would be handed a copy of the admittance, which would describe his name, the land he held, and the terms on which it was held. These terms were usually to the effect that the land was held at the will of the lord according to the custom of the manor, at the yearly rent, suit of court, customs and other services due and of right accustomed. Thus copyholders, like leaseholders, would pay rent; while customs and other services would mean those feudal incidents of heriots and fines which in many surviving manors attached to copyhold until its abolition. A heriot was a death duty payable to the lord from the deceased's estate, which by custom was his best beast (increasingly commuted to money);[53] while a fine was a sum payable to the lord as condition for the new tenant's admittance to occupation of the land. The court roll copy not only gave its name to the tenure but acted as proof of

---

51 Scriven, p.53, citing *Kempe and Carter's Case* (1586) 74 ER 51, 1 Leonard 55

52 In this context, the term 'to the use of X or Y' means 'for X or Y'.

53 The decision in *Garland v Jekyll* (1824) 2 Bing 273; 130 ER 311 is of particular interest for Best CJ's explanation of the origins of the heriot: see at 294, 319.

ownership for the tenant and the lord, and the terms on which the copyhold tenancy was held. It operated in practice as a means of registration. By contrast, the conveyance of freehold land was carried out by livery of seisin and then, after 1 October 1845, also by deed. If copyhold and freehold land within a manor were adjoining and a lord who had obtained possession of a copyhold wished to convey both to a purchaser, the different methods of land transfer meant that copyhold had first to be enfranchised so that it could be conveyed as freehold.

Copyhold tenure, despite its inferior status to freehold, could benefit tenants because the customs associated with it provided security and inheritance to a greater or lesser degree. Moreover, the cost of feudal incidents was based on custom and in the event of dispute could be determined by judges in the royal courts. For lords, however, the benefits of copyhold tenure were mixed. As noted above, it was difficult to convey out of the manor, and while it provided an income from feudal incidents as well as rents, its customary basis could have a rigidity that denied the lord the level of profit that could be made from leasehold tenancies where rents could more easily reflect the market. The conversion of land from copyhold to leasehold by agreement between lord and tenant was a process which began from around 1600 and continued steadily thereafter. This diminished the extent of copyhold even though it moved in parallel with another process of copyhold creation by parliamentary enclosure under statute. The parliamentary enclosure movement, whose busiest period was the mid-18th to the early 19th centuries, enabled neighbouring landowners to divide, exchange and allot lands as freehold or copyhold. As a private act of Parliament, an Inclosure Act was a statutory conveyance. Parties to them were often wealthy landowners, and they or their descendants would have been amongst those 19th century copyholders who sought enfranchisement by private agreement or under the Copyhold Acts 1841 to 1894. The 1841 Act allowed voluntary enfranchisement to be made by compensation at once or by an annual rent charge. The 1852 Act allowed either the lord or the tenant to require enfranchisement. It was followed by amending Acts of 1858 and 1887 and a consolidating Act of 1894, which provided for compulsory enfranchisement in Part 1 and voluntary enfranchisement in Part 2.[54]

Valuation of freehold and copyhold

Writing in 1907 the barrister, surveyor and prolific textbook author Benaiah Adkin, noted that 'a copyhold of inheritance, though held in customary fee simple, is in many ways inferior to a freehold held in fee simple, and when subject to an arbitrary fine it is usually worth about three-quarters as much as the property would be if it were freehold.' He explained and illustrated the valuation point with a table comparing the respective characteristics of a freehold and the copyhold of inheritance, which was the most valuable species of copyhold.[55]

Copyhold of inheritance	Freehold
Base tenure	Free tenure
Held of the lord of the manor	Held of the Crown usually
Many payments and services due	Fealty to the Crown the only service usual, and that not actively performed

[54] There were exceptions to the requirement for compulsory enfranchisement in the case of (1) copyholds for lives where the tenant had no right of renewal; and (2) manors in which the Crown had an interest; see Copyhold Act 1894, s.96. For further discussion of the Copyhold Acts, see pp.266-267, 272-274, 280-283.

[55] Benaiah Adkin, *Copyhold and Other Land Tenures of England* (1907), pp.89-90. The book was published by the Estates Gazette and intended primarily for candidates for the examinations of the Surveyors' Institution and the Auctioneers' Institute.

Dealings with the property limited by custom and to some extent subject to the lord's will	Dealings with property unrestricted
Powers of leasing very limited, only one year possible by general custom	Powers of leasing unlimited
Timber and minerals usually belong to the Lord	Timber and minerals belong to the freeholder
Forfeiture possible for waste or failing to observe the custom of the manor	Forfeiture now unknown
Costs much to enfranchise or make free	Is free already
Improvements largely for benefit of lord if fines assessed on annual value	Improvements solely for tenant's benefit
Descent to customary heir	Descent to heir-at-law[56]
Customary curtesy and freebench by special custom	Common law dower and curtesy[57]

56 So far as descent was concerned, where a copyholder tenant died intestate his estate escheated to the lord. The lord's right of escheat was abolished for the benefit of the Crown: see LPA 1922 Sch 12, para 1(c); Sch 13, para 15; and Administration of Estates Act 1925, s 46(1)(vi).

57 Freebench was a widow's interest due from copyholds to which she was entitled by the custom of some manors. Dower was the freehold equivalent. Curtesy was a tenancy of land which had formally devolved on a widower after his wife's death, so long as she had been in possession of the land and there was a child of the marriage capable of inheriting her land. On dower and curtesy, see J.H.Baker, pp.289-91. Freebench, dower and curtesy were abolished in the legislation of 1922-1925.

Inclosure Acts: purpose, nature and content

The heyday of parliamentary enclosure ran from the 1750s to the 1820s, when a significant amount of parliamentary time was taken up by Inclosure Acts. The purpose of enclosure was to reorganise landholdings within a manor so that they could be cultivated more profitably, and reorganisation involved exchange of lands and the creation of freehold allotments granted to tenants who may not have held freehold tenancies before. Judicial recognition of these matters was quickly established and remained constant. An Act of 1777 'for Dividing and Inclosing the Common and Waste Grounds, and Certain Common Fields, and also Two Mosses ... within the manor of Yealands, in the ... county Palatine of Lancaster' came before the court of King's Bench in 1788 in the leading case of *Townley v Gibson*.[58] Speaking of Inclosure Acts generally, Ashurst J said:

> The object of an inclosure is, that the lord of the manor in respect of his seignory and waste should have some part of the ground to be allotted to himself in lieu of his manorial rights; and the other lands are allotted to the proprietors of the inclosed lands within the manor; and these are not made copyholds, but the grantees take them as freeholds of inheritance. Therefore *prima facie* they are entitled to all mines, & c [sic], belonging to the land.[59]

Putting the matter somewhat differently in *Love v Bell* in the House of Lords in 1884, Lord Selborne LC described an Inclosure Act in terms of a statutory agreement: 'a case of mutual considerations resulting in the apportionment of land to which the parties may be taken to have agreed, or have had determined for them by the authority which made

58 2 TR 701; 100 ER 377.

59 At 706; and at 380.

the award.'[60] In the Court of Appeal in 1890 in *Duke of Devonshire v O'Connor*,[61] Fry LJ dealing with an act of 1798 but speaking of Inclosure Acts generally, said:

> '[It] begins with a preamble in the usual form, which shows the object of the Inclosure Act. It recites that the waste lands were in their present state yielding but little profit to the persons interested therein, and therefore, of course, it followed that it was in the interest of those persons that the lands should be inclosed and allotted; that was the general object of all contracting parties who came before Parliament for the purpose of obtaining an Inclosure Act.'[62]

Manorial land comprised demesne, tenanted land whether freehold or leasehold or copyhold, common and waste. The lord owned the freehold of all land within the manor except that owned by other freeholders, but the process of exchange and allotment of his own freehold land was only possible by agreement with the tenants, which could more easily be secured within the framework of a parliamentary statute because it required only majority approval from the tenants rather than the unanimity which would otherwise be needed were the reorganisation by private agreement alone. The lands involved in exchange and allotment were of different tenurial status as well as being different in kind and in actual or potential agrarian productivity, and the amount and proportions of different kinds of land subject to an enclosure would vary. Every manor had developed customs of its own which affected individuals, whether lord or tenant, and which also affected distinct lands within the manor to which those customs applied. A lord was not going to renounce rights or advantages which he enjoyed as freeholder by virtue of his ownership of the soil; equally,

---

60 9 App Cas 289 at 290, followed by Farwell J in *Bishop Auckland Industrial Co-operative Society Limited v Butterknowle Colliery Company Limited* [1904] 2 Ch 419 at 425.

61 [1890] 24 QBD 468.

62 At 479-480. Bowen LJ concurred (at 485).

his tenants would be unwilling to renounce such rights or advantages as they had as copyholders and commoners by virtue of custom or prescription.

There were, therefore, two specific issues to address in any enclosure process. First, the value of lands exchanged or allotted had to be calculated and agreed. Second, the status of rights which the participants in the process had enjoyed over lands before the enclosure had to be preserved or, if not, compensated. The resolution of these issues was dealt with in the Inclosure Act and then in the Award made pursuant to the Act.

Valuation, exchange and allotment were provided for in the Act, with the appointment of commissioners and valuers whose expenses would normally be paid for by the wealthier parties to the enclosure. The Act would usually involve the lord giving up the freehold to part of his wastes or commons, over which tenants had rights, and in return the lord would receive a percentage of the area he had given up – usually a seventh or a sixteenth in the Midlands, Durham or Devon,[63] but it could be more or less – which he continued to hold as freehold but no longer subject to commoners' rights. The percentage would normally

---

63 Roger Kain, John Chapman and Richard Oliver, *The Enclosure Maps of England and Wales 1595 – 1918* (Cambridge, 2011). See p.7, where the authors also point out, on the basis of analysis of enclosure agreements and acts from Durham, the Midlands, and Devon: 'In general, lords of the manor had to make a judgement whether to take their full allocation of land, normally one-seventh, and lose any rights to minerals which might be found subsequently, or to take a smaller amount, usually one-sixteenth, and retain their rights to anything which might be exploited in the future.' In Yorkshire, the Campsall, Norton and Askern Inclosure Act of 1814 (54 Geo 3 c.136) provided the lords with one-eighteenth: see *Thomson v Saint Catharine's College, Cambridge* [1919] AC 468 at 485. In Montgomeryshire in mid-Wales, the Arwystli Inclosure Act of 1816 provided for allotments to the lord to be either one-fourteenth or one-twentieth of the value of the land being enclosed, depending on its location: see *Wynne-Finch v NRBW* at [27] and [50] (Falk J); and at [52] (CA).

be the result of calculation by the valuers, whose 'chief business upon an inclosure is valuing – the assessing of equivalents'.[64] There would also be exchange and allotment of lands both freehold and copyhold. It had been held by the courts that copyhold land had existed 'time out of mind' and could not be created by operation of law because it was not a creature of law but a creature of fact and must have custom to support it.[65] At common law it was impossible for new copyhold plots to be created out of freehold, and since *Townley v Gibson* the rule, on allotment, was that the grantee received a freehold in fee simple.[66] Thus allotment following exchange under Inclosure Acts had the consequence of enfranchising land that had formerly been copyhold. Parliament, however, notwithstanding the provision against sub-infeudation in *Quia Emptores* of 1289, was capable of creating new copyhold tenure if an act, including a private act, clearly said so.[67] But not all Inclosure Acts did; and where they did not, the intended effect of the clause saving the lord's manorial rights that was typically inserted towards the end of the act was to reserve to the lord over the grantee's new freehold the rights which the lord had formerly had over what had been their copyhold.[68] This mechanism was adopted by Parliament under the General Inclosure Act 1845 which provided that all land taken in exchange or on partition or allotment under the Act should be held by

---

64 *Jacomb v Turner*, [1892] 1 QB 47 at 50 per Collins J. The action concerned an allotment under the General Inclosure Act 1845 but the valuers' task of assessing equivalents for exchange within the land subject to the award was no different from that carried out under private inclosure acts. Valuers had no jurisdiction under the 1845 Act to deal with title, which was left to the commissioners.

65 *Revell v Joddrell* (1788) 2 TR 424, 100 ER 224

66 The grantee had formerly been a copyholder. See *Doe v Davidson* (1813) 2 M&S 175, 105 ER 348; at 186, 352 per Lord Ellenborough CJ (Le Blanc, Bayley, Dampier JJ concurring).

67 Ibid; and at 189, 353 (Le Blanc J), 192, 354 (Bayley and Dampier JJ).

68 Ibid. at 189, 353 (per Lord Ellenborough CJ (Le Blanc, Bayley, Dampier JJ concurring). Before the LPA 1922, mineral rights were not seignorial rights but rights incidental to ownership of the soil.

the person to whom it was given under the same tenures, rents, customs and services as the land in respect of which it had been given.[69]

No two Inclosure Acts were precisely the same, but their content and structure tended to follow a common form because their draftsmen used existing acts as precedents. By the early 1800s if not before, they began with a recital naming the relevant lord or lords (or lady or ladies) of the manor and their ownership of or claim to entitlement to the soil of the commons and waste grounds in a particular parish. Then would follow the names of other local landowners, and an assertion that the commons and waste lands were of little value but could be improved by division, enclosure and allotment effected by the authority of Parliament.[70] The operative clauses or sections of the act came next, dealing with the appointment and powers of commissioners and valuers, of an umpire in case of disagreement between commissioners, provisions about notice of meetings, maps and their inspection, costs and expenses, and allotments remaining subject to the same tenures as the lands in respect of which the allotments had been made. Towards the end of the act would come a series of reservations in favour of the lord of the manor and their successors. Typically, there would be a reservation in favour of the lord of mines and minerals in the waste lands allotted to others, together with free liberty of powers of working and extraction, with provisions about compensation to the owners of allotted lands if they were damaged in the process. The minerals reservation might form part of or would be followed by a clause frequently entitled 'general saving of manorial rights' or, more briefly, 'saving of manorial rights'.[71] This was drafted very broadly and stated that nothing in the act should prejudice, lessen or defeat the right, title or interest of the lord to a series of manorial and other rights, and that the lord should continue to enjoy them in as full, ample and beneficial a manner as if the act had never been passed. A final savings clause protected the rights of the crown in

69 See s.94.

70 See *Duke of Devonshire v O'Connor* [1890] 24 QBD 468.

71 A minerals reservation might not be included if the lord was granted a larger proportion of the waste. See above, n.63.

respect of the lands allotted. The savings clauses relating to manorial rights and mineral rights provided fertile ground for disputes.

Inclosure Acts: construction

Inclosure acts were private acts which the courts construed as contracts and in accordance with the intention of the parties. The identity of the parties was to be found in the preamble to the act. In 1788 in *Townley v Gibson*, Lord Kenyon CJ said 'that private Acts of Parliament are to be construed according to the intention of the parties, but then that intention must be collected from the words used by the Legislature, without doing violence to their natural meaning.'[72] In 1867 in *Lord Leconfield v Dixon*, all six judges of the Court of Exchequer Chamber held: 'The inclosure act [of 1808] was passed with the assent of the lord, and of those who were entitled to commonable rights over the wastes of the Manor; it is in the nature of a contract between the parties, and should be construed according to the fair and ordinary meaning of the language employed.'[73] It follows that Inclosure Acts are not to be construed as a public general act but as a contract.[74] As Lord Esher MR pointed out in 1889, this meant that judges 'have to construe it .... as we have so often said, as if we had to construe it a day after it was

72 At 705; and at 379. Lord Kenyon CJ gave the leading judgment.

73 (1867) Law Rep 3 Exch 30 at 31 (Bovill CJ, Willes, Blackburn, Mellor, Shee, and Montagu Smith JJ).

74 One of the principles of construction for a public general act is that 'every word in the Act should be given a meaning. ... On the presumption that Parliament does nothing in vain, the court must endeavour to give significance to every word of an enactment.' See *Bennion on Statutory Interpretation* (5th edition, 2008), p.1157. The current (8th) edition of what is now known as Bennion, Bailey and Norbury on Statutory Interpretation (2020) makes the same point at section 21-2: 'There is a presumption that every word in an enactment is to be given meaning', and the basis of the presumption is that the legislature does nothing in vain. This section has been judicially approved: *Densham v Charity Commission for England and Wales* [2018] UKUT 402 at [61].

passed'.[75] The process of construction will therefore involve taking account of the context, of what was known to the parties, and of the relevant law as it stood at the time.[76] This is unlikely to be a quick or straightforward exercise. Where an Inclosure Act affects third parties, it is to be read strictly against those who promoted it and their successors is title.[77]

During the 19th and early 20th centuries, questions on the construction of Inclosure Acts frequently came before the courts. Although each case depended on the wording of a particular act, there was sufficient similarity between them to warrant the deduction of some general principles applicable to all such acts, settled by numerous decisions with many of them in the House of Lords.[78] The principles mostly concerned the status of the new freehold granted in exchange for former copyhold land, and the relationship between a lord of the manor who had reserved mines and minerals and powers of working for himself out of that grant and the owner of the new freehold tenement. Disputes over reservations extended to sporting rights as well, but it was in relation to mines and minerals that most of the disputes were fought.

---

75 *Consett Waterworks Company v Ritson* (1889), reported at [1922] 2 Ch 187 at 188 (Lord Esher MR, Lindley and Lopes LJJ.

76 *Duke of Sutherland v Heathcote* [1892] 1 Ch 475 at 483 per Lindley LJ (sitting with Bowen and Fry LJJ). On the construction of mineral reservations in Inclosure Acts, see chapter 7 below; and the decision of Parke and Alderson BB in *Earl of Rosse v Wainman* (1845) 14 M&W 858, 153 ER 724, upheld on appeal in the Court of Exchequer Chamber (1848) 2 Ex 799, 154 ER 714 (Lord Denman CJ, Wilde CJ, Patteson, Coleridge, Maule, Cresswell and Williams JJ).

77 *Harper v Hedges* (1924) 93 LJKB 116 at 117 per Scrutton LJ. The act in question here was not an Inclosure Act but a private act passed in 1749 which provided that manorial land in a parish should be charged with all such taxes as would in future be charged upon the parsonage house and its accompanying glebe lands.

78 *Bishop Auckland Industrial Co-operative Society Limited v Butterknowle Colliery Company Limited* [1904] 2 Ch 419 at 424 (Farwell J).

In 1848 in *Earl of Rosse v Wainman* the seven judges of the Court of Exchequer Chamber unanimously approved the following passage from the judgment of Parke B in the Court of Exchequer when construing a minerals reservation in an Inclosure Act of 1805:[79]

> The term 'minerals' here used, though more frequently applied to substances containing metals, in its proper sense includes all fossil bodies or matters dug out of mines... Beds of stone, which may be dug by winning or quarrying, are therefore properly minerals, and so we think they must be held to be in the clause in question, *bearing in mind that the object of the act was to give the surface for cultivation to the commoners, and to leave in the lord what it did not take away for that purpose*' [emphasis added]

Although the words emphasised must have related to the particular act before the court, they were capable of being read as applying to Inclosure Acts generally and, so far as the meaning of minerals was concerned, for at least fifty years following were understood by courts and practitioners in that sense. That understanding altered as a result of concerns that mineral reservations, if coupled with powers of working (as they usually were), could interfere with a freeholder's enjoyment of the surface by denying his common law right to subjacent support. It was one thing to require support for grazing as a commoner, who as a copyholder had received a freehold allotment. But it was another to require it as a freeholder of land which had been an allotment under an Inclosure Act but had since been built on. In 1881 in *Love v Bell*, Lord Selborne established the principle that when the nature of a commoner's interest was changed by an Inclosure Act then, unless otherwise provided, his right to support changed as well. The change came about because the commoner's interest was extended by giving up the rights of common and taking instead a freehold allotment. The lord of the manor as minerals owner had to work the minerals in a way so as not to damage the extended interest which the commoner had acquired under

79 *Wainman v Earl of Rosse* (1848) 2 Ex 800, affirming Parke B (later Lord Wensleydale) and Alderson B in the Court of Exchequer (1845) 14 M&W 858 at 872.

the Act.[80] Provisions in an act to pay compensation for damage made no difference.[81] However, it did not follow that ownership by another of all sub-strata beneath the topsoil was incompatible with a surface owner's right to support, and the current state of the law on this point appears uncertain.[82]

Lord Esher MR dealt with a significant number of appeals involving Inclosure Acts and appreciated that such acts were in a category of their own and of a common form which had existed for many years. Inclosure Act cases frequently went to the Court of Appeal and the House of Lords, and he tried to identify rules of construction or, as he put it, 'a mode in which you are, primarily or *prima facie* to look at [them]', which other courts could follow.[83] In *Consett Waterworks Company v*

---

80 *Butterknowle Colliery Company v Bishop Auckland Industrial Co-operative Company* [1906] AC 305 at 311 per Lord Loreburn LC (Lords Macnaghten and Robertson concurring), identifying and approving Lord Selborne's principle in *Love v Bell* (1884) 9 App Cas 286 at 292. Lindley LJ, a member of the CA in *Love v Bell,* discussed the case dealing with an Inclosure Act of 1771) in *Consett Waterworks Company v Ritson* (1 May 1889 but reported at [1922] 2 Ch 187), saying (at 194): 'Before the Act the lord of the manor lets down the surface and makes no compensation. Why? Because nobody is injured, but the moment you come to allot the surface and he lets down the surface somebody is injured. That was the whole controversy. Is he then to make compensation to the allotees who are injured, or is he to be relieved from all liability to damage in that respect because of the words which I have mentioned.' The words in question were those in the minerals reservation clause of the 1771 Inclosure Act. These reserved to the lord the minerals and rights of working them 'in as full, ample, and beneficial manner to all intents and purposes as they could or might have held and enjoyed the same in case this Act had not been made.' The relevant part of the reservations clause is set out in the headnote of the CA decision in *Love v Bell* (1883) 10 QBD 547.

81 [1906] AC 305 at 312 (Lord Loreburn), 314 (Lord Macnaghten), 3-15-16 (Lord Davey).

82 See chapter 7 for the discussion of the *Wynne Finch* case.

83 *Consett Waterworks Company v Ritson* at 189.

Ritson he expressed as rules two propositions of Lindley LJ in the Court of Appeal in *Bell v Love*.[84] First, 'that an inclosure act is not to be construed so as to allow the lord of the manor to let down the surface of allotments by working mines under them unless the language of the Act is clearly and unmistakably to that effect'. And second: 'that the absence of all provision for compensation for injury sustained by letting down the surface tends strongly to indicate that the legislature did not intend by general words to reserve to or confer upon the lord of the manor the right to work his mines so as to let the surface down.' He added a third rule of his own: once an inclosure act was made, 'the allottees had become freeholders, and unless we can find something in [the Act] to say that they are not to have the right to have the surface unmolested, they ought to have it unmolested.'[85] This something had to be expressed in the clearest possible terms, or to arise by necessary implication from language necessarily leading to such a conclusion.

The third rule applied also to shooting rights as the Court of Appeal, with Lord Esher again presiding, held in 1890 in *Duke of Devonshire v O'Connor*. 'When the part of the waste which is allotted to a person in respect of his former rights of common is allotted to him expressly as his own freehold, the fact of the allotment being granted to him as his freehold gives him, *prima facie*, the right of shooting game upon that freehold as fully as any owner of land in this country has the right of shooting game upon his own land.' For a reservation to be effective, 'the right of shooting must not only be reserved generally, but must be reserved over the lands enclosed under the Act, and declared in the Act to be the freehold of the allotee.'[86] The reason for giving the freehold allottee this degree of protection, similar to that given against minerals

84 (1883) 10 QBD 547.

85 *Consett Waterworks Company v Ritson* at 189, 191.

86 (1890) 24 QBD 468. The draftsman of the act had succeeded in framing an effective minerals reservation but had failed to use similar or sufficient language to do the same for sporting rights.

extraction, was that sporting rights over land were 'a burden of a feudal and onerous character inconsistent with the ownership in fee.'[87]

Further remarks by Lord Esher in the same case about his third rule provide important insights into his thinking about Inclosure Acts which may be useful when construing such acts today. The Act in *Duke of Devonshire v O'Connor* was of 1798. 'Now the application of the rule to any one of these statutes can seldom or ever be quite clear, having to the want of care with which they are generally drawn. It would seem that the draughtsman, without inquiring into the facts of the manor with which he is about to deal, puts in every possible word, whether applicable to the particular case or not, which he thinks may possibly apply: this makes the construction of these statutes a matter of some difficulty.' The failure to frame a clear reservation for sporting rights, which the draftsman had succeeded in doing for mineral rights, was a blunder which 'occurs with great frequency in these Inclosure Acts; whether that blunder consists in applying the claim of the lord, as owner of the soil, to manorial rights, or whether it is the opposite blunder, I cannot say. There is therefore a difficulty in construing this exception [for sporting rights], for from one point of view it may reserve the right claimed for the lord, whereas from another it does not; and its meaning not being clear, it does not by necessary implication reserve the right.'[88] Clearly, the problem for draftsmen was to recognise and understand the implications of the difference between seignorial rights and rights which the lord of the manor had as a landowner – in other words, those rights incident to ownership of the soil. This was what the draftsman in *Townley v Gibson* had failed to do because he confused a manorial right with right to ownership of the soil.

87 At 473-74 (Lord Esher MR).

88 At 478-479.

The 1845 General Inclosure Act: sporting reservations

When the General Inclosure Act 1845 came into force, the responsibility for drafting legislation for particular enclosures rested with the Inclosure Commissioners, who were government officials. The legislation took the form of their provisional orders which were made subject to the 1845 Act (and its subsequent amending acts) and each year were submitted in tranches to parliament for approval as an Annual Inclosure Act. Inclosures under the 1845 Act generated less litigation than their private act predecessors, but reservations of sporting rights and mineral rights in favour of the lord still proved disputatious.

Section 25 of the 1845 Act provided that, on application made to the commissioners by those who represented at least one third in value of the interests in the lands proposed to be enclosed, the commissioners could make inquiries in the locality and hold meetings to hear objections which might be made and receive evidence about it. Section 26 allowed the commissioners to specify any terms or conditions which appeared to them 'proper for the protection of any public interest and of any mineral property or peculiar rights in relation to the land proposed to be enclosed.' Section 27 required the commissioners, if they thought enclosure expedient, to prepare a provisional order on terms they thought appropriate and to determine the size of the allotment to the lord of the manor in respect of his right and interest in the soil either exclusively or inclusively of his right or interest in all or any of the Mines, Minerals, Stone and other substrata ... or any other right or interest... in the land to be enclosed.' The provisional order was then to be sent to the locality and, if two-thirds in value of the parties interested agreed, could be placed in the commissioners' annual report before parliament so that, if no successful objection were made, the enclosure could proceed. Notably, section 29 of the 1845 Act gave the lord an absolute veto on the enclosure of his waste. He could refuse his consent unless the parties interested agreed that the right to take the game be severed from the right to the soil in the land proposed to be enclosed. There was no obligation on the lord to assent, and he had a perfect right to make a stipulation to that effect.[89] Once the right was severed from the soil, it became an incorporeal right in gross.[90]

In *Musgrave v Forster* the question was whether the lord of the manor was entitled to the exclusive right of shooting over lands formerly part of the waste of the manor but enclosed and allotted to the defendants by a provisional order ratified by the Annual Inclosure Act of 1853. The provisional order for enclosing the waste contained the following term: 'that one-sixteenth part in value of the lands be allotted to the lords of the manor in lieu of their right and interest in the soil of the lands, exclusively of their right and interest in the game, and in all mines, minerals, stone, and other substrata in and under the said lands.'[91] Were the commissioners authorised by legislation to make it a condition of enclosure that the right of sporting should be severed from the right in the soil and the tenement thus created remain with the lord, whilst the soil was allotted to others? On 12 August 1868 the defendants, on their own land, had shot and carried away a grouse and were sued for disturbing the lord's right and liberty of shooting and killing game upon lands which formerly constituted the waste of the manor.

Blackburn J, in the Court of Queen's Bench found for the lord. He doubted that the 1845 Act gave the commissioners power to reserve shooting rights because 'the right of the owner of the soil to take game is a general incident to the property in the soil, a mode of enjoying the property, and is not therefore aptly described as a 'peculiar right' under section 26 or 'another right or interest in the land' under section 27. However, this gap concerning rights of game was covered by section 1 of the General Inclosure Amendment Act of 1848[92] which gave the commissioners power 'to set forth any special agreement or matter

---

89 *Musgrave v Forster* (1871) LR 6 QB 590 at 594.

90 *The Overseers of the Townships of Hilton and Walkerfield v The Overseers of the Township of Bowes* (1866) 1 QB 359 at 369 per Cockburn CJ (Blackburn and Lush JJ agreeing).

91 *Musgrave v Forster* (1871) LR 6 QB 590.

92 11 & 12 Vict. c.99

concerning or affecting the lands to be enclosed, and to make the same a condition of such inclosure.'[93]

A shooting right, where severed from the land, is an incorporeal hereditament in gross and may be subject to the provisions of the LPA 1925 relating to freehold land.[94]

The 1845 General Inclosure Act: minerals reservations

While any doubt about the commissioners' power under the 1845 Act to propose gaming reservations was resolved by the 1848 Amendment Act, there had never been such doubt with mineral reservations. Consistently with the express power granted to the lord to veto the terms of a provisional order,[95] the 1845 Act took the greatest of care to protect his pre-enclosure rights to the sub-surface where, following enclosure, his land was allotted to others. Those rights could be reserved beneath such land; or, if they were not reserved, they could be valued and compensation provided to the lord for loss of them. The statutory formula describing the extent of the lord's sub-surface rights was drawn in very wide terms, referring to his right or interest in 'Mines, Minerals, Stone and other Substrata beneath such land.'[96] The scope of the formula was broader and different from earlier terms found in mineral reservations in private Inclosure Acts, such as 'all mines and minerals, of whatever nature or kind so ever',[97] as well from the words of the statutory mineral reservation of 'any mines of Coal, Ironstone, Slate, or other Minerals under any Land' contained in the Lands Clauses

93 LR 6 QB 590 at 595.

94 See s 201(1); p.59 below.

95 See s 29, which bore the sub-heading 'Consent of the lord of the manor'.

96 See ss 27, 76, 97, 98 and 116. *Jacomb v Turner* [1892] 1 QB 47 (Collins J) and *Simcoe v Pethick* [1898] 2 QB 255 (CA) contain judicial analysis of the scheme and working of the 1845 Act.

97 The words used in *Earl of Rosse v Wainman* (1845) 14 M & W 858; affirmed at (1848) 2 Ex 800.

Consolidation Act and the Railways Clauses Consolidation Act also passed in 1845. The implications of this difference have not been worked out in the courts.

Manorial boundaries

Identifying the boundary of a manor at any particular date depends on surviving documentation and can be a difficult exercise. The key point is that a manor was not necessarily a single block of land with a defined boundary running round its edges. Manors could be and often were inter-mixed lands, with other owners (or lords) holding land between separate parts of the manor. The normal evolution for a manor was to decline in size as time passed because land was sold off by the lord. There were two notable consequences of this in terms of understanding the subsequent manorial boundary. First, if land sold off did not lie around the edge of the manor, the unsold land within the manor became fragmented so that the line of the manorial boundary could assume the configuration of an island chain. As copyhold enfranchisement progressed, that fragmentation increased. Second, if the land sold was later re-acquired by the lord, it could not come back into the manor again: the lord merely held it in fee simple.[98] This was a rule stated in *Delacherois v Delacherois*, an Irish case decided in the House of Lords in 1864 and regarded as binding in England and Wales. However, in 1704 in *R v The Duchess of Buccleugh* it was held by Holt CJ and the whole court of Queen's Bench that 'lands once severed from a manor, can never after become parcel of it in reality, but it may in reputation; as if lands, part of a manor, be aliened away absolutely, and re-purchased, and an unity of possession for a considerable time after.'[99] There must have been many instances both before and after the *Buccleuch* decision

98 *Delacherois v Delacherois* (1864) 11 HL Cas 62 at 102-103. Equally, land acquired by the lord adjoining the manor could not come into the manor, except perhaps by statute under an Inclosure Act.

99 (1704) 6 Mod 150; 87 ER 909. The HL in *Delacherois* was aware of *Buccleuch* and did not consider it wrong: see Lord St Leonards at 106.

where exactly this occurred, although the 1894 edition of Scriven refers to no case later than *Buccleugh.* At all events, if manorial land is sold off but re-acquired with unity of possession in the lord in circumstances where the land is regarded as becoming part of the manor, then the land apparently comes once again within the manorial boundary.

The key manorial documents for investigating boundaries are the extent and the perambulation. An extent was a survey of a manor and may show not just its fields and boundaries but the names of tenants. Extents do not usually date from before the late 16th or early 17th century and are particularly good if made during the later 19th century, when surveyors and draftsmen of estate plans paid great attention to detail. A perambulation is a written account of the process of beating the bounds – i.e. a walk by officials or the homage of the manor around its boundaries to inspect them. Perambulations of the same manor may be difficult to interpret if landmarks or features mentioned in them no longer exist, or if perambulations at different dates appear inconsistent in the sense that the later record indicates a larger manor than the earlier. If so, then it may be necessary for the party asserting the later boundary to explain how the size of the manor had increased since the earlier perambulation.

If lands within a manor were ever subject to an Inclosure Act, another useful source for identifying manorial ownership and boundaries are the maps produced for any Award or Awards made pursuant to the Act. Although these may not give the entire boundary of the manor, they will identify parts of it, together with their occupants and their tenures, at the date of the Award. Since they will have been prepared by surveyors and valuers at the end of the enclosure process, they are likely, depending on the date, to have a reasonable or high degree of accuracy.

Conveyancing of manors

The prospective purchaser of any manorial title, land or right should take particular care when making pre-contract investigations and enquiries; and the same may also apply to a prospective purchaser of land which was formerly part of a manor and may be subject to rights reserved on a previous sale.

The conveyancing of manors before 1882 was subject to a strict rule that distinguished between real manors and reputed manors, and the rule applied not just to deeds of conveyance but also to settlements and wills. The rule was that where a manor had become a reputed manor by its reduction to less than two free tenants and loss of its court baron, a conveyance which was expressed to pass the manor, whether described as a manor or reputed manor, in fact passed nothing at all unless there was specific mention of freeholds in the wastes or of particular tenements. In 1843, giving judgment in *Clayton v Williams*, Lord Abinger CB said:

> Now, although the wastes and demesnes will pass by a conveyance of the manor, if nothing more be said, yet, if the manor be lost, and have become only a manor by reputation, there is no case which I am aware of that goes to the length of deciding, that, under the words 'reputed manor' the freehold interest in wastes, or in any specific tenement that is possessed by the grantor, will pass. A man may grant a certain tenement and his reputed manor by such a name; but if there be no real manor, I cannot conceive that anything would pass but that tenement, and the right (although, perhaps, that may be questionable) to appoint a gamekeeper, within certain limits, of that which was formerly the manor. But there being nothing substantial in the word 'manor', I cannot, as at present advised, suppose that anything passed by that word where there is only a manor by reputation.[100]

---

[100] (1843) 11 M&W 804 at 807-808.

The consequence of the rule was that conveyances, settlements and wills were drafted in comprehensive terms to identify all demesnes, wastes, mines and minerals and other rights that the grantor sought to pass to the grantee. This increased the cost and difficulty of drafting and was necessary if there was any uncertainty about whether the manor was real or reputed. This position only changed when the Conveyancing Act 1881 provided that the term 'manor' was deemed to include lordship, reputed manor and reputed lordship;[101] and that the transfer of the manor was deemed to include all those lands and rights appertaining or reputed to appertain to the manor or, at the time of conveyance, demised, occupied or enjoyed with it.[102] Before the Act's introduction it had been necessary to identify all these individually to ensure that each one of them passed.

The modern conveyancing of manors dates from the 1881 Act whose general words and interpretation provisions were substantially re-enacted in the Law of Property Act 1925.[103] The 1925 Act impliedly allows manorial lordships, land and rights to be conveyed individually or in combination; and in this respect it continues the position at common law before the 1881 Act. The 1925 Act also raises an important point concerning the formalities of transfer for a lordship in gross. Although the Act regards a lordship in gross as an incorporeal hereditament,[104] which at common law can be transferred by contract rather than by deed of conveyance, section 201(1) makes no distinction between lordships and lordships in gross: it treats them, along with manors and reputed manors, as freehold land.

---

101 See s 2(iv).

102 See s 6(iii).

103 Compare sections 2(iv) and 6(iii) of the Conveyancing Act 1881 with sections 62(3) and 205(1)(ix) of the LPA 1925.

104 See section 201(1). But this was not always so. In *Tyrringham's Case* (1584) 4 Co Rep 63a; 76 ER 973, the court expressly regarded a manor as land.

> The provisions of this Act relating to freehold land apply to manors, reputed manors, lordships, advowsons … perpetual rentcharges, and other incorporeal hereditaments, subject only to the qualifications necessarily arising by reason of the inherent nature of the hereditament affected.

Lordships in gross have become more important in recent years due to the growth of the market in lordship titles. They are now commonly bought and sold. However, the implications of section 201(1) for the lordship in gross are not straightforward due to the closing words 'subject to the necessary qualifications arising by reason of the inherent nature of the hereditament affected'. A lordship in gross is not land but it is inherent within the lordship right that its owner may become entitled to waste, which is land, or to mines and minerals, which are deemed under s 205(1)(ix) of the 1925 Act to be included within the meaning of land. This suggests that an unregistered lordship title should be transferred by deed because, if the transferee lord subsequently claimed waste or mineral rights, there could be doubt as to whether he had title to do so.

Registered lordship titles are the subject of contract and transfer using Land Registry form TR1 and are subject to compulsory registration.

So far as unregistered manorial land is concerned, that too should be the subject of contract and conveyance, followed by application for first registration. The purchaser of registered manorial land will proceed by contract and transfer. So too will the purchaser of registered manorial rights. For the prospective purchaser of unregistered manorial rights,[105] it will be necessary before purchase to examine not only the devolution of those rights to the vendor but also the title or titles of land over which those rights are said to be exercised.

---

105 Whose priority was at risk if they were not registered by 12 October 2013: see chapter 3 on registration.

Coastal manors

Where manors adjoin the sea or tidal estuaries there may be questions about ownership of the foreshore and fundus along the seaward or estuarial boundaries of the manor, particularly where the extent of the foreshore has increased by the retreat of the sea.[106] The foreshore is the area of land between high water mark and low water mark. The fundus is the seabed in a tidal river below the low water mark. There is a presumption that foreshore and fundus are owned by the Crown and, in Cornwall, by the Duchy of Cornwall. The critical question is the strength of the presumption where, as a matter of fact, the theory of *prima facie* title is one on which little reliance can be placed. The presumption is now of less weight than it was;[107] and, in relation to Cornwall, a respected practitioners' text by an author particularly well-placed to know the documents states that the Crown had probably parted with all the foreshore prior to its grant of the foreshore to the Duchy in 1337.[108] A lord of the manor claiming title to foreshore, or to foreshore and fundus, will have the burden of displacing the presumption. To succeed in establishing the title, the lord will require either evidence from which a grant from the Crown may be inferred or, alternatively, possession for a period of over sixty years.[109]

---

106 See *Baxendale v Instow Parish Council* [1982] 1 Ch 14.

107 *Halsbury's Laws*, vol 29 (2024), para 161, n.2. See *Le Strange v Rowe* (1866) 176 ER 903 at 905; 4 F&F 1048 at 1051-1052 per Erle CJ: '[T]he soil between high and low water mark, that which is left dry by the ebb of the tide, and which is covered by the full tide, is presumed to be in the Crown, unless the Crown at some time or other has parted with it. In a great number of cases the Crown has parted with it. There are some manors that remain in the Crown that are the property of the Crown, as in Cornwall; but I take it that in the great majority of cases the right to the foreshore between high and low water mark is in the lord of the manor.'

108 Halsbury's Laws, vol 29, para 166, n.1; and Stuart Moore, *A History of the Foreshore and the Law relating thereto* (Third edn, 1888).

109 Halsbury's Laws, vol 29, para 171. See *Le Strange v Rowe* (1866) 176 ER 903 at 906; 4 F&F 1048 at 1054 per Erle CJ: 'the grant of a manor with

The commercial significance of the right to ownership of foreshore or fundus (or both) may be great. The vesting of the shoreline or estuarial riverbed in the lord will enable him to build jetties, charge mooring fees, and to develop oyster grounds and other activities. Claims of this nature are likely to be easier for long-established owners, with private records and long family memories, than for those who acquire lordships for commercial exploitation. In *Roberts v Swangrove Estates*, the owner of a newly acquired lordship claimed title to the fee simple in the adjacent parts of the northern foreshore and fundus of the Severn estuary to the centre of the deep-water channel.[110] The area in question comprised thousands of acres of sand, mud flats and similar land. Had the claim succeeded, the lord would probably have been able to exploit the commercial uses of the estuary: dredging sand; fishing, wildfowling and shooting, with the prospect of future use extending to wind farms or tidal barrage. It failed because the court found that the Crown had established title to the foreshore and fundus by adverse possession, and the effect was to extinguish any lordship title over them.

---

anchorage, groundage and wreck is good presumptive evidence …that the soil of the foreshore is in the party to whom that manor belongs.'

110 [2007] EWHC 513 (Ch); [2007] 2 P & CR 17; [2008] EWCA Civ 98; [2008] Ch 439 (CA). The lordship was of Magor in south Monmouthshire.

CHAPTER THREE

REGISTRATION

Introduction

The law of property in England and Wales has, since the introduction of the Land Registration Act 1925, been profoundly changed by the development of land registration. Writing in 2016, the Chief Executive and Chief Land Registrar said that HM Land Registry's 'main purpose is to register ownership of land in England and Wales and to record dealings with land once it is registered'.[1] Registration is intended to provide certainty and security of title, and to facilitate the process of transferring land and interests in land. The ultimate objective of registration is the creation of a register which is complete in the sense that it covers all land in England and Wales. As every property lawyer knows, the register itself is intended to embody three principles: the mirror principle, the curtain principle, and the insurance principle, which underlie the policy of the 1925 Act and its successors. The mirror principle is that the register, with its constituent parts dealing with proprietorship, the extent of the property and any charges over the land, should accurately reflect all facts material to the title. The curtain principle is that the register should be the only and definitive source of information for intending purchasers while not revealing information of a sensitive nature. The insurance principle is that if, because of error by the Land Registry, the title transferred is later proved to be defective in any way, then the person suffering loss as a result should be indemnified by the state.[2]

The development of land registration since 1925 has proceeded slowly and unevenly. There was a piecemeal extension of compulsory first

---

1 See Land Registry, *Consultation to amend the Land Registration Rules 2003* (2016), p.4. The words are those of Professor Graham Farrant.

2 See LRA 1925 s.8, and LRA 2002, s.103 and Sch.8.

registration on sale from 1925 but it did not become compulsory until 1 December 1990, when first registration of land was required when it was sold.[3] It was only from 1 April 1998 that first registration was required when land was gifted, or when there was an assent of land on death, or when land was mortgaged.[4] So intending purchasers were and still are faced with land that is either registered or unregistered when they are investigating title. Unregistered land requires significantly more investigation than registered land because title must be established historically by production and examination of conveyances and other title documents. And once unregistered land is acquired, there is no certainty that it is not subject to rights which pre-contract enquiries had failed to reveal. With registered land the uncertainty is reduced but real nevertheless. A major source of that uncertainty is that land can be subject to manorial rights or rights of manorial origin which were not required to be on the register because the LRA 1925 treated them as overriding interests. The term 'overriding interests' applies to 'estates, rights and interests which are not protected on the register in any way, but which nevertheless override first registration or, as the case may be, a disposition of a registered estate'.[5] Thus where registered land is subject to overriding interests, any purchaser of the land holds it subject to those interests even though they are not on the register and the purchaser has no knowledge and perhaps no means of acquiring knowledge of them before acquisition. As a species of overriding interests with a previous track record of erratic registration before 1926, and no incentive to register after 1925, manorial rights are a significant obstacle to the mirror principle's implementation.

---

3 SI 1987/1347.

4 Land Registration Act 1997, s.1; SI 1997/3036.

5 *Megarry and Wade: The Law of Real Property* – Tenth Edition (2024) by Martin Dixon, Janet Bignell KC, and Nicholas Hopkins, p.160, para 6-008, citing LRA 2002 Sch 1 and Sch 3.

Section 70 of the Land Registration Act 1925

Section 70 dealt with the liability of registered land to overriding interests and, in relevant part, provided:

> (1) All registered land shall, unless under the provisions of this Act the contrary is expressed on the register, be deemed to be subject to such of the following overriding interests as may be for the time being subsisting in reference thereto, and such interests shall not be treated as incumbrances within the meaning of this Act, (that is to say):—
>
> (a) Rights of common, drainage rights, customary rights (until extinguished), public rights, profits a prendre, rights of sheepwalk, rights of way, watercourses, rights of water, and other easements not being equitable easements required to be protected by notice on the register....
>
> (b) Liability to repair highways by reason of tenure, quit-rents, crown rents, heriots, and other rents and charges (until extinguished) having their origin in tenure....
>
> (d) Liability in respect of embankments, and sea and river walls....
>
> (j) Rights of fishing and sporting, seignorial and manorial rights of all descriptions (until extinguished), and franchises;

Sub-sections (1)(a), (b) and (d) included specific rights and liabilities of manorial origin while sub-section (1)(j) referred to manorial rights generally.[6] The words in brackets 'until extinguished' referred to the

6 Not all rights in s 70(1)(a), (b) and (d) were of manorial origin. Most obviously, the rights in (a) could easily have non-manorial origins.

effect of those sections within Part VI of the Law of Property Act 1922 which extinguished manorial incidents on payment of compensation.[7]

Although no new manorial rights could be created after 1925, what is striking about section 70 is how wide a range of manorial rights continued, without registration, as overriding interests unless and until they were noted on the register. Since there was no requirement to register such rights, or to register the lordship itself, the impact and even the existence of a manor were difficult for any intending purchaser or owner of land to identify from existing title documents. It made no difference whether the land was registered or unregistered. The position was not helped by the rules about manorial documents introduced under the Law of Property Act 1922 which enabled their transfer to local record offices. While the rules were necessary to preserve manorial documents for future use, their removal over time from local lords or stewards of the manor[8] led to a loss of memory within neighbourhoods about matters relating to land that were relevant to proposed transactions and liabilities that the land was subject to.

A more informative list of the 'manorial rights of all descriptions' referred to in section 70(1)(j) had appeared in the Law of Property Act 1922 at paragraphs (5) and (6) of Schedule 12. The contents of those paragraphs, the parts of them of continued relevance, and how manorial rights appeared in the register, were set out in 1987 by the Law Commission in their Third Report on Land Registration:[9]

> As well as the sporting rights of the lord, certain other manorial incidents were preserved for an indefinite period (unless

---

7 See ss. 138 to 143 of the LPA 1922.

8 Lords or stewards were often solicitors. The plaintiff in *Beaumont v Jeffery* [1925] 1 Ch 1 was a solicitor who by the time of trial 'had already acquired between thirty and forty manors and was the steward of about 120 manors': see the report at 2.

9 Law Com 158, *Property Law: Third Report on Land Registration* (laid before Parliament on 31 March 1987), para 2.97.

> extinguished by agreement) under the legislation which enfranchised copyholds on 1 January 1926. Many manorial incidents have ceased to exist. Those which may still remain are:
>
> (a) The lord's or tenant's right to mines and minerals;
>
> (b) The fairs, markets and sporting rights of the lord;
>
> (c) The tenant's rights of common;
>
> (d) The lord's or tenant's liability for the construction, maintenance, cleansing and repair of dykes, ditches, canals and other works.
>
> Where land has been enfranchised and the deeds or abstract of title show the rights of the lord which were saved, it is the practice of the Land Registry to repeat this information on the register when the title to the land comes to be registered.

As noted above, first registration on disposition became compulsory in 1990; and in their Consultative Document of 1998[10] the Law Commission and the Land Registry were able to report on the more visible profile which manorial rights were having on the register.[11]

> Where enfranchised copyhold has been registered, these manorial rights are almost always apparent from the deeds affecting the property. Should the property in question be registered, they will therefore be entered on the register in most cases.[12] In practice therefore, few such rights will be overriding interests. However, because we cannot be completely confident

---

[10] The subject of the consultation was the content of legislative proposals for what became the Land Registration Act 2002.

[11] Law Com 254, *Land Registration for the Twenty-First Century – A Consultative Document*, paras 5.84 and 5.85.

[12] The authority given for this statement was the then current edition of Ruoff & Roper, *Registered Conveyancing*, 6-24.

> that this is so, we consider that— (1) they should be retained as overriding interests; but (2) the wording should be simplified. We therefore provisionally recommend that any subsisting manorial rights which have not been noted on the register should remain as overriding interests.

This provisional recommendation was generally endorsed by those who responded to the consultation, and was included in the bill which became the Land Registration Act 2002. The bill was published in a further report by the Law Commission and Land Registry, where the thinking behind its proposals for manorial rights registration was explained.[13]

> The Bill provides that franchises and manorial rights can be overriding interests, as indeed they are under section 70(1)(j) of the Land Registration Act 1925. In the Consultative Document, we recommended the retention of this category of overriding interests and this was supported by most of those who responded. However, we consider that it is reasonable that such rights should be protected on (and therefore apparent from) the register for the following reasons –
>
> (1) Those who enjoy such rights tend to know that they have them.
>
> (2) Such rights can be very valuable and must therefore detract from the value of the land which is subject to them.
>
> (3) Many manorial rights are of a kind that could have been the subject of an express grant, such as a right to fish, shoot or take minerals. It is not apparent to us why their manorial origin should give them a special status when it

[13] Law Com 271, *Land Registration for the Twenty-First Century: A Conveyancing Revolution* (9 July 2001), para 8.40.

> comes to the issue of whether or not they should be registered.
>
> (4) Similarly ... franchises originate in a royal grant, actual or presumed. There is no reason why such rights should not be registered.
>
> For these reasons, we have concluded that the overriding status of franchises and manorial rights should be phased out over a period of 10 years.

This passage from the further report signified a movement away from the position taken in the Consultative Document and a more restrictive approach, consistent with the mirror principle, towards the retention of manorial rights as overriding interests. The bill when enacted contained provisions which limited the status of manorial rights as overriding interests to a period of ten years. If, by that date – 13 October 2013 – the rights had not been entered on the register by their owner, they would not take priority over the rights of the registered owner of the land where that owner had, on or after 13 October 2013, purchased by way of disposition for valuable consideration and completed registration of their own title.[14] The Land Registration Act 2002 did not use the term 'overriding interests' and preferred to describe them, more informatively, as 'unregistered interests' which override first registration or registered dispositions, as the case may be.[15]

14 However, if a manorial right is not protected by a notice entered before 13 October 2013, it can still be exercised against the person who is proprietor on that date, and against his successors in title, other than successors under a disposition for valuable consideration which is registrable and completed by registration: see LRA 2002 s 29(1) and (2); and HMLR PG 66 at paras 3.6.3 and 5.

15 See LRA 2002, Schedules 1 and 3. Nevertheless the words 'overriding interests' do appear in the LRR 2003 at rr. 28 and 57 and are still in use on Land Registry forms FR1 and AP1, as well as Practice Guides.

Registration of manors under the Land Registration Act 2002

As the Land Registry Practice Guide points out, there are three separate elements of manors that can affect land registration under the Land Registration Act 2002:[16]

- lordship of the manor: whoever owns the lordship of the manor is entitled to refer to themselves as lord of that manor.
- manorial land: because a manor was a defined area it included the physical land within that area. Such land could either be freehold or leasehold.
- manorial rights: rights which were part and parcel of the manorial title and which were usually kept by the lord on disposal of parts of the manorial land, for example, the right to hunt, shoot or fish.

These different elements may exist separately or they may be combined, and it is important to keep this firmly in mind whenever the word 'manor' appears in legislation. A lord may have no more than his lordship title. Or he may have both land and rights, or either of them, together with his lordship. Where a lord owns historic manorial land he will very likely have all the rights of a freehold owner of that land, although those rights may be subject to those of third parties. A lord may also have rights over land not his own, but which once was part of the historic lands of the manor. Land and rights may be divided into separate ownerships but a lordship title today is indivisible and can exist without land or rights attached to it.[17]

---

16 HM Land Registry Practice Guide 22: *Manors*. At the time of writing, the latest edition is dated 24 June 2015.

17 In which case it is known as a lordship in gross. It should be noted that a lordship in gross may entitle its holder to the ownership of manorial waste, which is incidental to the title: *Scriven on Copyhold*, p. 397.

Registration of lordship title

Registration of lordship title has never been compulsory. Before the Land Registration Act 2002 came into force on 13 October 2003, it was possible voluntarily to register a lordship title.[18] But since there was no requirement to do so, most lordship titles were unregistered. However, the Act made no provision for first registration of title for a manor,[19] and so after 12 October 2003 such registration has become impossible.[20] The rationale for this state of affairs is not easily understood. While a lordship title is an incorporeal hereditament and therefore an interest having no physical existence, the Act does allow for first registration of title for a franchise and a profit à prendre in gross. Like manors, these too are incorporeal hereditaments and interests without physical existence. More problematically, a lordship title confers on the holder a *prima facie* right to the freehold of any manorial waste which remains unregistered.[21] Although an incorporeal hereditament, a lordship therefore has the potential to acquire something with physical existence in the form of an estate in land. Improvements in digital technology and greater access to that technology have made it simpler to locate and interrogate manorial records. In consequence, it is now easier for a lordship owner to identify unregistered land and to bring a claim for ownership of waste.

The Index of registered lordship titles

The Land Registry kept and maintains an index of those lordship titles registered before 13 October 2003. The Practice Guide states that each registered title has an individual register, which contains the name and

---

18 Land Registration Rules 1925, rr. 50 and 51.

19 See Law Com 271, para 3.21.

20 See ss. 2 to 4 of the LRA 2002 dealing with the scope of title registration (s. 2), when title may be registered (s. 3), and when it must be registered (s. 4).

21 Subject, of course, to any claim for adverse possession by a squatter.

address of the current registered proprietor who can be contacted with any enquiries about the manorial interests (if any) that affect the land in question. The Practice Guide adds that, because of their nature, lordship titles do not have title plans and that the Land Registry holds no definitive record of the extent of the original manor.[22]

The absence of any title plan at the Land Registry is a problem because the name of a manor by itself may afford little help in identifying its location. Since manors could not be created after 1289, the absence of any definitive record showing the extent of the original manor is not surprising. The boundaries of manors contracted (and never expanded) over time, but from the late 16th century onwards the development of surveying led to the production of estate maps known as extents. An extent was intended to show the boundary of a manor at the date of the extent, and a named lordship title (whether registered or not) can be searched for at a local record office to see whether an extent exists for the manor. For those investigating lordship title and manorial boundaries it is important to remember that enquiry at the Land Registry will almost certainly need to be further supplemented by further enquiries at the National Archives and local record offices. Procedures for searching the Land Registry index of registered lordships are explained in the relevant Practice Guide.[23]

De-registration of lordship title

Section 119 of the Land Registration Act 2002 makes specific provision for manors to be de-registered: 'On the application of the proprietor of a registered manor, the registrar may remove the title to the manor from the register.' Once the title is removed, the lordship continues in

22 HMLR PG 22 at paragraph 2.1.

23 HMLR PG 13: *Index of relating franchises and manors.*

existence but no longer as a registered estate, and the Land Registry will hold no record of it.[24]

Leases of registered manors

Section 27 and Schedule 2 of the LRA 2002 set out those circumstances where dispositions of registered estates are subject to compulsory registration. These circumstances include those where a registered manor is leased, with slightly different requirements applying depending on whether the term exceeds seven years or not. Although not free from doubt, the content of the Land Registry Practice Guide[25] and the fact that the relevant provisions treat manors and franchises in the same way suggests that the word 'manor' in this context could in principle apply to a lordship, or manorial land or manorial rights or any combination of the three. In practice, however, the grant of such a lease is likely to be very rare. The relevant provisions are at Schedule 2, paragraphs 4 and 5:

> 4 (1) This paragraph applies to a disposition consisting of the grant out of a franchise or manor of a lease for a term of more than seven years from the date of the grant.
>
> (2) In the case of a disposition to which this paragraph applies—
>
> (a) the grantee, or his successor in title, must be entered in the register as the proprietor of the lease, and

---

24 For the process of application for de-registration, see LRPG 22 at paragraph 2.3. The fact that s.119 exists at all is surprising because the newly introduced power to remove existing registered lordship titles from the register on the application of the owner undermines the mirror principle. It creates unnecessary complexity and risks causing confusion because other elements of the manor – i.e. historic manorial land and manorial rights – are now subject to compulsory registration requirements of various kinds. See below.

25 HMLR PG 13.

(b) a notice in respect of the lease must be entered in the register.

5 (1) This paragraph applies to a disposition consisting of the grant out of a franchise or manor of a lease for a term not exceeding seven years from the date of the grant.

(2) In the case of a disposition to which this paragraph applies, a notice in respect of the lease must be entered in the register.

Transfer of registered manors

When a registered manor is transferred, it is a registrable disposition and it must be completed by registration if it is to operate at law.[26] This will apply to the transfer of a registered lordship, or of manorial land where that land has not yet been separated from the manorial (i.e. lordship) title.

Many manorial titles include no physical land. But for those that do, title to the land may pass on transfer of the lordship. The compulsory registration provisions of the Land Registration Act 1925 made an express exception for land that was parcel of a manor 'and included in the sale of a manor as such'.[27] There is no such exception in the Land Registration Act 2002. So if a manor includes physical parcels of land, the title to the land concerned must be registered following a transfer. That registration is required even though an unregistered lordship itself can no longer be registered.[28]

---

26 LRA 2002 s.27 and Sch. 2, Part I, para 7. A lordship, despite being an incorporeal hereditament, was 'land' for the purposes of LPA 1925, s 205(ix) and therefore fell within s. 1(2)(a) of the LPA 1925 as an interest in land capable of being conveyed.

27 LRA 1925, s.120(1).

28 See HMLR PG 1: *First Registration* at para 1.1.2.

Mortgage of a manor

If a protected first legal mortgage is created against unregistered manorial land which is included within a lordship title, first registration is compulsory.[29]

Registration of manorial rights

The Land Registration Act 2002 made the protection of manorial rights after 12 October 2013 dependent on registration. The rights in question were not defined in the Act but in their further report accompanying the bill the Law Commission and the Land Registry stated:

> As regards manorial rights, we explained in the Consultative Document that –
>
> (1) the meaning of "manorial rights" was a precise one: the rights in question were listed in some detail in paragraphs 5 and 6 of Schedule 12 of the Law of Property Act 1922, provisions that have since been repealed;
>
> (2) such rights could no longer be created after 1925; and
>
> (3) on first registration, the existence of such rights is normally apparent from the deeds so that the burden of them is noted on the register in most cases.[30]

The scope of manorial rights was therefore to be found at paragraphs 5 and 6 of Schedule 12 of the Law of Property Act 1922. The further report added:

> Because the provisions of the 1922 Act have been repealed, it has not been possible in the Bill to define "manorial rights" by

[29] LRA 2002, s.4(1)(g).

[30] Law Com 271, para 8.41. Para 5 re-enacted s 23(1) of the Copyhold Act 1894 and is set out below at p.280. Para 6 is set out at p.287.

> reference to them. However, it may be taken that the list found in Schedule 12 of the 1922 Act is a comprehensive statement of these rights.[31]

The Land Registry, which with the Law Commission was responsible for this further report, is on record as continuing to hold this view.[32] On the assumption that the Land Registry has acted consistently with it, any court considering the question of what comprises a manorial right under the Land Registration Act 2002 is likely to agree that the scope of such rights is as set out in the 1922 LPA.[33]

Manorial rights, both before and after the 2002 Act, were overriding interests. In other words, in the 1922 LPA they had been legal interests to which land which had formerly been copyhold was subject and binding on the owner of that land. They were not noted on the register or, in the case of unregistered land, did not necessarily appear on those conveyances conferring good title on the owner of the land. Once interests are noted on the register they cease to be overriding, and a key feature of the 2002 Act was to encourage owners of manorial rights to get them registered within ten years or risk losing the priority of those rights to a registered proprietor of the land on a first registration or registrable disposition once the ten years had passed. The land would then no longer be subject to manorial rights. Would that mean that they were extinguished? Extinguishment of manorial rights was not a stated objective in the Consultative Document or the further report, and any provision to that effect in the Act could well have been in breach of the Human Rights Act 1998 because a manorial right is a property right. But there can be no doubt that in many instances manorial rights may over time become extinguished by the back door because the cost and trouble of asserting them are too great.

---

31 Law Com 271, para 8.41, n.147.

32 HMLR PG 66: *Overriding interests that lost automatic protection in 2013* (updated 6 April 2018), para 3.6.3.

33 At LPA 1922, Sch. 12, paras 5 and 6.

The Act achieved this result by providing that manorial rights would lose their overriding status after 12 October 2013 in relation to both registered and unregistered land.[34] Thereafter, the rights were not extinguished and continued to exist but their owners would have to have them noted on the register if they were to take priority in the event of a first registration or registrable disposition of the land subject to them. In March 2003, in advance of the Act's entry into force later that year,[35] the Land Registry offered three points of guidance to owners of manorial rights which remain relevant today.[36] First, they have a duty to disclose those rights on all first registrations or dispositions of registered land.[37] Second, such owners can apply for the existence of manorial rights to be recorded on a notice on the register of a title that is subject to them, and will have the burden of persuading the Land Registry that such rights exist. Third, if the land subject to the rights is not registered, then the rights can be protected by a caution against first registration. What may still happen where a notice or caution has not been registered before 13 October 2013 is set out later in this chapter.[38]

Registration of manorial mineral rights

For purposes of registration, the term 'manorial mineral rights' has no precise meaning but in practice needs to be considered when registering or examining minerals title in relation to the specific class of rights preserved in favour of the lord or the tenant by the LPA 1922. These rights arise in relation to copyhold land, of which the freehold was in

34 See LRA 2002 ss.11, 12, 29, 30, 117; Sch.1, para 11; Sch.3, para 11; r. 2 LRA 2002 (TP) (No 2) Order 2003.

35 The LRA 2002 came into force on 13 October 2003.

36 HMLR PG 22, para 4.3. The owners of manorial rights will often be lords of the manor concerned. However, an owner will not be lord if they have simply purchased specific rights (such as sporting rights).

37 This would apply in all those cases where the landowner was applying for first registration of the land or was the disponor.

38 See p.85.

the lord, but which was enfranchised in 1926 so that the freehold then passed from the lord by what was in effect statutory conveyance to be vested in the former copyholder. Paragraph 5 of schedule 12 of the Act had the effect of preserving such rights as the lord or tenant had in or to any mines and minerals immediately before enfranchisement. In its report proposing the draft bill subsequently enacted as the LRA 2022,[39] these particular rights were identified by the Law Commission as one of four kinds of 'manorial rights' which survived the 1922/1925 legislation, and were to be treated as overriding interests for a period of ten years from the date the LRA 2002 came into force (13 October 2003). After ten years they were not extinguished but ceased to be overriding interests with the consequence that, if they remained unregistered on 13 October 2013, they no longer had priority in the event of a registrable disposition of the land in question for valuable consideration. However, for so long as the land remained in the same ownership after 12 October 2013, the rights could still be registered and would therefore retain priority.

Distinct from these rights, and apparently unaffected by the 2002 Act, are proprietary rights to minerals which derive from other manorial sources unconnected with paragraph 5 of schedule 12. Thus rights to a freehold minerals estate created by a minerals reservation under a conveyance continue to exist and can be registered at any time because there is no requirement under the 2002 Act (or any other legislation) for minerals to be registered. Also unaffected are easements or profits à prendre which may have been excepted or reserved under a conveyance of manorial land because in these circumstances a conveyance by a lord of land granted as freehold is no different from one by a grantor who is not a lord.[40]

---

39 See Law Commission 271, *Land registration for the 21st century: A Conveyancing Revolution* (2001), paras 8.40 and 8.41.

40 According to a Land Registry consultation paper of 2016, most of the problems surrounding the registration of minerals (and mines) relate specifically to estates in minerals as opposed to rights in mines and minerals flowing from easements or profits à prendre (such as the grant of

Notices to protect manorial rights over registered land

A notice is an entry in the register in respect of the burden of an interest affecting a registered estate or charge.[41] The entry of a notice is to be made in relation to the registered estate or charge affected by the interest concerned.[42] Notices come in two types: unilateral and agreed. Neither guarantees that the lord's interest it protects is valid or that it even exists; it will only ensure that the priority of that interest, if it is valid, will not be postponed on the registration of a subsequent registrable disposition for valuable consideration of the land subject to the interest.[43] Once the interest has become the subject of a notice, its overriding status is lost and cannot be regained even if the notice is cancelled. An agreed notice will not be cancelled unless the registrar is satisfied that the interest protected has come to an end or is otherwise invalid.[44] There is a duty to act reasonably when applying for a notice, and when objecting to an application to the registrar.[45] The duty is owed to any person who suffers damage in consequence of its breach.[46]

---

a right to enter on land and extract minerals). These are not classified as an estate in fee simple and therefore cannot be registered with their own title. As HM Land Registry PG 65 points out at section 10, such a right *may* be registered if it is in gross, and it *must* be registered where the grant is out of registered land (except where the right can be registered under the Commons Registration Act 1965). The non-registration of a right in gross may cause similar confusion to the non-registration of an estate. See Law Commission LC 227, *Updating the Land Registration Act 2002: A Consultation Paper* (2016) at para 3.20; LRA 2002 s.3(1)(a); HM Land Registry PG 65 'Registration of mines and minerals'; HM Land Registry PG 16: 'Profits à prendre', at section 3.

41 LRA 2002, s.32(1).

42 LRA 2002, s.32(2).

43 LRA 2002, s.32(3).

44 HMLR PG 22, paras 3 and 3.1; LRA 2002, s.29(3).

45 LRA 2002, s.77(1).

46 LRA 2002, s.77(2).

Unilateral notices

According to Land Registry Practice Guide 66, a unilateral notice may be entered without the consent of the relevant proprietor.[47] The applicant is not required to satisfy the registrar that their claim is valid and does not need to support their claim to the interest with any evidence. The registrar will however check that the interest claimed is of a type that may be protected by unilateral notice. If so, there will be entered against the subject title the details of the unilateral notice specifying what right (or liability) it relates to, its date, its beneficiary and their address.[48]

The relevant proprietor is not notified of the application until after the entry has been made and therefore will not usually be able to object to the application. However, they will always be notified after the application has been completed. They can then apply at any time to cancel the notice and, by doing so, require the beneficiary of the protected interest to prove the validity of their claim.

Not surprisingly, the ten-year deadline prompted a large number of applications from manorial rights owners to the Land Registry in the period shortly before its expiration. The Land Registry's practice of notifying registered proprietors of the subject land only after the application had been completed and the unilateral notice entered was not well received by those proprietors.[49] The impact of a unilateral

---

47 HMLR PG 66, para 3.1. This appears to be the curtain principle in operation.

48 A liability may arise because of the situation created by para 6 of Sch.12 of the LPA 1922. Enfranchisement triggered by the Act did not affect any liability existing at the commencement of the Act for for the construction, maintenance, cleansing or repair of 'any dykes, ditches, canals, sea or river walls, piles, bridges, levels, ways and other works required for the protection or general benefit of any land within a manor or for abating nuisances therein'.

49 They complained to their parliamentary representatives who initiated an investigation bv the House of Commons Justice Select Committee into

notice on the subject land will depend on the nature of the right and whether the right can be later established. Although an unsuspecting proprietor would be understandably alarmed to be told by the Land Registry that a lord had registered a unilateral notice in respect of mines and minerals beneath his property, in practice the lord is unlikely to be able to exploit the right without the proprietor's consent. But that may not always be the case and, if so, the proprietor can challenge the unilateral notice by applying for its cancellation.

Cancellation of a unilateral notice

Section 36 of the LRA 2002 provides that a person may apply to the registrar for the cancellation of a unilateral notice if they are the registered proprietor of the estate or charge to which the notice relates, or if they are entitled to be registered[50] as the proprietor of that estate or charge.[51] If such an application is made, the registrar must inform the beneficiary of the notice that the application has been made; [52] and unless the beneficiary objects to the application within 15 working days of receiving the information or such longer period (up to 30 working days) as may be allowed, the registrar must cancel the notice.[53]

---

the question of whether manorial rights should be abolished. See: https://publications.parliament.uk/pa/cm201415/cmselect/cmjust/657/65702.htm

50 HMLR PG 19 at para 2.5.2 identifies common examples where someone may be entitled to be registered as proprietor. These are (1) where they have recently taken a transfer of the estate or charge but have not yet become registered as proprietor. For example, where form AN1 is lodged at the same time as the application for registration; (2) where the sole relevant proprietor has died and they are the personal representative; (3) where they are the trustee in bankruptcy of the relevant proprietor and the estate or charge forms part of the bankrupt's estate.

51 LRA 2002, s.36(1).

52 LRA 2002, s.36(2).

53 LRA 2002, s.36(3); and Land Registration Rules 2003, r. 87.

Where the beneficiary does object, they must set out their grounds of objection to the registrar who will decide whether the objection has any chance of success. If not, the objection will be cancelled under section 73(6) of the LRA 2002. To succeed, the beneficiary will need to provide details of the law or facts which entitle them to the notice. Once the registrar has decided that an objection is not groundless, details of that decision will be given to the applicant. Any dispute about whether the notice should be cancelled that cannot be resolved by agreement will be referred to the First-tier Tribunal of the Land Registration division of the Property Chamber.[54]

Removal of unilateral notice

The procedure known as removal of a unilateral notice from the register is available under section 35(3) of the LRA 2002 where the beneficiary of the notice wants to remove it. The applicant is therefore the beneficiary or their personal representative, trustee in bankruptcy or conveyancer acting on their behalf.[55]

Agreed notices

While a unilateral notice is by its nature provisional and vulnerable to challenge, an agreed notice is a permanent fixture on the register against the entry of the subject property. It can be entered on the register either by, or with the consent of, the relevant proprietor of the subject property (or someone entitled to be registered as such). But it can also be entered if the applicant can satisfy the registrar that the interest clamed is valid.[56]

---

54 HMLR PG 66, para 3.8.1.

55 See LRR 2003, r. 85.

56 See HMLR PG 66, para 3.5.

According to the Land Registry Practice Guide, 'we are not obliged to serve notice on the relevant proprietor before approving an application for an agreed notice made without the proprietor's cooperation. In most cases we will determine the application on the basis of the evidence lodged without involving the proprietor. However, if the application is one based on evidence rather than proprietor cooperation, we will always notify the proprietor that the entry has been made when we complete the application.' The Practice Guide adds that if the registrar decides that an agreed notice can be entered, details of the protected interest will be given on the register and that this is often achieved by referring to a document that describes, or that created, the interest.[57]

The rubric of the Practice Guide can be read as suggesting that an applicant may be able to register an agreed notice against a subject property without the knowledge of the registered proprietor – effectively behind their back. Whether or not this is so, the registrar retains a discretion to accept or reject the application, and there is nothing to prevent the registrar from involving the registered proprietor in advance of any final decision to approve the application and enter it on the register.

While the evidential burden for registering a unilateral notice is light, in the case of an agreed notice it is formidable. The Practice Guide states that, to establish the validity of a claim for the purposes of an agreed notice, the applicant will normally need to produce:[58]

(1) evidence that the land in question was previously copyhold of the manor in question (this will usually be provided by producing a copy of the deed of enfranchisement or compensation agreement);

---

57 This appears to be another example of the curtain principle in operation.

58 See HMLR PG 66, para 3.6.3.

(2) evidence that it was the custom of the manor in question that the lord had the rights claimed, for example by evidence from the court rolls;

(3) evidence that the rights in question survived enfranchisement (this will usually be provided by producing a copy of the deed of enfranchisement or compensation agreement);

(4) evidence of the applicant's title to the particular manorial rights claimed (this will usually consist of an abstract or epitome of title showing the applicant's title to the lordship of the manor and that the rights have not been severed from the lordship).

These requirements, if observed, are stringent and will involve providing extensive historical documentation from (at least) the 19th and 20th centuries. They are also indicative of the points that the beneficiary of a unilateral notice will need to establish if a registered proprietor decides to challenge it.

Cancellation of an agreed notice

An agreed notice can be cancelled by application supported by appropriate evidence that the protected interest has come to an end. There is no restriction on who may apply to cancel the notice. If the interest protected by the notice has only come to an end in part, the registrar must make an appropriate entry to that effect.[59]

Caution against first registration

This procedure is available where the subject land is unregistered. The person with the benefit of the interest affecting the land can apply to enter a caution against first registration. The cautioner must provide details of the nature of the interest claimed, together with sufficient

59 LRR 2003, r.87.

particulars to enable the extent of the land affected by the caution to be identified on an Ordnance Survey map. In most cases this will involve providing the registrar with a clear and suitably scaled plan.[60] As with a unilateral notice, a person must not lodge a caution without reasonable cause. If they do, they owe a duty to, and can be sued by, anyone who suffers damage.[61]

Manorial rights left unprotected before 13 October 2013 by notice or by caution against first registration

This currently appears to be a grey area. Although the effect of section 117 LRA 2002 was to remove overriding status from manorial rights that were not registered before 13 October 2013, the Act did not provide that such rights automatically cease to exist on that date. They continue but they are not on the register. If the land subject to them has neither been the subject of first registration nor the registration of a disposition for valuable consideration before the date when the owner of the manorial rights seeks to protect those rights,[62] there is no problem. The owner of the rights can still apply by notice or by caution against first registration, and a successful application will enable the owner to preserve the priority of those rights if their validity can be established.

However, even where the land has been the subject of first registration or of registration of a disposition for valuable consideration after 12 October 2013 and the owner of the manorial rights seeks subsequently to register them, the Land Registry will continue to accept the application. HMLR Practice Guide 66 says this:

> The courts have still to consider if and when it may be possible after 12 October 2013 for the holder of the interest to have the

60 HMLR PG 66, paras 4 and 4.3.2.

61 LRA 2002, s.77.

62 Necessarily after 12 October 2013.

> register altered so that a notice is entered where the registered proprietor has taken free of the interest following first registration or following the registration of a disposition for valuable consideration. They have also still to consider whether indemnity may ever be payable where the register cannot be altered in this way.
>
> HM Land Registry will still accept applications for the registration of notices to protect overriding interests that lost their automatic protection after 13 October 2013 and will not check whether the registered proprietor has changed since this date before proceeding with the application.[63]

It is striking that the Practice Guide contains this passage, for it may indicate a view that loss of overriding status for manorial rights does not lead to their ultimate extinction even where the subject land is registered free of them.[64] How such rights should be treated, whether or not they can be entered on the register, and what may be the implications for indemnity, all appear to remain open questions. The reason for the inclusion of the passage apparently relates to the issue of whether an

---

63 HMLR PG 66, para 5.

64 Such a view would be consistent with an interpretation of s. 117 consistent with Article 1 of the Human Rights Act 1998. A manorial right is a property right. Article 1 of the HRA 1998 is headed 'Protection of Property'. It provides: 'Every natural or legal person is entitled to the peaceful enjoyment of his possessions. No one shall be deprived of his possessions except in the public interest and subject to the conditions provided for by law and by the general principles of international law. The preceding provisions shall not, however, in any way impair the right of a State to enforce such laws as it deems necessary to control the use of property in accordance with the general interest or to secure the payment of taxes or other contributions or penalties.' However, the Law Commission's view (see the text immediately below) is that the normal effect of s 117 will be to eliminate the overriding interest if it is not registered before 13 October 2013. If so, it raises the question of whether s 117 falls within or outside the UK's margin of appreciation under human rights law.

overriding interest whose priority has been postponed under section 29 LRA 2002 can be revived on a subsequent section 28 transaction affecting the burdened land. Sections 28 and 29 both deal with the effect of dispositions on priority. Section 28 sets out the basic rule for estates (and charges), which is that, except as provided by section 29,[65] the priority of an interest affecting a registered estate is not affected by a disposition of the estate. Section 29(1) provides that if a registrable disposition of a registered estate is made for valuable consideration, completion of the disposition by registration has the effect of postponing to the interest under the disposition any interest affecting the estate immediately before the disposition whose priority is not protected at the time of the registration. The question here is what happens to the overriding interest which is postponed. In its 2018 report *Updating the Land Registration Act 2002*,[66] the Law Commission acknowledged that there were academic questions about this but concluded that there was no real doubt about the effect of s 29(1).[67]

> It remains our view that the effect of postponement in section 29(1) is clear. "Postpone" means that the disponee will take free from the interest under the registrable disposition. As explained by Mr Justice Norris in *Halifax Plc v Curry Popek* [2008] EWHC 1692 (Ch) at [49], a registered disposition for valuable consideration "wipe[s] the title clean of any prior unprotected equitable interests".[68]
>
> The word "postpone" captures the idea that the interest is not necessarily destroyed; it may remain valid against interests other than that of (and those created by) the disponee.... [There are] examples of cases in which a postponed interest is not destroyed. The most common example is when the disposition that

---

65 And section 30, for charges.

66 Law Com 380 and HC 1336, ordered by the House of Commons to be printed on 19 July 2018.

67 See paras 8.17 to 8.18, and 8.20 to 8.21.

68 [2008] EWHC 1692 (Ch) at [49].

> postpones the interest is the grant of a lease: the lessee will take free of the interest, but the interest will continue to affect the freehold reversion once the lease expires. Because a leasehold estate is an estate that is time limited, the postponed interests will revive at the end of the term of the lease.
>
> ....
>
> In most cases, the practical effect of section 29(1) is that the postponed interest will be eliminated. The interest will not revive on a subsequent disposition of the disponee's interest, whether or not that subsequent disposition engages section 29.
>
> Despite some academic discussion, we disagree that there is any real question about what "postpone" means in section 29(1) of the LRA 2002.

Alteration of the register is governed by the provisions of Schedule 4 of the LRA 2002, and any attempt by a manorial rights owner to apply for registration of their rights after 12 October 2013 is likely to generate an objection to the application from the registered proprietor.[69] If so, the registrar may well refer the matter to the First-tier Tribunal of the Property Chamber.

[69] There is a useful Land Registry discussion of Sch 4 case law in HMLR PG 77 (updated 16 March 2020): *Altering the register by removing land from a title plan.*

CHAPTER FOUR

WASTES AND COMMONS

Introduction

As Thomas Scrutton pointed out in 1887, 'the origin and history of common lands in England are inseparably bound up with the history of the Manor.'[1] The colonisation of England and Wales by the Normans after 1066 saw land progressively acquired and brought into use by the king's tenants-in-chief and their own tenants and sub-tenants.[2] Within the manor and under the jurisdiction of the lord, cultivated land and other land used by the lord for his house and grounds were demesne whereas uncultivated land included waste and common. Those with free tenures held of a lord had rights of common over his waste. Not all waste was common but the extent of waste and common steadily declined as lords brought more land into cultivation by approvement and assarting. Approvement, which was later more frequently known as enclosure, usually involved the lord enclosing lands within his manor, which then became demesne. Assarting was the creation of small areas out of the waste which the lord leased to tenants for a money rent. From

---

1 Thomas Edward Scrutton, *Commons and the Common Fields: The History and Policy of the laws Relating to Commons and Enclosures in England* (Cambridge, 1887), p.1. At the time of publication, Scrutton was Professor of Constitutional Law at University College, London, and his book had been the Yorke Prize Essay of the University of Cambridge for 1886. Although better known as a commercial lawyer both as a judge and for his work on Charterparties and Bills of Lading (which he had already published), Scrutton was a formidable property lawyer as well. His Prize Essay is a powerful work of legal scholarship and deserves attention from anyone concerned with the law of commons.

2 This paragraph follows the analysis of Professor T.F.T. Plucknett in his Ford lecture on 'The Incidents of Feudalism' delivered in the University of Oxford in 1947. It was published in *Legislation of Edward I* (Oxford, 1949): see pp.83-85.

the early 13th century, when royal courts recognised that the soil of waste and common lands belonged to the lord, the shortage of land available to lords for cultivation led to an increase in approvement and in disputes between them and their freehold tenants with rights of common over the lord's waste. Those rights extended over the whole of the common lands and were protected by the royal courts so that, if the tenants objected, the lord was unable to approve. After complaints by the barons to the King, the statute of Merton was enacted in 1235,[3] giving lords power to approve waste but on condition that sufficient was left to satisfy the requirements of their tenants with rights of common. For lords this provided only a partial remedy because their waste was still subject to rights of common over it by tenants of other lords on neighbouring lands. In 1285 the statute of Westminster II addressed this with a similar remedy: lords could approve waste over which neighbours had rights of common on condition that sufficient waste was left for them to exercise their rights of common.[4] The two statutes were re-enacted in 1549.[5] The statute of Merton was repealed in 1953,[6] and the statute of Westminster II in 2006.[7]

---

3 20 Hen 3 c.4.

4 13 Edw 1 c.46.

5 3 & 4 Edw VI, c. 3. Known as the Improvement of Commons Act, this was repealed by the Civil Procedure Acts Repeal Act 1879.

6 The Statute Law Revision Act 1953.

7 Commons Act 2006, Sch 6, Part 3. Gadsden notes that 'by the end of the 18th century approvement seemed to have fallen into almost total disuse': see p.303 at para 6-41. Since at least the 17th century, lords had proceeded by way of private agreement (usually sealed in court), or by parliamentary legislation through a private act.

Wastes, commons and rights of common

The modern understanding of the courts about the relationship between commons, waste and manor was set out in Lord Templeman's speech in *Hampshire County Council v Milburn*.[8]

> The remainder of the land [in the manor, apart from demesne and copyhold] consisted of uncultivated land, referred to as the waste of the manor. The waste land was the natural source of grazing, fodder and fuel for all the inhabitants of the manor. The waste land belonged to the lord of the manor subject to the rights of the tenants to enjoy in common the fruits or some of the fruits of the soil in the manner of a "profit à prendre". The rights of the commoners varied from manor to manor. The extent of the right of any particular commoner depended on the origin of the right and might depend on the size and situation of land held by the commoner. A grant of arable land to a freeman prior to 1290 entitled him by common law to the use of the manorial waste for such purposes as were necessary for the maintenance of his husbandry. Common rights could also be acquired by grant, custom or prescription. The right of a commoner was the right "to eat the grass with the mouths of his cattle, or to take such other produce of the soil as he may be entitled to:" 1 Roll Abr. 406 as adopted in 1 Saund. 353(a) (Halsbury, 2nd ed., vol. 4, para. 1134). There were four main categories of common rights, namely the common of pasture, being the right to feed cattle, horses, sheep and other animals; the common of estovers, namely the right to take wood to build and maintain houses and fences and for fuel and other agricultural purposes; the common of piscary, being the right to fish and the common of turbary, being the right to dig peat. Whatever the rights of a commoner he could enforce his rights against the lord of the manor who owned the soil but could not obstruct the exercise of the rights so that Watson B. was able to

---

[8] [1991] 1 AC 325 at 338C-H.

say in *Attorney-General v. Hanmer* (1858) 27 L.J. Ch. 837, 840 that:

> "The true meaning of 'wastes,' or 'waste lands,' or 'waste grounds of the manor,' is the open, uncultivated and unoccupied lands parcel of the manor, or open lands parcel of the manor other than the demesne lands of the manor."

Hanmer decided that a Crown grant of minerals under the waste of the manor includes the minerals under the foreshore which formed part of the manor.[9] The facts were that the Crown, by letters patent as lord of the manor of Englefield on the Dee estuary, made a grant of 'all those coal mines found, or to be found, within the commons, waste grounds, or marshes within the said lordship'. There was, unusually, a proviso that the grant should be construed strictly against the Crown and strictly in favour of the grantees. The court was therefore dealing with a coastal manor whose waste included foreshore as well as open lands adjoining the foreshore, and Baron Watson's words should be considered in that context. 'Open' is to be understood as unenclosed because a lord's 'inclosure of waste is probably the most unequivocal act possible to indicate an intention that it should cease to be waste.'[10] 'Uncultivated' appears to be a question of fact and degree of cultivation: land which has been put to arable use or forestry will be regarded as cultivated whereas potential use or the planting of a few trees will probably not.[11] 'Unoccupied' is perhaps easier to understand by saying what it is not rather than what it is. In *Hanmer* the wastes were being used by the

---

9 *Hanmer* is reported at (1858) 22 JP 543; 27 LJ Ch 837; 4 Jur NS 751; 6 WR 804; 31 LTOS 379.

10 Gadsden, p.108 at 3-28.

11 Gadsden, p.107 at 3-29; *Re The Drives, Puncknowle, Dorset* (1972) 10/D/7; *Re Norris Mill Moor etc, Puddletown, Dorset* (1973) 10/D/35-7; Re *(1) Huntsham Hill and (2) the Old Quarry both in Goodrich, Herefords* (1973) 15/D/1-3, 6; *In the matter of Carn Brea, Cornwall* (1981) 206/D/720.

tenants of the manor for grazing purposes, and therefore 'unoccupied' is not simply non-use of the waste, while the letting or leasing of manorial land even if vacant gives it status as demesne.[12]

The definition of manorial waste in *Hanmer* was followed and applied by subsequent courts,[13] and in 1980 by Megarry V-C in *Baxendale v Instow Parish Council.*[14] There, the Devon County Council as commons registration authority under the Commons Registration Act 1965 had provisionally registered as common several areas of land that had been waste of a manor. [15] This they were entitled to do on the basis that section 22(1)(b) of the Act provided that 'common land' meant 'waste land of a manor not subject to rights of common'. The land was not subject to rights of common but for some years its owners had used part of it as car parks. Megarry V-C found that this had deprived the car park areas of the 'quality' or character of waste. He said:

> The commissioner found that hardcore had been put down and fencing had been erected; and that, coupled with the actual use as car parks and the consequent occupation of them by the trustees, seems to me to exclude the car parks from the category of waste.... [Neither] at the time of registration nor at any other material time do they appear to have had the quality in law of being "waste". They must therefore be excluded from the registration.[16]

---

12 See the discussion in Gadsden, pp.108-10, at sections 3-30 to 3-33.

13 *Ecroyd v Coulthard* [1898] 2 Ch 358 at 367 per Lindley MR; *In re Britford Common* [1977] 1 WLR 39 at 46H-47B (Slade J)

14 [1982] Ch 14.

15 See the first instance decision of commons commissioner A.A. Baden Fuller in *In the matter of sands, sandhills and grass areas above high water mark in Instow, North Devon District, Devon* (24 September 1979) Ref 209/D/156, 209/D/157 and 209/D/158 at p.3.

16 *Baxendale v Instow Parish Council* at 18.

While rights of common could be, and usually were, established over waste, they could also be established over demesne either by grant or by custom. Demesne was land within the manor which the lord actually had, or potentially had, in *propriis manibus* (i.e. in his own hands).[17] This extended to land that was leased or let, and such land could not become waste unless it was abandoned by the lord.[18] Equally, waste could not become demesne, even if the lord of the manor cut the grass for hay and silage, in the absence of inclosure.[19] If the lord sold waste or demesne to others so that the land went out of the manor, it made no difference to the commoners' ability to enforce their rights against the new owner: 'no lord of the manor could, by selling the manorial lands, deprive the tenants of the manor of their rights of common over them, no matter whether those lands were originally part of the demesne lands or the waste land of the manor.'[20]

---

17 See *A-G v Parsons* (1832) 2 Crompton & Jervis 279; 149 ER 120 per Lord Lyndhurst CB, delivering the judgment of the Court of Exchequer: 'we think we are fully warranted in saying, that, though the word "demesne" may in some cases be applied to any fee-simple lands a man holds, yet it is more correct and usual to apply it to the lands of a manor, which the lord of that manor either actually has, or potentially may have, in *propriis manibus*.' This definition was applied by the Chief Commons Commissioner in *Re Waste Land, Carperby, N Yorks.* (1977) 268/D/96 and by Slade J in *In re Britford Common* [1977] 1 WLR 39 at 47H-48B.

18 See Gadsden, p.108 at 3-30; and the commissioner decisions in *Re Hardown Hill, Whitechurch, Canonicorum and Chideock, Dorset* (No.1) (1974) 10/D/45-55; *Re Land to the north of Pipers Green, Brockley Hill, Stanmore, Greater London* (1974) 59/D/7; and *Re Waste Land, Carperby, N Yorks.* (1977) 268/D/96.

19 *In re Britford Common* [1977] 1 WLR 39 at 47H-48B (Slade J). There is further discussion of this point in Brown v Edwards (24 March 2025) REF 2022/0271, 0272, 0273.

20 *President and Scholars of Corpus Christi College, Oxford v Gloucestershire County Council* [1983] 1 QB 360 at 365G-H per Lord Denning MR.

Ownership of waste

The lord was before 1926 and remains *prima facie* entitled to all waste lands within the manor, and it is not necessary that he should show acts of ownership over them.[21] The right to ownership is incidental to the title: as Scriven puts it, 'the lord's ownership of waste lands is involved in his ownership of the manor, the wastes being as much parcel thereof as the demesne lands are'.[22] The lord's right to ownership of waste was not taken away by the Law of Property Acts 1922 and 1925, although his ability to use the waste was restricted by public rights of access over those commons to which s.193 of the LPA 1925 applied.

Ownership of the soil of the waste is therefore vested in the lord. As owner of the soil, the lord has the same rights in relation to the land as any freehold owner of land. However, statute has imposed significant limits on the freedom with which those rights can be exercised.[23] If waste is common and is registered as such, it will almost certainly come within the definition of 'access land' under section 1(1) of the Countryside and Rights of Way Act 2000 ('CROW'), and under section 2(1) of that Act any person is entitled to enter and remain on access land for the purposes of open-air recreation.[24] A registered common may also be subject to local acts or to byelaws made by the local authority and, in areas where the Commons Act 2006 ('the 2006 Act') applies, to management and control by a commons council for that common created by the appropriate national authority (i.e. the Secretary of State in England or by Welsh ministers in Wales).[25] In areas where the 2006 Act applies, if waste is unregistered or unregistered as common, it may now be registered as common by any person or by the

---

21 Scriven, p.397; *Doe on the demise of the Earl of Dunraven v Williams* (1836), 7 Car & P 332; 173 ER 148.

22 Scriven, p.397.

23 See Part 3 and s 38 of the CA 2006.

24 The entitlement to enter and remain on access land is itself subject to conditions. See CROW 2000 s 2.

25 See CA 2006, s 26.

commons registration authority for the area where the land is situated.[26] In this respect the 2006 Act continues the policy of the 1965 Act that manorial waste which had never been common may now be registered as common, with the consequence under CROW that it is thereby open to public access.[27] Section 2 of CROW extended the rights of access for air and exercise which the public were given under s 193 of the LPA 1925.[28]

Questions about ownership of waste arise today in situations where manors were dissolved, becoming reputed manors,[29] and land remains unregistered. Nearly all manors now are reputed, and their ownership will have devolved either by settlement or by will or by sale and purchase. Historically, knowledge of the extent of land within the manor was maintained through documentation held by lords, and this made it possible to identify manorial boundaries and holdings whenever ownership of the manor was transferred. However, with the passage of time that knowledge was eroded as lords no longer had the means or inclination to maintain the documentary record which proved their ownership of land. The manorial courts baron and customary courts, which together had delivered an early form of land registration, gradually ceased to operate; and their records – despite the belated efforts of legislators through the Manorial Documents Rules of 1925 – were diminished or destroyed. The failure of the 1925 property legislation to make land registration compulsory, or to make registration of manorial title compulsory, created a gap in the documentation of

---

26 CA 2006, Sch 2, para 4.

27 Lords who wish to exploit waste must keep in mind the statutory consequences of registration and public access.

28 Section 193 has been amended and partly repealed, albeit differently and at different times in England and in Wales. For the details of amendments and the statutory narrative creating them, see the current text of the LPA 1925 on the National Archives website at legislation.gov.uk

29 A reputed manor is one where there are no longer two or more freeholders holding their tenements of the manor subject to escheat: *Glover v Lane Clerk* (1789) 100 ER 699 per Lord Kenyon CJ; and see p.27 above.

land ownership in relation to manorial waste, whether or not the waste was common. Subsequent registration acts have done much to close this gap; but open, uncultivated and unoccupied land which remains unregistered may well be subject to ownership claims by lords on the basis that the land is manorial waste.

In *Burton v Walker*, the waste in question was in two distinct locations which the courts treated differently. The claimant had acquired a house and land from a vendor purporting to convey with them the lordship of Ireby in Lancashire. [30] He was successful in his application to the Land Registry to register the lordship title and then embarked on what he understood to be a manorial mapping process. This involved investigating the registered titles and title plans of houses in Ireby village and claiming that those plots of land within the village and not in the registered ownership of others were waste belonging to him as lord. This aspect of the claimant's attempt to reconstruct manorial title failed because the court found that the legal manor had been extinguished at least 250 years earlier and that the chain of devolution of title to what at most was the lordship of a reputed manor was broken long before the claimant took his conveyance. The Land Registry was accordingly mistaken in registering the lordship title, and the register was altered accordingly. However, had the court found that the lordship title was a good one correctly registered, it is not easy to see how the claims to plots within the village could have been resisted except for those which were occupied and used for a purpose, and where it was also possible to argue adverse possession.

The second location said by the claimant to be waste of the manor comprised 362 acres of moorland near the village and adjoining his own property. Known as Ireby Fell, this had been registered as common after a hearing before the chief commons commissioner in 1978, and the defendants had used it for many years for air, recreation and exercise. The claimant, after the Land Registry had registered his title as lord of

---

30 See the first instance First-Tier Tribunal Property Chamber decision of the Deputy Adjudicator (Mr Simon Brilliant), 10 December 2010 (REF 2007/1124).

the manor, applied in that capacity to register ownership of the hitherto unregistered fell in his name on the ground that it was waste of the manor and that as lord of the manor he was entitled to it. The Land Registry agreed. It registered his title to the fell, and the claimant thereafter spent money on its maintenance, entered into grazing agreements with local farmers so that they could pasture sheep on it, and prevented the defendants and other villagers from using it. The court at first instance, having found that the claimant was not entitled to the lordship and that registration of the lordship had been a mistake, refused to order alteration of the register in respect of the fell. This continued in the claimant's ownership. The court rejected the argument that registration of the fell was a mistake consequential upon the first mistake which should be treated similarly by rectification of the register.[31] Instead it found that as the claimant was a registered proprietor in possession of land, any order to amend the register in respect of that land was subject to paragraph 3(2) of Schedule 4 of the Land Registration Act 2002.[32] Under that provision, the court was not required to order amendment of the register unless *inter alia* it was unjust not to do so, and in the particular circumstances of the case there was no injustice in leaving the claimant in possession: he had spent money on the fell while the defendants had waited two years before objecting to his ownership and were not themselves claiming title. The

---

31 The author understands that the current practice of the FTT judges is to regard this part of the tribunal's decision (upheld in the Court of Appeal) as confined to its own facts and to regard entries in the register that are consequential upon an earlier mistake in the register as capable of rectification: see next footnote.

32 At [72]. Schedule 4 of the LRA 2002 provides for alteration of the register. Where an alteration involves the correction of a mistake and prejudicially affects the title of a registered proprietor, it is known as rectification and can only be ordered by a court if certain requirements are met. Under paragraph 3 of Schedule 4, rectification cannot be ordered without the proprietor's consent in relation to land in his possession unless he has by fraud or lack of proper care caused or substantially contributed to the mistake, or it would for any other reason be unjust for the alteration not to be made.

Court of Appeal upheld this reasoning, finding that the Crown or Duchy of Lancaster was probably the true owner of the fell but that neither of them wanted to claim it, and that it was a relevant consideration that the land should be owned by someone rather than left in limbo with continuing uncertainty about title to it.[33]

The facts of *Burton v Walker* are unusual, and it would be rash to suggest that a newly acquired lordship offers a green light to the further acquisition of unregistered land within the historic boundary of the manor as manorial waste. As noted earlier, the ownership of waste is incidental to lordship title, and if title later turns out not to be valid there must, at least, be a question about whether it is just for an owner of land possessed and registered on the basis of that title to retain it.

Verges and roads

Roads, historically, ran across wastes.[34] As they evolved from unmade tracks to public highways with metalled surfaces, they continued to have waste on either side. This was the origin of the roadside verge, which originally was waste owned by the lord of the manor. When a plot of land fronted a road, and the document of title granting the land was unclear on the point, the question arose whether the land adjoined the road or whether it was separated from it by a strip of waste belonging to the lord of the manor. In other words, did the right to ownership of the verge vest in the landowner or in the lord of the manor? This was a question of great practical importance which the courts answered in the early 19th century by finding that there was a *prima facie* presumption of law that waste adjoining a road belonged to the owner of the adjoining land, whether he was a freeholder, leaseholder or copyholder,

33 [2013] EWCA Civ 1228; [2014] 1 P&CR 9.

34 There is a valuable examination of this subject and its historic development through the case law in Jessel, pp.95-103.

and not to the lord of the manor.[35] The presumption remains good law today and can be rebutted by evidence of acts of ownership by the lord.[36] There is a further presumption, again rebuttable, that the owner of land adjoining the highway owns the subsoil beneath it to the mid-point of the highway.[37]

The ownership of a roadside verge may have significant financial value. Where the verge provides access between the highway and adjoining land, ownership of the verge may be critical for the adjoining landowner. If they do not own the verge, or have no adequate right of way across it, then a price may be extracted from the landowner who wants to buy it or secure a right of way over it. In addition to landowners and developers who own land adjacent to a highway but not, where one exists, the verge between them, questions about the ownership of verges typically involve lords of the manor and highway authorities.

The Highways Act 1980, based on statutory provisions stretching back to the Highways Act 1835, provides for the statutory vesting of highways. Section 263(1) of the 1980 Act provides that 'Every highway maintainable at the public expense, together with the materials and scrapings of it, vests in the authority who are for the time being the highway authority for the highway.' The materials and scrapings appear to be whatever is used to make the surface of the road, such as tarmac, gravel or sand.[38] Statutory vesting of a highway in the highway authority operates to vest in the highway authority a determinable fee simple in the surface of the land.[39] Thus the extent of the land vested in the

---

35 *Doe d Pring v Pearsey* (1827) 7 B & C 304; 108 ER 737; *Steel v Prickett* (1819) 2 Stark 463, 171 ER 706; Scriven, p.497.

36 *Doe d Pring v Pearsey* at 308 per Littledale J.

37 Jessel, p.98, citing *Commissioners for the New Towns v JJ Gallagher Ltd* [2003] P&CR 3 (Neuberger J).

38 *Regina (Smith) v Land Registry (Peterborough)* [2011] QB 413 at 419A-B (Arden LJ); [2010] EWCA Civ 200 at [10-11].

39 Ibid, at 419F and at [13], following *Tithe Redemption Society v Runcorn Urban District Council* [1954] Ch 383.

highway authority is the surface of the road and its foundations; and the fee simple comprising the land is not absolute but terminates when the highway ceases to be a highway. It follows from this that the sub-soil beneath the highway normally remains in ownership distinct from the highways authority, and that the owner of the sub-soil has a reversionary interest in the surface of the land if it ceases to be used as a highway.

Section 130(1) of the 1980 Act provides that 'It is the duty of the highway authority to assert and protect the rights of the public to the use and enjoyment of any highway for which they are the highway authority, including any roadside waste which forms part of it.' Whether roadside waste forms part of a highway is a question of fact, and will depend on whether the highway authority[40] has taken possession of or asserted ownership over the waste for the use and maintenance of the highway. It may, for example, have hardened the surface of the waste as part of the highway[41] or it may have let the herbage.[42]

Lords and commons: origins

A common, historically, was a particular kind of waste. Like a waste, it was open, uncultivated and unoccupied; and its freehold was in the lord. At that point however, the similarity ends because, unlike a waste, a common was land where others exercised rights of common over it. Those others were known as commoners, and their rights consisted of entering upon the land to take or use some natural thing found on it. A right of common was therefore in the nature of a profit à prendre; and

40 Or an authority other than the highway authority. See Section 130(2) of the HA 1980 : 'Any council may assert and protect the rights of the public to the use and enjoyment of any highway in their area for which they are not the highway authority, including any roadside waste which forms part of it.'

41 *East v Berkshire County Council* (1911) 106 LT 65.

42 *Coverdale v Charlton* (1878) 4 QBD 104, CA.

it was an incorporeal hereditament. The right had its origins in custom or, if there were long user, was presumed to lie in grant.

A right of common was enforceable in the courts by commoners against the lord if the lord sought to deny it or restrict it. A common was a place where rights of lords and commoners existed alongside each other and could be in competition. 'The lord, by granting rights of common upon his waste, does not thereby exclude himself or his tenants from all use of the waste on which the grant of common is to be exercised, but merely grants to others, in common with himself or his tenants, certain rights upon that waste. All that the lord has not granted remains in him. He may therefore apply the waste to any purpose not inconsistent with the rights which he has previously granted to the commoners.'[43] Thus the lord, as owner of the common, had the same rights over it as the commoners;[44] and he could also do things on it or under it which commoners could not.[45] He could plant trees,[46] dig for sand and gravel, quarry for stone and mine for minerals beneath the waste as well as sport over the waste so long as none of his activities (nor those of his tenants) deprived the commoners of their rights.[47] Those rights could be inconvenienced or abridged to an extent by the lord; and if they were, and the commoners questioned it, they had the burden of proving that the inconvenience or abridgment left them insufficiency of common.[48] By contrast, where the lord (or his tenant, or grantee if the lord had sold the freehold), erected fences to enclose the waste, the burden lay with

---

43 *Arlett v Ellis* (1827), 108 ER 752; 7 B&C 346 at 362-363 per Bayley J.

44 These were not rights of common as such but quasi-rights because a lord could not have rights of common over his own land: see Joshua Williams, *Rights of Common and other Prescriptive Rights* (1880), p.150.

45 A lord could grant any of his rights to be exercised by tenants.

46 *Kirby & Sadgrove* (1797) 126 ER 751; 1 Bos & Pul 13 at 17; *Arlett v Ellis* (1827) 108 ER 752; 7 B&C 346 at 362 per Bayley J.

47 *Arlett v Ellis*, at 362.

48 *Hall v Byron* (1876) 4 Ch D 667 at 680 (per Hall V-C).

the lord (or tenant or grantee) to establish that sufficiency of common remained for the commoners.[49]

Most commons rights owed their existence to and were attached to the homes and land of manorial tenants, whether the tenants were freeholders or copyholders. Entitlement to rights passed with the occupant of the tenancy. In a manor with demesne, arable common fields (worked by tenants), meadows, commons, and waste not amounting to a common, the general effect of the custom of the manor would be that -

- the tenants had individual rights to turn beasts out to graze on the commons (and on the meadows and arable fields when not enjoyed in severalty for growing and harvesting hay and other crops) for defined periods of the year;

- the number of beasts which could be turned out by any tenant was restricted to the number which their holding could support over the winter, described as *"levant and couchant"* on the holding;

- those rights were exercisable in common with other tenants and the lord of the manor;

- the tenants' rights of common *levant and couchant* were 'annexed', 'appurtenant' or 'appendant' to[50] their respective holdings and alienable only as part of their respective holdings.

It was also possible for rights of common to exist in gross, i.e. as a separate (incorporeal) item of property not attached or appurtenant or appendant to any holding; and such rights were freely alienable, and

49 *Arlett v Ellis*, at 370 per Bayley J; and 376 per Littledale J. *Hall v Byron*, LR 5 Ch D 667 at 680; *Robinson v Duleep Singh* (1879) LR 11 Ch D, 798 at 831.

50 In plain language: 'part of'.

exercisable for a fixed number of beasts, there being *ex hypothesi* no dominant tenement by reference to which the *levant and couchant* test could operate.

The 2006 Act describes such rights as being 'attached' to land, but books, reports or documents may describe them as 'annexed', 'appurtenant' or 'appendant' to land. Any distinction now is for most purposes immaterial. However, *appurtenant* rights, which had their origin in express grant, are capable of severance and can, in limited circumstances, become rights in gross.[51] By contrast, *appendant* rights, with their origin in custom, cannot be severed from the land to which they are attached. Some rights were either never attached to land or became severed from the land to which they were attached and became rights in gross, which can generally be freely bought or sold as incorporeal assets.

---

[51] In *Bettison v Langton* [2002] 1 AC 27 the House of Lords held that the Commons Registration Act 1965 placed no restrictions on the common law rule that grazing rights appurtenant to land, if limited to a fixed number of animals, could be severed from the land to which they were attached, thereby converting them from rights appurtenant to rights in gross; and that, on registration under s 15 of the 1965 Act, grazing rights formerly limited by levancy and couchancy became rights to graze a fixed number of animals as noted on the commons register, and could be severed from the dominant tenement and separately disposed of. However, s 9 of the Commons Act 2006 modified the position created by *Bettison v Langton*. It applies to a right of common which is registered as attached to land and, apart from s 9, could be severed from that land. Section 9(2) provides that, as from 28 June 2005, such a right cannot be permanently severed except for the purpose of being transferred, on its own, to any commons council for the relevant land, or to Natural England or the Natural Resources Body for Wales, or as authorised by other legislation. Any instrument which would contravene that prohibition is modified or avoided so as to prevent such contravention (s 9(3) and (4)); and if the dominant tenement is divided, the right of common must be apportioned rateably (s 9(5)). Provision is also made for authorising temporary severance in certain cases of leasing or licensing (Sch 1, para 2).

Lords and commons: from inclosure to regulation

From the mid-17th century, with changes in animal husbandry and the developing pace of the agricultural revolution, lords and landowners sought to improve the productivity of common land by inclosing it. Initially, this was achieved by agreement and then increasingly by private Acts of Parliament; but public general statutes were passed as well. The first was the Inclosure Act 1773, which relaxed the protective regime created by the Statutes of Merton and Westminster II and enabled lords to lease a twelfth of their waste and common with the consent of three-fourths of those with rights of common on the commons or wastes of the manor.[52] After this hesitant and modest start, Parliament next intervened with the Inclosure (Consolidation) Act 1801 which was passed to save parliamentary time and to facilitate enclosure by reducing the cost of private acts. It contained standard terms to go into all private acts but those terms were only effective and binding to the extent that they were not otherwise provided for in a private act.[53] The third major public general statute was the General Inclosure Act 1845, whose importance is less well understood than it deserves to be. The Act introduced procedural changes to reduce time and cost in Parliament but it also brought enclosure, for the first time, under official supervision and enabled officials to make local investigations and impose conditions on enclosure applications which the lord was obliged to accept if he wanted the application to proceed.[54] Official powers included the ability to allot for public purposes a portion of the land contained within the enclosure application.[55] A further Inclosure Act of 1857 protected such land from nuisances or encroachment on pain of criminal sanction (which remains in force

[52] 13 Geo. I c. 81.

[53] 41 Geo III c.109; and see section 44.

[54] The lord could by section 29 veto any proposals made by officials, but if he did then his application would not proceed. See further the discussion of these statutes in chapter 8.

[55] Section 30.

today).[56] From the 1860s the legislative focus saw a change away from enclosure and towards the regulation of commons, in recognition of their value as open space and for recreation. This change denoted a policy whereby the powers and freedoms of lords of the manor to deal with their freehold commons as they wished were progressively diminished, and the process which this change initiated has continued to the present day.

The Metropolitan Commons Act 1866 and the Commons Act 1876 were the first general legislative measures largely intended to protect and manage common land in the interest of local communities rather than inclose it in the interest of lords and landowners. The 1866 Act allowed local authorities within the area of the Metropolitan Police District around London to use income from rates to protect and maintain common lands in their areas.[57] The 1876 Act was more far-reaching. It provided for a measure of statutory regulation whenever common land was inclosed, and parts of it remain in force today. Section 7 required the Inclosure Commissioners to consider whether inclosure applications made to them would be for the benefit of the neighbourhood and to include regulatory terms and conditions about specified matters to ensure that they were.[58]

---

[56] See Inclosure Act 1857 c.31, section 12.

[57] 29 & 30 Vict. c. 122.

[58] 39 & 40 Vict. c.56. Section 7, which remains in force, is set out in chapter 8 at pp.275 below. The Inclosure Commissioners were to prepare a provisional order for submission to Parliament for statutory approval. Perhaps not surprisingly, only 28 enclosures under the 1876 Act took place before 1914. The matters specified under section 7 about which the commissioners could make regulations were "(1) That free access is to be secured to any particular points of view; and (2) That particular trees or objects of historical interest are to be preserved; and (3) That there is to be reserved, where a recreation ground is not set out, a privilege of playing games or of enjoying other species of recreation at such times and in such manner and on such parts of the common as may be thought suitable, care being taken to cause the least possible injury to the persons interested in the common; and (4) That carriage roads, bridle paths, and footpaths over

Two acts at the end of the Victorian era gave significant powers to local authorities to intervene in commons matters in ways that, if not openly challenging lords, imposed further limitations on their ability to use common land within their manors. The Local Government Act 1894 enabled councils in England and Wales to aid persons in maintaining rights of common the extinction of which would, in the opinion of the council, be prejudicial to the inhabitants of the district, and to institute or defend legal proceedings, or take other expedient steps, for that purpose.[59] The Commons Act 1899 extended the scope for intervention further.[60] Section 1 enabled a council to 'make a scheme for the regulation and management of any common within their district with a view to the expenditure of money on the drainage, levelling, and improvement of the common, and to the making of bylaws and regulations for the prevention of nuisances and the preservation of order on the common.' The scheme could 'contain any of the statutory provisions for the benefit of the neighbourhood mentioned in section 7 of the Commons Act 1876.' Section 6 provided for payment of compensation to be made to anyone whose estate, right or interest in a common was taken away or injuriously affected by the scheme. There followed a further Commons Act of 1908, more limited in scope, enabling commoners to apply collectively to the Minister for regulations as to the turning out of entire animals on a common so that it could be better managed.[61]

---

such common are to be set out in such directions as may appear most commodious; and (5) That any other specified thing is to be done which may be thought equitable and expedient, regard being had to the benefit of the neighbourhood."

59 See s 26, which remains in force.

60 62 & 63 Vict, c.30. Section 1, as amended by the Local Government Act 1972, s 179(3), remains in force.

61 See s 1 of the Act, which remains in force.

The Law of Property Act 1925: wastes and commons

The 1925 Act legislated for wastes and commons in terms of title, public rights of access, and restrictions. Its impact on title was described by Lord Templeman in *Hampshire CC v Milburn*:[62]

> The lord of the manor remained entitled to the waste land in fee simple subject to the rights of the commoners. Section 62(3) of the Law of Property Act 1925, repeating section 6(3) of the Conveyancing Act 1881 (44 & 45 Vict. c. 41), provided that a conveyance of a manor should be deemed to include all the manorial rights vested in the lord of the manor, including rights and incidents abolished by the Act of 1922 and including 'commons' which were 'to the manor appertaining or reputed to appertain, or, at the time of conveyance, demised, occupied, or enjoyed with the same, or reputed or known as part, parcel, or member thereof.' So after 1925 it was possible to convey waste of the manor by a conveyance in fee simple or by a conveyance of the manor itself so that the waste passed under section 62(3) of the Act of 1925.

Public rights of access and restrictions were dealt with at sections 193 and 194. The object of section 193, which (unlike section 194) largely remains in force,[63] was explained by the editor of *Wolstenholme and Cherry's Conveyancing Statutes* in these terms: 'to give to the public rights of access to commons and wastelands, which they have assumed in defiance of the law, but to regulate those rights by conditions to be imposed by the Minister of Agriculture with a view to securing a reasonable user of the land.'[64] This suggests the existence of a significant

---

62 [1991] 1 AC 325 at 339-340.

63 Section 193(2) is repealed. The text of s.193 as currently in force is set out in chapter 8 at p.289.

64 *Wolstenholme and Cherry's Conveyancing Statutes* (13th edition (1972) by J.T. Farrand), vol 1, p.321. This interpretation is supported by the terms of (the now repealed) sub-section (2) which gave the lord of the manor or other person entitled to the soil of the common the power to declare by

degree of trespass and perhaps encroachment at the time the statute came into force which the section was designed to control and regulate in the interests of those who owned the freehold, many of whom would have been lords of the manor. Sub-section (1) gave members of the public the right of access for air and exercise to any land which was a metropolitan common,[65] or manorial waste, or a common wholly or partly situated within a borough or urban district,[66] and to any land which at the commencement of the Act was subject to rights of common. This grant was subject to four limitations. First, such rights of access were subject to existing statute or schemes, provisional orders, regulations, byelaws or orders made pursuant to statutory authority. Second, if the lord of the manor or other person entitled to the soil or to commonable rights affecting it applied to the minister, the minister could regulate rights of access to protect existing interests for the purpose of securing reasonable user of the land. Third, rights of access did not include any right to bring vehicles onto such land, or to camp or light fires on it. Fourth, rights of access would end over any land where commonable rights were extinguished by statute or otherwise and where, in the latter case, a local authority, with the minister's consent, decided to exclude the operation of section 193.[67] Sub-section (4) made it a criminal offence for anyone 'without lawful authority' to introduce a vehicle onto the common, or to camp or light fires on it, or to fail to observe any limitation or condition imposed by the minister.[68] Sub-

deed that s 193 applied to the land. Where s 193 applied, the common could be subject to locally imposed regulations and bylaws.

65 Within the meaning of the Metropolitan Commons Acts 1866 to 1898.

66 Immediately before 1 April 1974.

67 Commonable interests could be extinguished otherwise than by statute where commoners agreed a release with the lord of the manor, or where there was an enfranchisement by deed before 1926 where the rights of common were not re-granted and the remaining rights were subsequently released.

68 It may be possible to justify driving on the common as a legitimate exercise of commonable rights if done reasonably and for the purpose, for example, of tending animals or gathering wood or turf.

section (5) stated that nothing in section 193 'shall prejudice or affect the right of any person to get and remove mines or minerals or to let down the surface of the manorial waste or common.' Mining and minerals extraction, and the rights of those entitled to carry out those activities, who would have included lords of the manor, were therefore expressly preserved.

Section 194 of the LPA 1925 imposed restrictions on works on commons and made unlawful without ministerial consent the erection of any building or fence or the construction of any other work which could prevent or impede access to specified commons.[69] The matters which the minister was required to consider before giving consent were those set out in the Commons Act 1876, section 10(3), (4) and (5). Although section 194 was repealed by the Commons Act 2006, authority dealing with it may be useful in considering the application of section 38 of the 2006 Act, which is the successor section to section 194 but defines restrictions differently and in greater detail.

The Commons Registration Act 1965

In 1955 the Royal Commission on Common Land in England and Wales was set up to enquire whether changes in the law were needed to balance the rights of landowners, commoners and the public and 'to recommend what changes, if any, are desirable in the law relating to common land'. The 1965 Act was passed following the Royal Commission's report of 1958.[70] The Act established a scheme for ascertaining what lands were commons and what rights of common were claimed still to exist over them, registering them and extinguishing from 1 August 1970 those rights that were not by then registered with

---

69 LPA 1925, s 194 was repealed by CA 2006, s.56, Sch 6 Pt 2 (with s.60), with effect from 1 Oct 2007 for England and 1 April 2012 for Wales; SI 2007/2584, art. 2(d)(ii) (with art. 3); S.I. 2012/739, art. 2(h) (art. 4). Section 193 has also been partly repealed and amended, albeit differently and at different times in England and in Wales.

70 Royal Commission on Common Land 1955-1958 – Report, Cmnd 462.

the county and county borough councils that were designated as registration authorities.[71] Section 1(1) of the Act made registrable:

- Land which was common land or a town or village green;
- Rights of common over such land;
- Persons claiming or found to be owners of such land.

The Act had no effect on the ownership of title to land, and the process of registering title and charges at HM Land Registry remained unaffected. Section 4 provided that registrations could be made supported by a statutory declaration; no evidence of title was required. Registrations under section 4 were provisional only[72] but if no objection was made by the end of the prescribed period (31 July 1970), then the registration became final.[73] However, if there was an objection it could be referred to commons commissioners for determination. The commissioners were lawyers with extensive property law experience. Under the jurisdiction of the Act, they conducted not a judicial hearing but an inquiry.[74] They presided over hearings between registrants and objectors and gave reasoned decisions that were subject to appeal on a point of law by way of case stated to the Chancery Division of the High Court.[75] If the registrant won, the provisional registration became final;

---

71 Section 2(1). Following the Local Government Act 1972, Sch 30 (which amended the 1965 Act in relation to designation of registration authorities) and later local government re-organisations, the registration authority is normally the county council for the area in which the common land is situated.

72 Section 4(5).

73 Section 7.

74 *In re Yateley Common* [1977] 1 WLR 840 at 843H (Foster J). In practice, an inquiry before the commissioners was like a judicial hearing but without the strict procedural rules that would have applied in court proceedings governing pleadings, evidence and representation.

75 See reg 31 of the Commons Commissioners Regulations 1971.

if the objector won, the provisional registration was not confirmed. Provisional registrations were often withdrawn in the light of objections or earlier decisions of commissioners or the courts. The commissioners did not finish their work until 2010, and their decisions about registration were often based on an understanding of the Act which subsequent court decisions made obsolete after it was too late to re-open the commissioner's decision.

Apart from the question of ownership of land, the Act treated registration of land and registration of rights of common differently. Unless application to register had been made by 31 July 1970, the Act operated to extinguish after that date all existing unregistered rights over common land, including statutory rights of common derived from enclosure awards and public rights of access. Whether the land itself was registered as common or not made no difference to the extinguishment of rights.[76] The status of land and rights once registered was conclusive and could not be challenged. If land was common land at the time the 1965 Act came into force but was not registered, its status as common land was lost.

The definition of 'common land' came in section 22(1) of the Act which defined it as embracing two mutually exclusive types of land: '(a) land subject to rights of common (as defined in this Act) whether those rights are exercisable at all times or only during limited periods; (b) waste land of a manor not subject to rights of common.[77] Section 22(1)(b) was unhappily drafted. It had, and was meant to have, the effect of creating common from land which was manorial waste but had never been subject to rights of common. This definition was of concern to landowners, who were often lords of the manor, because if land which had previously been waste became registered common, it was liable to be made subject to regulations, byelaws and various statutory provisions. This would interfere with the landowner's use and potential

---

76 *Central Electricity Generating Board v Clwyd CC* [1976] 1 WLR 151, Goff J.

77 Section 22(1) is set out below at p.293.

uses of the land and render it less valuable to them. Not surprisingly, landowners made frequent objection to applications for provisional registration. However, if they were unaware of them because they had received no notification from the registration authority,[78] a provisional registration would become final so that the land was subject to unchallengeable rights of common. Rights of common, if not apparent on a reasonable inspection of land, may be a latent defect in title that fall within a vendor's duty of disclosure on sale of the land.[79] This is a problem on sale and purchase transactions because rights of common are overriding interests.[80] Although registrable under the 1965 Act, they cannot be registered under the Land Registration Act 2002.[81] It is therefore important that all parties to any transaction which may involve the sale or purchase of land that was formerly manorial waste should carry out a search of the local commons register.[82]

The 1965 Act permitted unjustified claims to become final if they were not challenged in time. It drew heavy criticism from the Court of Appeal in *Corpus Christi College (Oxford) v Gloucestershire CC* for omissions and obscurities, including the unduly heavy burden of proof placed on commoners, tight time limits, the lack of sufficient provision to amend the register, and the failure to require registration authorities to notify

78 The Act placed no obligation on a registration authority to provide such notification, and in many instances registration authorities did not notify owners of the land because they did not know who the owners were.

79 A defect in title is latent if it is not obvious on a reasonable inspection of the land affected by it: see *Re Gloag and Miller's Contract* (1883) 23 Ch D 320 at 327.

80 They were under the Land Registration Act 1925, s 70(1)(a); and remain so under the LRA 2002: see Sch 1 at paras 3 and 4.

81 See s 1 of the 1965 Act as amended by LRA 2002, Sch 11, para 7(2).

82 See *G&K Ladenbau (UK) Ltd v Crawley and de Reya* [1978] 1 All ER 682, where solicitors investigating title had found no defect but were held negligent for failing to make a search in the Commons Register where a previous conveyance had indicated that part of the land had previously belonged to a lord of the manor.

landowners that an application to register rights of common had been made in respect of their property.[83] Oliver LJ said that the Act and its regulations contained what he described as a 'concealed trap'.[84] If an application was made to register commons rights over land and resulted in provisional registration, it had the further consequence of making the land subject to provisional registration as common land. However, if a successful objection was made to the application to register commons rights, it did not automatically lead to the undoing of the provisional registration of the land as common land. 'So the land is now conclusively presumed to be common land although it is not conclusively presumed to be land subject to rights of common, since those rights have not yet been established.'[85]

Waste land of a manor: the *Box Hill* and *Milburn* cases

The 1965 Act had further consequences. The first and most important was the uncertainty over the definition of common land within section 22(1)(b), which described it as 'waste land of a manor not subject to rights of common'. Did this apply only to waste land of a manor at the time of the application for registration? Or did it apply more widely so that it also included land which had been waste land of a manor in the past but no longer was at the time of the application? Commons commissioners interpreted it in the first, narrower sense; but the courts were initially less certain. In *Re Box Hill Common*, a local authority provisionally registered land which had formerly been part of the manor of Box. The owner objected and the dispute was referred to the chief commons commissioner. He found that the land was open, uncultivated and unoccupied, that it had become severed from the lordship of the manor in 1878, and that no rights of common existed

[83] See Denning MR in *Corpus Christi College (Oxford) v Gloucestershire CC* [1983] QB 360 at 370; Oliver LJ at 370-373; and Carnwath J in *R v Suffolk CC ex p Steed* (1995) 70 P&CR 487 at 489-494.

[84] *Corpus Christi College (Oxford) v Gloucestershire CC* at 372B.

[85] See Oliver LJ at 372B-373B.

over the land. He refused to confirm the registration, finding that the plain meaning of the words in section 22(1)(b) could only apply to land that was owned by the lord of the manor at the time of the application to register.[86] On the local authority's appeal by case stated, Foster J set aside the commissioner's order and confirmed the registration, holding that the land was waste land of a manor within section 22(1)(b). His reason was that, if the land had at some time in the past been waste of the manor, it need not at the date of registration be in the same ownership as the lordship of the manor; and, being such land, it was registrable under section 1(1)(a). On the owner's appeal to the Court of Appeal, the commissioner's decision was restored on the basis that the true construction of the words 'waste land of a manor' in section 22(1)(b) excluded land no longer connected with a manor before the date of registration, with the result that it could not be registered as common land under section 1(1)(a).[87]

The *Box Hill* decision was itself overturned in 1990 in *Hampshire County Council v Milburn* where the House of Lords held that 'waste land of a manor' in section 22(1)(b) meant 'waste land *now or formerly* of a manor' or 'waste land of manorial origin.'[88] The decision frustrated a landowner's attempt to undo the impact of registration on waste land of which he was the lord and freehold owner by the device of severing the ownership of the waste from ownership of the lordship of the manor and then applying to de-register it.[89] The case raised the question of whether land which was registrable at the time of the 1965 Act and was registered could subsequently be de-registered by ceasing to be waste of the manor. The House answered this question in the negative by relying on points that had not been canvassed in *Box Hill.* First, the word 'of'

---

86 *In the matter of Box Hill Common, Box, Wiltshire*, Ref 241/D/56-60 (17 Jan 1977), Mr G.D. Squibb QC.

87 [1980] Ch 109, CA (Stamp, Ormrod and Bridge LJJ)

88 [1991] 1 AC 325 at 344A.

89 The total area of waste was 365 acres of land in north-east Hampshire which would have been more valuable to the owner if its registration as common could be undone.

in the term 'waste land of a manor' should be considered not a genitive of possession but, in the context of the 1965 Act where possession of a manor had become irrelevant to ownership, as a genitive of origin. And second, it was 'impossible to read the [1958] report of the Royal Commission without reaching the conclusion that Parliament intended to prevent waste land ceasing to be common land, so that existing public rights of access would be preserved and so that provision could be made in the future for public access to be granted and schemes of management introduced.'[90] Thus land which was open, uncultivated and unoccupied, held by the lord or anyone else and which *had* been waste but was no longer part of the manor, was registrable as a common and subject to the Act.

Before the *Milburn* decision, the prevailing view of section 22(1)(b) was that it was to be interpreted in accordance with the narrower, more literal sense that had been settled law since 1978. As the Explanatory Notes to the 2006 Act put it, 'Many provisional registrations of common land were cancelled by the Commons Commissioner solely on the grounds of the *Box Hill* judgment or were withdrawn by the applicant for registration in anticipation of cancellation and were out of time or ineligible for appeal following the decision in *Milburn*.'[91] Recognising that the drafting of section 22(1)(b) and its interpretation through the courts had prevented final registration of many areas of common land, government decided to address the problem in further commons legislation. It would do this by introducing measures to enable provisional registrations that had been cancelled or withdrawn to be resuscitated.[92] There was no need to redefine the term 'common land' because it had been done already by way of judicial amendment in *Milburn*.

---

90 [1991] 1 AC 325 at 343C and 343F.

91 See Commons Act 2006, Explanatory Notes at para 120.

92 See p.293 below.

Countryside and Rights of Way Act 2000

The future provision for public access referred to by the House of Lords in *Milburn* came about in the Countryside and Rights of Way Act 2000. The relationship between this Act and the earlier and later Commons Acts needs to be clearly understood by owners of lordships and their advisers. By section 1 of the Act, any land that is a registered common is access land for the purpose of the Act, and by section 2 any person has a right to enter and remain on access land for open-air recreation. Thus a landowner whose waste gets registered as common will find that the public have a statutory right of access to it and over it.[93] A lord who successfully claims unregistered land as manorial waste will find that anyone can register it as common,[94] so that the Act will apply and the public have access to it and over it. If the lord wishes to develop the waste it is therefore important to act quickly before the waste is registered as common. If the waste is registered as common, then any development proposals the lord may have will be subject to the Commons Act 2006, and in addition the lord will probably find it necessary to work with the local authority and other local bodies. If, before the application to register waste as common is made, the land has been developed, improved and brought in hand so as no longer to have the character of manorial waste, it is unlikely to be registered.[95]

The Commons Act 2006

<u>Application</u>

In 2006 a further Commons Act was passed to correct the registration problems in the 1965 Act. It also provided for further regulation of commons by way of protection and management. The registration provisions in Part 1 of the 2006 Act apply to all land in England and

---

[93] Whether the waste was previously common or not.

[94] See p.295 for para 4 of Sch 2 of CA 2006.

[95] See Commons Act 2006 Explanatory Notes at para 118.

Wales except the New Forest, Epping Forest and the Forest of Dean.[96] In England, the registration provisions are at present fully in force only in nine pioneer areas.[97] In Wales, most though not all sections of Part 1 are in force in all areas.[98] The intention is that the whole 1965 Act will be repealed when the 2006 Act is fully in force, but it is unclear when that will be and until then it is necessary to take account of both. For areas in England which are outside the pioneer areas, there is an obligation to interpret references to the registers in Part 1 of the 2006 Act as references to the register in the 1965 Act though without there being any obligation on a registration authority to keep the register up to date.[99] Subject to any local government reorganisation in the interim,

---

[96] CA 2006, s 5. Whether they also apply to land exempted by ministerial order under s 11(3) of the 1965 Act is not yet the subject of any judicial determination. The Explanatory Notes to the 2006 Act say at para 117: 'It may be possible for commons exempted from registration under section 11(3) of the 1965 Act (a list of which appears in annex B) to be registered under paragraph 2 [of Schedule 2 of the 2006 Act]'. The editors of the current edition of *Gadsden* (2020) include Mr Hugh Craddock, who was the official at Defra responsible for the bill which became the 2006 Act. The text of *Gadsden* at pp.162-63 states that Part 1 of the 2006 Act 'contains no provision for exemption of land by order of the Minister. Any land exempted by order under the 1965 Act ceases to be exempted under Part 1, and such land is very likely to be eligible for registration as common land … on an application or proposal under Part 1.'

[97] The areas are (from 1 Oct 2008): Blackburn and Darwen BC; Cornwall Council; Devon CC; County of Hereford DC; Hertfordshire, Kent, and Lancashire CCs; and (from 15 Dec 2014): Cumbria CC and North Yorkshire CC now (following local government re-organisation) North Yorkshire Council.

[98] See https://www.gov.wales/sites/default/files/publications/2021-02/commons-act-2006-sections-in-force.pdf

[99] See Commons Act 2006 (Commencement No.2, Transitional Provisions and Savings) (England) Order 2014 (SI 2014/3026) art.4; Commons Registration (England) Regulations 2014 (SI 2014/3038), Sch 8 para 3. The latter reads: 'For the purpose of this Schedule, any application made to a 1965 registration authority, and any action subsequently taken by that authority, in relation to its register of common land or town or village

there is substantial continuity between the registration authorities appointed under the 1965 Act and the commons registration authorities appointed under the 2006 Act, which are now the London Borough councils or county or county district councils in England and county or county borough councils in Wales.[100] These authorities are to continue to keep the 1965 Act register for the purpose of registering land as common land and for registering rights of common exercisable over land registered as common land.[101]

Regulations introduced in 2014 provided for the maintenance of the registers of common land, including the procedure for applications to amend them under Part 1 of the 2006 Act.[102] The registers can be amended to add new information or amend or remove existing information. Amendments can be made to reflect contemporary changes, mistakes and anomalies, and historic unregistered events.[103] The Regulations apply in full to the nine areas who are required to review their registers to identify anomalies and to process fifteen types of applications. The Regulations partially apply elsewhere in England to allow five types of applications to correct mistakes in the registers. The five types of applications are those for the correction of mistakes made by an authority when it made an entry in the register,[104] and for the removal of certain types of land that was wrongly registered as common

greens before section 1 of the 2006 Act has come into force in relation to the area in which the land is situated shall apply in relation to that land and to any registration made in respect of it in such a register that is maintained for that area under the 1965 Act.' For the introduction of Part 1 to non-pioneer areas, see also Gadsden, pp.150-151, paras 4-02 and 4-03.

100 CA 2006, s 4.

101 CA 2006, ss 1 and 2.

102 Commons Registration (England) Regulations 2014 (SI 2014/3038). The regulations extend to town and village greens. See also the Explanatory Memorandum to the regulations, on which this paragraph is based.

103 See CA 2006, ss 6-15, 19, Sch 2 and Sch 3.

104 CA 2006, s 19(2)(a).

land.[105] The Regulations require applications to be submitted to commons registration authorities, who must refer them to the Planning Inspectorate for determination where the authority has an interest in the outcome of an application. Applications to correct a mistake, or add land to, or remove land from, the registers must also be referred to the Planning Inspectorate if objections have been received from persons with a legal interest in the land.

The legal position created by the registration and other aspects of these statutory arrangements is at best confusing and at worst bewildering.

Registration of new common land and new rights of common

Under the 2006 Act, common land can still be registered;[106] but the Act restricts the circumstances where a right of common can be created in the future. It cannot be created by prescription[107] but can be created by express grant if the right is attached to land.[108] However, it will not operate at law until the right is registered as a right of common and the land is registered as common land. The register remains, as under the 1965 Act, conclusive as to both the status of land as common land and the existence and nature of rights of common over it.[109] The extent of a right of common is left open, and nothing in the 2006 Act affects the

105 Or town or village green. See CA 2006, paras 6, 7, 8 and 9 of Schedule 2.

106 CA 2006, s 3(1).

107 In *R (Littlejohns) v Devon CC* [2016] EWCA Civ 446; [2016] QB 1092 the Court of Appeal held that the effect of section 1(2)(b) of the Act was that, after 31 July 1970, no unregistered rights of common could be exercised over land which was registered as a common, and no effective, exercisable, right of common could be granted over such land; and that, therefore, no right of common over land registered as common land could be acquired by prescription after that date.

108 CA 2006, s 6(3)(b).

109 CA 2006, s 18.

existence of any constraint upon it if the constraint does not appear in the register.[110]

Correcting the commons register

Section 19 of the Act allows anyone who is aggrieved by the register to challenge it by applying to a commons registration authority for the correction of a mistake made by the authority in making or amending an entry in the register, or any other mistake where the amendment would not affect the extent of any land registered as common land or what can be done by virtue of a right of common.[111] 'Mistake' has no precise definition but includes a mistaken omission or an unclear or ambiguous description.[112] An amendment may be made by a commons registration authority either on its own initiative or on the application of any person.[113]

Non-registration or mistaken registration under the 1965 Act

Section 22 of the Act gives effect to Schedule 2, and both are headed 'Non-registration or mistaken registration under the 1965 Act'. Schedule 2 applies only to land and not to rights and contains detailed provisions intended to correct omissions from registration and mistaken registration under the 1965 Act. It is one of the most important parts of the Act for lords of the manor and the paragraphs within Schedule 2 of particular relevance to them are those dealing with

- non-registration of common land (paragraph 2);

---

110 CA 2006, s 18(5).

111 CA 2006, s 19(1) and (2). There is a detailed discussion of the application of s 19 in *Gadsden*, pp.170-74, from which it appears that the scope of a mistake capable of correction under s 19 is likely to be narrow.

112 CA 2006, s 19(3).

113 CA 2006, s 19(4).

- waste land of a manor not registered as common land (paragraph 4);
- other land wrongly registered as common land (paragraph 7).[114]

Amendment of the register under these paragraphs may be made on the application of any person or on a proposal by the commons registration authority itself, and the application or proposal (as the case may be) must be published.[115] Where the application or proposal are disputed, the registration authority may refer the dispute to a planning inspector, whose decision will be amenable to judicial review.[116] Any dispute is likely to turn on whether the conditions required by the relevant paragraph are met: if they are met, the registration authority must alter the register accordingly and has no discretion to do otherwise.

As the Explanatory Notes to the Act point out, paragraph 2 enables 'the registration of land which was specifically recognised by or under an earlier statute as being common land … but which was not registered under the 1965 Act. The criteria for registration as common land under paragraph 2 are set out in sub-paragraph (2) and include the requirement that the land is regulated under the Commons Acts 1876 or 1899, the Metropolitan Commons Act 1866, or a local or personal Act, or is otherwise recognised as common land by or under any other enactment.'[117] There is no specific reference to manorial waste in paragraph 2, but manorial waste which statute has previously recognised

---

[114] Other paragraphs deal with wrong registration or non-registration of town or village greens, or of buildings registered as common land or as town or village greens.

[115] See para 2(3); para 4(6); and para 7(3).

[116] A planning inspector appears to be an unusual legislative choice for resolving what may be a technical legal dispute. However, the relevant Commons Registration (England) Regulations 2014 (SI 2014/3038) do not prevent a planning inspector from appointing a legal assessor. Nor do they prevent a lawyer from being appointed as a planning inspector.

[117] CA 2006, Explanatory Notes, para 116.

as common land is covered by the provision and *prima facie* can be registered.[118]

Paragraph 4 requires a commons registration authority to register as common land any land which at the time of the application or proposal is waste land of a manor. 'Consequently, land which is otherwise eligible for registration under paragraph 4, but which has been developed, improved and brought in hand, or otherwise fails to fulfil the character of waste land of the manor, cannot be registered.'[119] The land must have been provisionally registered as common land under section 4 of the 1965 Act and an objection must have been made in relation to the provisional registration so that the provisional registration was cancelled. That cancellation must have taken place in any of three particular circumstances.

First, the provisional registration was referred to a commons commissioner under Section 5 of the 1965 Act who determined that, although the land had been waste land of a manor at some earlier time, it was not such land at the time of the determination because it had ceased to be connected with the manor, and for that reason only had refused to confirm the provisional registration.[120]

---

118 There may, however, be some doubt in relation to common land exempted under s 11(3) of the 1965 Act. Para 117 of the Explanatory Notes reads: 'For example, a local Act may have defined the extent of a common in a plan deposited with the House authorities during the passage of the corresponding Bill through Parliament, but part (or all) of the lands defined in the plan were overlooked and not registered under the 1965 Act. The amendments will enable the land to be registered, subject to any criteria specified in regulations (which may, for example, restrict application to the owner of the land, or require that the land remains common land at the date of the application). It may be possible for commons exempted from registration under section 11(3) of the 1965 Act … to be registered under paragraph 2.'

119 CA 2006, Explanatory Notes, para 118.

120 Sch 2, para 4(3).

Second, the provisional registration was referred to a commons commissioner under Section 5 who determined that the land was not subject to rights of common and for that reason refused to confirm the provisional registration and did not consider whether the land was waste land of a manor.[121]

Third, the person on whose application the provisional registration was made requested or agreed to its cancellation (whether before or after its referral to a commons commissioner).[122]

Paragraph 7 requires a commons registration authority to remove land from its register of common land where the land was provisionally registered under section 4 of the 1965 Act, was not referred to a commons commissioner under Section 5 so that the provisional registration became final, and immediately before provisional registration the land was neither subject to rights of common, nor waste land of a manor, nor a town or village green within the meaning of the 1965 Act, nor land of the very broad common law description of common specified in section 11 of the Inclosure Act 1845.[123]

<u>Commons Act 2006: Part 2 – Management</u>

Part 2 of the Act deals with the establishment and functions of commons councils, whose overall purpose is to improve the management of commons by way of permanent oversight and regulation. In practical terms, familiarity with Part 2 is important for the owner of the soil of the common, whether lord of the manor or not, because the owner is given opportunity for a role in commons council deliberations and there are matters for which the owner's consent is required. If that opportunity is left unused, the owner's voice is likely to be ignored and decisions may be taken that will leave the land less valuable to the owner than it would have been with their full

121 Sch 2, para 4(4).

122 Sch 2, para 4(5).

123 Sch 2, para 7. See also the commentary in *Gadsden*, p.21 at 1-31.

participation in the statutory process. Where a commons council is established, it is of particular importance for an owner to seek membership of it and then play an active part in it.

In relation to any registered common land, the appropriate national authority may by order establish a body corporate to act as a commons council.[124] For the purpose of doing this it must first publish a draft of the proposed order, invite representations about it, and may cause a local inquiry to be held. It cannot make the order unless satisfied that the representations and the result of any local inquiry indicate 'substantial support' for making the order. In particular, it must have regard to representations received from those having rights in relation to or occupying the land specified in the order, from those entitled to exercise rights of common over the land, and from those with statutory functions relating to maintenance or management of it.[125] The appropriate national authority must by regulations prescribe standard terms as to the constitution and administration of commons councils,[126]

---

124 CA 2006, s 26. The appropriate national authority means the Secretary of State in England and Welsh Ministers in Wales.

125 CA 2006, s 27.

126 CA 2006, s 29. Note that s 29(3) gives the appropriate national authority the power to make an order under s 26 as to the constitution and administration of a commons council. See Defra and Natural England Guidance *Set up a Commons Council* (issued 28 Mar 2015; updated 22 Feb 2016). The Guidance points out that 'the establishment order will set out the categories of voter in your commons council, for example:

- active graziers – people exercising animal grazing rights on the common
- other commoners – people who have a right to graze but choose not to or whose right is not to do with grazing
- landowners

Each category elects or appoints people to represent them.

For example, active graziers and other commoners vote for their own representatives and can't vote in any other category, while landowners usually appoint their representative.' Those eligible to vote for members and can confer upon them functions including the management of agricultural activities, vegetation and rights of common on the land.[127] The commons council must discharge its functions having regard to any guidance given by the appropriate national authority and the public interest in relation to the land for which it is established. Matters of public interest include nature conservation, the conservation of the landscape, the protection of public rights of access to the land, and the protection of archaeological remains and features of historic interest.[128]

As for consent, section 33 provides that where the consent of a person with an interest in the land is required for the commons council to do anything on the land, nothing in Part 2 authorises it to do anything on the land without that consent. Thus if commoners acting collectively would require the consent of the owner to undertake works to improve the drainage on a common, then a commons council would also require the owner's consent to undertake the same activity. However, a commons council does not need the consent of a person with a right of common before doing anything on the land, and it does not need consent for any activity which commoners could themselves undertake without consent. If a person whose consent is required cannot be identified, a commons council can serve notice on them by posting a notice on the land, and if the owner fails to respond to such notice within the time and manner specified in the notice, then consent is deemed to have been given.

---

of commons councils are commoners, landowners or tenants, and 'anyone else with a legal interest in the land the council is responsible for, eg a club with sporting rights.' At the time of writing the Guidance is published online at https://www.gov.uk/guidance/set-up-a-commons-council#establishment-orders

127 CA 2006, ss 29 and 31.

128 CA 2006, s 31(6) and (7).

Commons councils and other bodies: overlapping jurisdictions

The Act recognises that it is legislating for commons at the end of a period of some 140 years where that same thing has been done by public and private acts, local byelaws, regulations, schemes and arrangements, and where some (albeit very few) manorial jurisdictions remain. Section 36 deals with the problem that long-established competing jurisdictions could cause a newly established commons council by giving the appropriate national authority the power to vary, abolish or revoke a very wide series of existing jurisdictions and to do so by ministerial order. Although the Act describes this as a 'Consequential Provision', it is remarkably wide in its potential scope and impact once a commons council has been established and its functions allocated.

The Explanatory Memorandum to the Act puts the matter this way: 'Section 36 addresses potential problems where the functions given to a council might overlap with those of some other body. One example might be a manorial court (*e.g.* a court leet) which still exists in relation to some commons. For example, if a council were to be established encompassing several commons and one of those commons was governed by a manorial court, the section enables the appropriate national authority to alter or abolish that court's jurisdiction in order to remove any conflict of functions. Similarly, an order might make provision for the abolition or curtailment of the functions of a board of conservators in relation to common land.... The power enables the appropriate national body to vary or revoke specific legislation, including any scheme or arrangement in or under a local or personal Act, which relates to the management or maintenance of common land or the exercise of rights over common land.'[129]

What is striking about this passage is the unfettered nature of the power given to ministers in England and in Wales to act by order to end historic local jurisdictions once a commons council is established. The Explanatory Memorandum lumps together manorial courts, boards of conservators and local Acts, but in the case of local legislation the

[129] CA 2006, Explanatory Memorandum, paras 81 and 82.

exercise of power is generally given to local authorities who are accountable to local people. Section 36 enables central government to remove that power from local authorities and to replace it with something else more acceptable to the minister.

Commons Act Part 3: Prohibition on works on commons

Part 3 of the 2006 Act introduces a regime for the control of works on commons which covers works both by private undertakers and by local authorities pursuant to a scheme under Part 1 of the Commons Act 1899.[130] In either case, such works may or may not involve lords of the manor. Lords are likely to be involved if they own the soil of all or part of the common or if they own mineral rights beneath its surface.

The 2006 Act enables anyone to apply to court to injunct prohibited works on common land.[131] There is no need for the applicant to be a commoner or to have any other kind of interest in the land. Specified works are prohibited unless they have received consent from the appropriate national authority; and Part 3 creates a consent procedure, similar to a planning inquiry, which must give approval before otherwise prohibited works can be carried out. Retrospective consent is possible.[132]

Section 38 provides that a person may not, except with the consent of the appropriate national authority, carry out any restricted works on common land. Restricted works are of two kinds. First are those which have the effect of preventing or impeding access to over common land, and such works include the erection of fencing, the construction of buildings and other structures, and the digging of ditches and trenches

130 CA 2006, ss 38-51.

131 CA 2006, ss 38 to 41. The main statutory features of the scheme are set out below. It is important to consult not only the full text of these sections but also any regulations made in England by the Secretary of State or in Wales by Welsh Ministers pursuant to s 40.

132 CA 2006, s 39(7).

and the building of embankments.[133] Second are works for the resurfacing of land which consist of the laying of concrete, tarmac, and coated roadstone or similar material. Works which consist only of the repair of an existing surface of the land made of such material are excluded.[134] Section 38 applies to any land registered as common land, and to any land not so registered which is regulated by an act made under the Commons Act 1876 confirming a provisional order of the Inclosure Commissioners.[135]

General provisions for getting consent for otherwise prohibited works are set out at section 39. Application has to be made to the appropriate national authority, and in determining that application the authority must have regard to four matters: the interests of persons having rights in relation to or occupying common land, and in particular persons exercising rights of common over it; the interests of the neighbourhood; the public interest; and any other matter considered to be relevant.[136] Public interest includes the public interest in nature conservation or landscape conservation, the protection of public rights of access to any area of land, and the protection of archaeological remains and features of historic interest.[137] Procedure for getting consent is not specified in the Act beyond its provision enabling regulations to be made dealing with issues such as the form and content of an application, the evidence and representations in relation to it, the appointment of a person to determine it, and the holding or hearing of a local inquiry.[138]

Power to exempt under section 43 of the Act is given to the appropriate national authority to provide by order that section 38 is not to apply in particular circumstances, where it is satisfied that the works are or are

---

133 CA 2006, s 38(1)-(3).

134 CA 2006, s 38(2)(b) and (4).

135 CA 2006, s 38(5).

136 CA 2006, s 39(1).

137 CA 2006, s 39(2).

138 CA 2006, s 40.

likely to be necessary for use of the land by members of the public for any one of the following purposes: open air recreation pursuant to any right of access, the exercise of rights of common, nature conservation, the protection of archaeological remains or features of historic interest, and the use of the land for sporting or recreational purposes[139] This power can apparently operate whether or not there has been any application for consent.

In the absence of either consent or exercise of the power to exempt, then section 41 provides that if restricted works are carried out on common land then any person may apply to the county court for an order for the removal of the works and restoration of the land to its condition before the works were carried out.[140] Alternatively, where section 38 consent has been given but the works have not been carried out in accordance with any term of that consent, the court may order that they should be and subject to such conditions as the order may specify.[141] The terms of the order are a matter for the court's discretion, and even if the works are held unlawful an order may still be refused. At the time of writing there is not yet any reported case law on section 41.[142]

Lords, vehicles, and restricted works

A lord's interest is likely to be affected in cases of proposed works on or over common land if he is owner of the soil or of mineral rights beneath it. If he agrees with others to enter into an arrangement for development, he needs to address not only the section 38 prohibition on works without consent but also the rights of commoners whose interests may be damaged and any questions about vehicular access over

[139] See s 41(1) to (4) as to what those circumstances are.

[140] CA 2006, s 41(1) and (2)(a).

[141] CA 2006, s 41(2)(b).

[142] The reason for that could be that the jurisdiction is exercised at county court level. It is hard to see why the High Court should refuse jurisdiction in a matter of sufficient value or weight.

the common. Section 34 of the Road Traffic Act 1988 prohibits the driving of mechanically propelled vehicles elsewhere than on roads. Under s 34(1), a person is guilty of an offence if without lawful authority he drives a vehicle onto or upon any common land not being land forming part of a road or on any road being a footpath, bridleway or restricted byway. The issue here is what is meant by 'without lawful authority'. In *Bakewell Management Ltd v Brandwood*,[143] a House of Lords decision concerning section 193(4) of the LPA 1925 (which has similar wording to section 34 RTA 1988),[144] Lord Walker said at [24]:

> The words in subsection (4) "without lawful authority" deserve careful attention. They have been taken, in cases like the present and like *Hanning v Top Deck Travel Group Ltd* (1994) 68 P & CR 14, to refer to an authority given by the owner of the common. They might also, if proviso (a) is applicable, refer to an authority given by some public official or public body pursuant to the Act, scheme, byelaw or regulation in question. But the ability of the owner of the common in question to give

143 [2004] 2 AC 519.

144 Section 193(4) read: 'any person who, without lawful authority, draws or drives upon any land to which this section applies any carriage, cart, caravan, truck, or other vehicle, or camps or lights any fire thereon, or who fails to observe any limitation or condition imposed by the Minister under this section in respect of any such land, shall be liable on summary conviction to a fine ... for each offence.' Despite Lord Walker's application and interpretation of the section, the ratio of the case is that LPA 1925 s.193(4), which made it an offence to drive without lawful authority on a common to which the section applied, did not prevent a person who had contravened it from acquiring an easement by prescription or the doctrine of lost modern grant. While a lost modern grant could not be presumed where an actual grant by the landowner would have been unlawful, there was no requirement of public policy that prevented the acquisition of an easement by long and uninterrupted user in breach of a statutory prohibition where it would have been lawful for the landowner to make such a grant and where such grant would have removed the criminality of the user.

> someone a "lawful authority" to do one or other of the things prohibited by subsection (4), or, indeed, to do one or other of those things himself, is subject, in my opinion, to an important qualification. The owner of a common cannot lawfully do anything on the common that would constitute an unreasonable interference with the rights of the commoners: see section 30 of the Commons Act 1876 (39 & 40 Vict c 56). To do so would be a nuisance: see *Clerk & Lindsell on Torts*, 18th ed (2000) para 31-27. Nor could the owner of a common lawfully authorise things to be done by others on the common that, if done, would constitute a nuisance. The reference to "lawful authority" in subsection (4) does not, therefore, mean that the owner of a common can authorise to be done whatever he pleases. Authority given to too many people to camp on the common and light too many fires could damage the sufficiency of grass on the common for the commoners' grazing rights. If that were so, the authority would not, in my opinion, be a lawful one. Similarly, authority to too many people to drive too many cars or other vehicles over the tracks on the common might not be lawful. It would depend on the facts. But, subject to that qualification, subsection (4) allows the owner of a common to which section 193 applies to authorise the doing of an act that if done without that authority would be an offence under the subsection.

There is, therefore, no lawful authority given for the purpose of RTA 1988 section 34 where a lord gives consent to works on a common which are otherwise unlawful either at common law or by contravening statute. However, there may be circumstances where consent for works is required from a lord who is owner of the soil of a common or of minerals beneath it. Where a local authority has proposed or is proceeding with works on a common which are not only restricted under section 38 of the 2006 Act but are also prohibited by or outside a scheme pursuant to Part 1 of the 1899 Act,[145] the works will require not only section 38 consent but also the consent of the landowning lord.[146]

Lords, legislation and land assembly for renewable energy projects

Developers of renewable energy projects requiring extensive land seek to acquire it from neighbouring landowners, usually by long lease. In the case of wind farms, standard lease arrangements between a landlord as the owner of the freehold estate and the tenant as the company operating the wind farm, will include provisions allowing the tenant to use existing roads, to construct new roads, to create a turbine protection zone, and to comply with the obligations on the landlord relating to third party rights to the extent that those affect the property. Land assembly of this nature may involve not just privately owned land, where the development infrastructure is to be created and sited, but common land as well. If the owner of the common land is identifiable, the developer can approach them to seek agreement. But where the owner is not identifiable, almost certainly due to lack of registration of title either on the land register or the commons register, this is impossible. Wherever access to proposed infrastructure sites is limited, and particularly in upland areas, access over common land may appear to be a convenient solution for the transport of equipment and material needed for the project.

The original ownership of what is now common land was, without exception (unless the land was allodial), vested in the lordship of a manor. If the current owner of the common is not identifiable on the land or commons registers, it may be necessary for anyone concerned with the development to investigate whether the common is or contains land allotted under an award in an annual Inclosure Act made pursuant to the General Inclosure Act 1845. Sections 30 and 31 of the 1845 Act

[145] See Commons Act 1899, s 1(3); and Commons (Schemes) Regulations 1982 (SI 1982/209) Schedule, Form 1.

[146] Commons Act 2006, s 42(5).

gave the Inclosure Commissioners powers to appropriate or allot for public purposes a proportion of the land included in the application for enclosure. These included power to require, as conditions of enclosure, allotments for exercise and recreation for the inhabitants of the neighbourhood[147] and allotments for the labouring poor.[148] Where a provisional order was drafted which did not make such requirements, the commissioners in their annual general report to Parliament had to explain why.[149] Where land was allotted for public purposes, the Act further empowered the commissioners to direct that is should be held on trust for those purposes by the Churchwardens and Overseers of the Poor for the time being in the parish where the land was situated.[150]

In 2018 in a case brought by an allotment holder, *Densham v Charity Commission for England and Wales*, the Upper Tribunal had to consider whether awards comprising allotments of land to the labouring poor made in 1855 and 1862 under section 31 of the 1845 Act had created charitable trusts over the land and whether subsequent legislation had extinguished any such trusts.[151] In holding that a charitable trust had been created and subsisted, the Upper Tribunal explained its reasoning thus:[152]

> Our consideration of the 1845 statutory scheme pursuant to which these inclosure awards were made leads us to the view that Parliament placed particular importance upon the allotment of land for the labouring poor in the social and economic circumstances prevailing at the time. We note that, if no allotment for the poor was to be made in the context of an

147 S.30.

148 S.31. Allotments for the labouring poor were described at s. 34 as 'field gardens'.

149 See ss.30 and 31.

150 S.73.

151 [2018] UKUT (TCC) (Falk J and Judge McKenna)

152 At [56], [57], [59], [64].

inclosure award, the Commissioners were under an obligation to explain publicly why this had not been done… In these circumstances, in the absence of a machinery for the enforcement of rights to land for the labouring poor within the 1845 Act itself, and about a century in advance of effective public law enforcement mechanisms, we can see why the legislative scheme may have permitted reliance on the enforcement of fiduciary obligations through the courts of equity to guarantee the continued availability of the land to those otherwise dispossessed by enclosure.

Such a policy would have to rely upon the creation of a charitable trust, because a non-charitable purpose trust would of course have been void.

The awards in this case were compensatory in nature. The land was derived from owners who would otherwise have benefited from the inclosure, and whilst not obviously a 'gift' in the conventional sense either from the Crown (because it was not Crown land) or from the owners (who may not have felt inclined to bounty, and also received at least some level of rent charge, albeit it seems not equivalent to a full rent), in a broad sense it is a case of Parliament requiring the owners to exhibit generosity in return for being permitted to enclose land.

In our view the 1845 Act established the necessary conditions for the creation of a charitable trust in an inclosure award made pursuant to its authority. Firstly, we note the element of beneficence referred to above. Secondly, we note the dedication of land to the relief of poverty, then being an accepted first-head charitable purpose. Thirdly, we note the express reference to a 'trust' in the act and awards and consider that the draftsman used that word in its technical sense. Finally, as equity does not want for a trustee, it seems to us that the transfer of land to the Churchwardens and Overseers of the Poor to hold 'in trust' had the effect of appointing them as trustees.

Thus the *ratio* of the decision is that land allotted under the 1845 Act to the labouring poor is held subject to a charitable trust. However, it is clear from the 1898 decision of the Court of Appeal in *Simcoe v Pethick* that the same applies, and for the same reasons, in relation to land allotted under section 30 for the purposes of recreation and exercise for the inhabitants of the neighbourhood.[153] When, after an award of 1848, a lord of the manor claimed that allotments for the purposes of exercise and recreation and for the labouring poor had left the land vested in him, the court had no hesitation in deciding that 'allotment' under the Act was part of the award and had the effect of taking the soil from the lord and vesting it in the Churchwardens and Overseers 'in trust for the parish'.[154]

The Commons Act 1876 was described in its long title as 'An Act for facilitating the regulation and improvement of Commons, and for amending the Acts relating to the Inclosure of Commons'.[155] Its preamble stated 'that inclosure on severalty as opposed to regulation of commons should not be herein-after made unless it can be proved to the satisfaction of the [Inclosure] Commissioners and of Parliament that such inclosure will be of benefit to the neighbourhood as well as to private interests, and to those who are legally interested in any such commons'. By section 7 of the Act, the principle of 'benefit to the neighbourhood' became integral to any provisional order in relation to a common that the commissioners were to lay before Parliament. They were required to take the principle into account on every application for enclosure; and when making any order, whether for enclosure or for regulation of a common, they could reserve a recreation ground or, if none was set out, 'a privilege of playing games or of enjoying other

153 [1898] 2 QB 555. There is no reference to *Simcoe v Pethick* in the *Densham* judgment and it does not appear to have been referred to in argument.

154 See 562 per A.L.Smith LJ and 563 per Rigby LJ (Vaughan Williams LJ agreeing).

155 1876 cap.56. The Act became law on 11 August 1876.

species of recreation at such times and in such manner and on such parts of the common as may be thought suitable'.

The consequence of allotments made by Inclosure Commissioners on provisional orders for enclosure under the Inclosure Acts 1845-1868 or the Commons Act 1876 was that, when those orders were confirmed by Act of Parliament, the freehold of the specified land formerly owned by the lord of the manor was conveyed to Churchwardens and Overseers of the Poor on charitable trust for the poor and other inhabitants of the neighbourhood. Where such allotments were made, the land became trust property. Land allotted for exercise and recreation was also protected from encroachment or interruption of its use by section 12 of the Inclosure Act 1857, which imposed (and continues to impose) criminal sanction on those responsible.[156] Now vested in the local parish council or, in Wales, the community council as trustees,[157] the trust comprising the land has from 1876 been subject to the state supervision of the Charity Commission. Section 19 of the 1876 Act imposed limitations on the powers of the Charity Commissioners, stating that 'it shall not be lawful … to authorise the use of or to use any such allotment, or any part thereof, for any other purpose than those declared concerning the same by the Act of Parliament and award, or either of them, under which the same has been set out'. The clarification of the law by the Upper Tribunal in *Densham* suggests that if any land allotted for public purposes under the 1845 General Inclosure Act or the 1876 Commons Act has been subject to encroachment or enclosure, the person responsible for the encroachment or enclosure will have intermeddled with trust matters and made himself a trustee de son tort. That will carry personal liability to account to the beneficiaries, in

156 Section 12 of the Inclosure Act 1857 is set out and discussed at chapter 8 below.

157 See s 189(3) Local Government Act 1972; and s 12 Inclosure Act 1857, making it a summary offence for any person to interrupt the use or enjoyment of land allotted under an inclosure act as a place for exercise and recreation, and giving churchwardens and overseers authority to lay an information before the justices so that such person can be tried before them.

addition to the trustee de son tort holding the trust property or its traceable product as constructive trustee for the beneficiaries.[158] Since the trust created by the 1845 Act is a public charitable trust, its enforcement would be by the Attorney-General.[159] The potential implications of interrupting the use and enjoyment of land allotted for public purposes under an award pursuant to the 1845 or 1876 Acts are clearly serious where, notwithstanding any planning or commons consents previously obtained, the interruption consists of renewable energy development. It is therefore important for those concerned with that development to ascertain the boundaries of the allotted land, the terms of any trust affecting it, and to act accordingly.

---

158 *Mara v Browne* [1896] 1 Ch 199 at 209 (A.L.Smith LJ); *Carl Zeiss Stiftung v Herbert Smith & Co* (No 2) [1969] 2 Ch 276 at 289-291.

159 *Gaudiya Mission v Brahmachary* [1998] Ch 341 at 350 (Mummery LJ); *Weth v Attorney-General* [1999] 1 WLR 686 at 691 (Nourse LJ).

CHAPTER FIVE

MANORIAL MINERALS

Introduction

The term 'manorial minerals' is capable of bearing a number of different meanings and it is important to be aware of the differences between them. While it may be said that all minerals, except those on allodial land, ultimately have manorial origin, the primary sense in which the term is now used relates to those minerals where the party asserting ownership of them claims to derive title from the lordship of a manor. All lands within a manor to which the lord had freehold title could have minerals underneath, and whenever the lord sold such lands privately, or enfranchised them at common law or under statute, or transferred them pursuant to statutory conveyance, the sale or enfranchisement or transfer documents would generally include a reservation of the minerals so that they remained in the ownership of the lord and did not pass to a buyer or transferee. The right of ownership to manorial minerals was, and remains, incidental to lordship title, and passes with the devolution of the title. Those claiming such ownership will need to show that the minerals have not been severed from the lordship title. Manorial minerals are therefore not the same as what may be referred to as 'freehold minerals' usually created by way of exception or reservation on a freehold sale where no manorial element is present.

The second and similar, but more limited, sense of manorial minerals arises in the context of the compulsory statutory enfranchisement of copyhold land under the LPA 1922. The Act provided that any enfranchisement which took place pursuant to it should not affect any right which the lord or tenant had at its commencement in or to any mines or minerals in or under the enfranchised land.[1] Mineral rights arising in this way are considered by HM Land Registry to be 'manorial

1 See LPA1922 Sch 12, para 5, which is discussed at p.287 below.

rights' within the meaning of section 117(1) of the Land Registration Act 2002,[2] with the consequence that they ceased to have effect as overriding interests and lost their priority on a registered disposition of the land if title to them had not been registered by 12 October 2013.

Practitioners dealing with manorial minerals need to start by considering both the value and importance of the minerals in question because the issues are likely to be complex and expensive to investigate. The investigation may begin with the tenurial status of the manorial land or former manorial land in which the minerals lie, and that status may have altered over time. The how, when and why of that alteration will almost certainly be relevant to the issues that practitioner is having to address, which are likely to involve the ownership of manorial minerals and registration issues. If the land is now freehold or leasehold, it may earlier have been copyhold which itself evolved from villein tenure through private Inclosure Acts and a process of common law and statutory enfranchisement until its abolition on 1 January 1926.

For owners and would-be owners of mineral titles, the devolution of title is critical and tracing it is likely to require more research and analysis than is usual on other conveyancing transactions. This is so because the law and practice of modern land registration is unsatisfactory in relation to minerals. The Land Registry's own uncertainty about minerals ownership is reflected in two striking facts: it rarely registers absolute title to mines and minerals,[3] and the scope of the minerals-related indemnity provided under the Land Registration Act 2002 is very limited.[4] An owner or prospective purchaser of

---

2 See HMLR PG 66 'Overriding interests that lost automatic protection in 2013' at para 3.6.3.

3 CP 227, para 3.24; LRPG 65, para 2.2.

4 Paragraph 8 of Schedule 2 to the Act provides: 'no indemnity is payable under this schedule on account of – (a) any mines or minerals, or (b) the existence of any right to work or get mines or minerals, unless it is noted in the register that the title to the registered estate concerned includes the mines or minerals.'

registered land may find evidence that before first registration the land was either copyhold or subject to the rights of a lord of the manor. If so, it may become necessary to investigate documents or private acts of Parliament up to several centuries old. The texts of those documents or acts need to be considered in their historic context, which includes the law as it then stood,[5] with particular attention given to the effect of savings clauses, exceptions and reservations. Lords of the manor were tenacious in defence of their mineral rights when making land grants or agreeing to allotments in Inclosure Acts and Awards, but they were less good at resisting encroachments which gave rise to adverse possession claims. Case law about manors is not easy to understand, dates mostly from the 18th and 19th centuries, and is best approached through the successive editions of 19th century textbook writers and decisions of the senior judiciary of the period who were well versed in it. Case law about minerals falls into two categories. The first is where issues about manorial minerals are involved, and the second is where they are not. When reading the cases, it is important to distinguish between these two categories because canons of construction derived from them may vary according to the category. This in turn could affect a court's approach to the construction of documents or private legislation in a later case.

Manorial mineral rights: creation

Three features of English property law set the context in which mineral rights can arise. First, at common law, the owner of the surface of land owns all the strata beneath as well as the sky above. This is the normal position with freehold ownership, and the consequence is that the surface owner is also entitled to the minerals beneath the surface. However, this is subject to a qualification resulting from the second

5 As Lindley LJ said giving the Court of Appeal's judgment (with Bowen and Fry LJJ) in *Duke of Sutherland v Heathcote* [1892] 1 Ch 475 at 483, 'In order to understand the effect of this deed, it is necessary to carry our minds back to 1783, and construe it as such instruments were construed at that date. We must not forget that in those days a grant did not pass lands, mines, or minerals, although it might confer a right to work them.'

feature: that the ownership of land can be divided vertically. It is possible therefore that a surface owner does not own all the strata beneath the surface. The third feature is that property law doctrines of tenure and estates allow a freehold owner to create concurrent interests in the same land which are less than his own. All three features are present in the Supreme Court's reminder in *Bocardo SA v Star Energy* that it is a well-recognised rule of law that the owner of the surface is the owner of the strata beneath it, including the minerals that are to be found there, unless there had been an alienation of them by a conveyance, at common law or by statute to someone else.[6]

Historically, all lords of non-Crown manors would have been freehold owners of the surface of the land, whether holding directly of the Crown or of a mesne lord. As time passed and lords disposed of land, a grant by a lord could include provision for exception and reservation of minerals. This was typically inserted into grants alienating copyhold land because the grantee received a freehold while the lord retained the value in anything which was known to lie or which might lie on or underneath the land: even loose flints were considered part of the soil, and the soil – i.e. the surface and everything underneath – was in the lord.[7] To later generations, the extent of what the lord retained and was

---

6 [2010] 1 AC 380 at [27] per Lord Hope, with whom the other justices agreed on this point. See also Lord Hope's review of English law and other authorities at [8] to [25] on the proposition derived from Roman law *cuius est solum, eius est usque ad coelum et ad inferos.* At [26] Lord Hope concluded: 'in my opinion the brocard still has value in English law as encapsulating, in simple language, a proposition of law which has commanded general acceptance. It is an imperfect guide, as it has ceased to apply to the use of airspace above a height which may interfere with the ordinary user of land: *Lord Bernstein of Leigh v Skyviews and General Ltd* [1978] QB 479.... But I think that the reasons for holding that the brocard has no place in the modern world as regards what goes on below the surface, even in England, are not by any means as compelling as they are in relation to the use of airspace.'

7 See below at p.151 and chapter 8 generally; Adkin, p.139; and *Dearden v Evans* (1839) 5 M & W 11

entitled to retain over enfranchised copyhold land may seem surprising. The position at common law on enfranchisement was that the grantee copyholder received a conveyance of the freehold, and such a conveyance would pass the minerals beneath the land unless there was a clear exception and reservation of them in favour of the grantor lord. This was the standard approach adopted by lords, and the common law position was reflected throughout the 19th and early 20th centuries in the Copyhold Acts 1841 to 1894 and again in the Law of Property Act 1922, each of which in relation to mines and minerals sought to preserve the situation of the lord and tenant as it was immediately before the enfranchisement. Copyhold tenure had evolved from villein tenure as a creation of the royal courts, and lords of the manor in pursuit of maximising value from their estates were adept at using minerals reservations on the alienation of either copyhold or freehold land or the carving out of leasehold interests.

Mineral rights may arise in different ways, but most commonly by express grant or reservation. HM Land Registry's Practice to the Registration of Mines and Minerals (LRPG 65) lists what the different ways are. There are two broad categories. First are minerals belonging to Crown and public bodies. These include Crown grants, usually with reservations in favour of the Crown; gold and silver; coal, which is vested in the Coal Authority; and oil and gas, which are vested in the Crown by s 1 of Petroleum Act 1998 (in the same terms as s 1(2) of Petroleum Production Act 1934).

Second are rights deriving from manorial ownership and copyhold, and these may give rise to manorial mineral rights which are only imperfectly recorded on HM Land Registry's surface title. There is a series of historic or manorial tenures which could give the owner of land the right to minerals beneath it. These are:

- Ancient demesne, which was confined to lands held in socage of manors belonging to the Crown in the reigns of Edward the Confessor and William the Conqueror;[8]

- Ancient freehold, which was 'a species of customary freeholds in which the freehold is in the tenant';[9]

- Customary freehold, which was a kind of privileged copyhold, with land held according to the custom of the manor but not at the will of the lord;[10]

- Tenant right, a kind of customary freehold found in northern England, where a copyholder had a right of renewal;[11]

- Copyhold

The first four of these will only occasionally be encountered and if they are, then, as LRPG 65 says, it is difficult to know which one. If the tenure was customary freehold, then property in the minerals was in the lord.[12] If the others are encountered, the probability is that the owner of the plot also owns the minerals beneath it, or that a predecessor-in-title once did. However, by far the most important of these tenures is copyhold.

---

8 To determine whether lands formed part of ancient demesne, it will be necessary to consult Domesday Book. See Scriven, pp.36-41; Jessel, pp. 401-03; *Merrtens v Hill* [1901] 1 Ch 842.

9 Scriven, pp.18-19; *Passingham v Pitty* (1855) 17 CB 299, 139 ER 1087.

10 Scriven, pp.14-15; *Duke of Portland v Hill* (1866) 2 Eq Cas 765 at 776 per Page-Wood V-C.

11 Scriven, pp.16-18; *Doe on the demise of Robert Reay v Huntington* (1803) 4 East 271, 102 ER 834 per Lord Ellenborough CJ.

12 *Bishop of Winchester v Knight* (1717) 1 P Wms 447 at 448 per Lord Cowper LC; *Duke of Portland v Hill* (1866) 2 Eq Cas 765 at 776.

Copyhold was a form of tenure affecting large areas of the country before its abolition, and its evolution from villein tenure provided a substantial measure of tenurial security to those who were copyholders, holding at the will of the lord but according to the custom of the manor, which could be upheld in the royal courts. Copyhold tenure was agricultural in origin and nature and gave the tenant the right to cultivate the surface and to graze his animals on the wastes and commons on the manor and to take certain types of specified minerals from beneath the copyhold land to use for the erection and repair of buildings and walls on the land. When lords sold land to copyholders so that the freehold, previously in the lord, was transferred to the tenant and the copyhold became extinguished, there were usually clauses saving and excepting out of the grant the mines and minerals and reserving to the lord and his successors the right to win them and take them away. The lord retained everything under the land, and typically the newly enfranchised freeholder would covenant that neither he nor his successors-in-title would dig for or get any of the specified minerals except for the purpose of improving or repairing the enfranchised premises or erecting new ones on the land.[13] Before the abolition of copyhold tenure in 1926, the most common situation governing the ownership of mines and minerals under copyhold land was that the property in the minerals and the sub-soil containing them were with the lord but the lord could not work them without the consent of his tenant. In 1876 in *Eardley v Granville*,[14] Sir George Jessel MR explained what he took as long-settled law:[15]

> The estate of a copyholder in an ordinary copyhold (for it is an estate) is an estate in the soil throughout, except as regards for this purpose timber-trees and minerals. As regards the trees and minerals, the property remains in the lord, but, in the absence of custom, he cannot get either the one or the other, so that the

13 See, for example, the precedent for a deed of enfranchisement in *Watkins on Copyholds* (4th edn, 1825), pp.455-64.

14 (1876) 3 Ch D 826

15 At 832-33, and at 835.

> minerals must remain unworked, and the trees must remain uncut. The possession is in the copyholder; the property is in the lord.... If a stranger takes the minerals, the copyholder can bring trespass against the stranger for interfering with his possession, and the lord may bring trover, or whatever the form of action may be now, against the stranger to recover the minerals.... [I]f the lord takes away the minerals, the copyholder becomes entitled to the possession of the space where the minerals formerly were, and he is entitled to use it at his will and pleasure.
>
> Where a freeholder grants lands excepting the mines, he intends first of all as a matter of construction, to except not merely minerals, but the portion of the subsoil containing the minerals; in other words, to retain a stratum of the property. And if he does that, of course the lessee or grantee has no title whatever to the portion of the stratum reserved. That is all that the case of *Duke of Hamilton v Graham*[16] decided. It decided that the same law applies to Scotland which applies to England. In a case like that the word mines meant subsoil containing the minerals, and not merely the minerals themselves.

Although copyhold was not abolished until 1926 the process of enfranchisement, by which copyhold was converted into freehold, had been operating for hundreds of years before that. Land could be sold out of a manor as freehold or retained and leased, and in the relevant grant there would almost certainly be a reference to ownership of mines and minerals. On enfranchisement of the copyhold, whether under the Copyhold Acts 1841-1894 or the LPA 1922, the position of the lord and tenant regarding mines and minerals was generally preserved by way of appropriate reservations implied by the relevant Act, but sometimes it was specifically dealt with by the parties at the time of enfranchisement in the enfranchisement deed. Enfranchisement of copyhold land at common law operated as a conveyance or release of

16 (1871) 9 M (HL) 98.

the fee simple to the copyholder, and the mines and minerals usually passed to the freeholder (formerly the copyholder) unless they were dealt with otherwise in the deed. It is not always apparent from deeds of enfranchisement whether the enfranchisement was at common law or under one of the Copyhold Acts.[17]

Thus with former copyhold land the source of rights to mines and minerals beneath the surface is either a deed made at common law or pursuant to one of the Copyhold Acts or, alternatively, to the statutory enfranchisement of the 1922 Act which expressly preserved the lord's and the tenant's then existing right to mines and minerals.

A further source of mines and mineral rights creation may be an Inclosure Act or Award. As LRPG 65 puts it:[18]

> Where land was the subject of an Inclosure Act or Award[,] the ownership of the mines and minerals may be dealt with by that Act or Award. The inclosure may have taken place as long ago as the 1700s and may not be referred to in later deeds but will still determine questions of ownership.

This brief statement from HM Land Registry guidance demonstrates the importance of the distant past in determining the ownership of mines and minerals today, but it makes no allusion to the difficulty of identifying and locating the relevant Inclosure Act and Award and the even greater difficulty in understanding it. The Parliamentary enclosure movement covered a period of over 300 years, and there were some 5,341 private acts in England and 229 in Wales. Most acts, though not all, were followed by awards which redistributed lands held within a manor, often including waste, and allotted it as freehold, leasehold or copyhold. Reading the text of an award and understanding its plans and annotations is hard enough, and matching the plans to modern maps or

---

17 LRPG 65 at 3.2.

18 LRPG 65 at 3.6.

plans is likely to require expert assistance from a surveyor skilled in Geographic Information Systems techniques.

Manorial mineral rights: devolution

The manorial system began its progressive decline in 1290 with the end of sub-infeudation and the introduction of the right to free alienation of land enacted by the *Quia Emptores* statute, which remains in force today. Land sold by a lord out of a manor went out of the manor for ever,[19] and there were instances of land grants where the property in mines and minerals was given to the grantee or where no reference was made to mines and minerals at all (which produced the same result). But more common was the situation where lords, on disposal of their lands by grant, sought to retain their property in the mines and the minerals by means of exceptions and reservations in the grant. Since the grantee was to have actual physical possession of the land in which the mines and minerals were or might be, clauses containing exceptions and reservations were of limited practical value should the lord wish to exploit the mines and minerals unless there was further provision in the

19 *Delacherois v Delacherois* (1862) 11 HL Cas 62 at 102, 11 ER 1254 at 1269 per Lord St Leonards: 'Now, as we have seen, this land was held by the lords in fee simple, and they conveyed it as such. If the demesne lands of a manor are treated by conveyance as a distinct property, they cease to form part of the manor, although the rents and dues may remain: for example, a fine formerly levied of them, and the same estate taken back, would have severed them. Where the fee was in a grantee originally, the lord had only the seigniory, which he held in common cases of the Crown. The land ceased to form part of the demesnes, and was held by a freehold tenant of the manor. If ultimately the lord repurchased the land, he thereupon became the fee simple owner of it; and he held not of himself (for a man cannot be lord and tenant), but he held this portion now of the chief lord. It had lost its character of demesne land, and there being no tenant of it, it is no longer held of the manor. There is no custom which attaches to it. The lord is simply seised in fee, as he was before the grant was made; but it is no longer really part of the manor, although in common parlance it may be so termed.'

grant for the lord to have access to and to work, win and get the minerals and remove them from the grantee's land. If there was such provision, then a question arose about compensation to be paid to the grantee if the mines and minerals were exploited and, if so, for how much. This question became acute when mining operations by A damaged the surface of B's land where, decades before, both their predecessors in title had received their lands and rights under the same instrument. Clauses dealing with these matters appeared not only in land grants but also in private Inclosure Acts, and their importance to the parties was such that their construction and effect were often litigated through the courts.[20]

The use of exceptions and reservations was made by lords because the devolution of ownership of manorial minerals took place through the devolution of the lordship title itself. Minerals were incidental to lordship title and not a separate asset from it. They only became so if the lord had specifically alienated the minerals or had sold land out of a manor without making exceptions or reservations. Investigation of ownership of manorial minerals today is very likely to involve tracing the devolution of the lordship by reference to grants or vesting assents passing landed estates down the generations.

---

20 See the decision of the HL in *Rowbotham v Wilson* (1860) 8 HLC 347 (Lords Wensleydale, Brougham, Chelmsford, and Kingsdown, with Campbell LC saying he agreed with the result, not after hearing argument in the case before the House of Lords, but because he had presided over the court of Exchequer Chamber below from which Mr Rowbotham had appealed without success). The case concerned the effect of a clause made under the award of freehold allotments under a private Inclosure Act of 1770 which entitled A to minerals under B's land and to carry out mining operations beneath it without liability for damage to the surface. On the wording of the clause concerned, the HL found that A's successor in title was not liable. Although the decision was not specifically about the construction of a minerals reservation clause, later courts looked at the compensation provisions in such clauses as a guide to the interpretation of words about mineral reservations and the meaning of the term 'mines and minerals'.

Inclosure Acts

Inclosure Acts would normally contain minerals reservations in favour of the lord, and as private acts are to be construed in the same way as private agreements.[21] The exercise of construction should take account of the intentions of the parties as collected from the words used by the legislature,[22] and the act must be 'construed as a whole, each part considered as it bears upon and affects every other, and should its language in any part of it not be clear and unambiguous, one must search in the preamble for a guide to the meaning of the obscure provisions.'[23] Account must also be taken of the surrounding circumstances at the date of the act [24] and the law, including the canons of construction used in the courts, as it stood at the time of the act.[25] Inclosure Acts had promoters who were named in the act. 'So far as persons not concerned in the Act are concerned, the Act is read strictly against the promoters; so far as the promoters themselves are concerned

---

21 *Rowbotham v Wilson* at 363 per Lord Wensleydale (Lords Brougham, Chelmsford, Kingsdown and Campbell LC agreeing).

22 *Townley v Gibson*, (1788) 2 Term Rep 701 at 705 (Lord Kenyon CJ).

23 *Thomson v St Catharine's College, Cambridge* [1919] AC 468 at 485 (Lord Atkinson)

24 *Rowbotham v Wilson* at 363.

25 *Duke of Sutherland v Heathcote* [1892] 1 Ch 475 at 483 per Lindley LJ (dealing with a minerals reservation of 1783). See also *Consett Waterworks Company v Ritson* (1889), reported at [1922] 2 Ch 187 per Lord Esher MR at 188: 'the Inclosure Act [of 1773] is passed and we have to construe it .... as we have so often said, as if we had to construe it a day after it was passed.' The question in *Ritson* was whether successors-in-title to freehold allottees of land under the act had the right to have the surface unmolested where the act gave power to the lord of the manor and his successors to search, win and work for reserved minerals under the land 'without paying any damages or making any satisfaction for so doing.'

it is read as a contract between them and is to be construed accordingly.'[26]

Together with these general principles of statutory construction, *Scriven* identified another that was applicable to Inclosure Acts. 'The general purpose of Inclosure Acts being to give to the commoners (or others) the surface for cultivation, what these acts do not for this general purpose take away from the lord, as incident to his ownership of the soil of the waste, remains in the lord, *nempe*, his right to the minerals within or under the waste, whether such minerals be workable by mines or by quarries, that is to say, whether they are mines of coal, iron, etc, or are freestone quarries.'[27] The text of the passage quoted appeared next to the marginal note: 'minerals under or within inclosed lands – right of lord to, when not expressly taken away.' The use here in *Scriven* of the term 'general purpose' assumed that the Inclosure Act in question contained effective provision for excepting and reserving the minerals in favour of the lord. If it did not, the transfer of land to allottees under the Act was of freehold and carried the minerals with it. This had been established in 1788 in *Townley v Gibson*.[28]

Savings, exceptions and reservations

In *Townley v Gibson* the Court of King's Bench had to interpret the savings clause in an Inclosure Act of 1777. The Act divided and enclosed the common, wastes and common fields of a manor, with part of them given to the lord in lieu of her right and interest in the soil, and the rest

---

26 *Harper v Hedges* (1924) 93 LJKB 116 at 117 per Scrutton LJ.

27 *Scriven*, p.308. The authorities relied on by *Scriven* for this passage were *Wainman v Earl of Rosse* (1848) 2 Ex 800 (Court of Exchequer Chamber) affirming Parke B (later Lord Wensleydale) at first instance in the Court of Exchequer (1845) 14 M&W 858 at 872; *Micklethwait v Winter* (1851) 6 Ex 644; *Pretty v Solly* (1859) 26 Beav 606 (Sir John Romilly MR); *Place v Jackson* (1824) 4 D & R 318 (Abbott CJ). The same passage had appeared in the 6th edition of *Scriven*.

28 (1788) 2 TR 701, 100 ER 377.

allotted to the several tenants of the manor in fee simple, discharged from all customary tenures. The savings clause reserved to the lord all seignories incident to the manor, and all rents, fines, services and all other royalties and manorial jurisdictions whatsoever in the common and waste grounds, in 'as full, ample, and beneficial manner, to all intents and purposes, as she or they [her successors-in-title as lord] might or could have held and enjoyed the same, in case this Act had not been made.' The question for the court was whether the lord was entitled to the mines under the savings clause allotting the enclosed lands to the tenants of the manor. Their answer was no. Lord Kenyon CJ, saying that private acts of Parliament are to be construed according to the intention of the parties, found that mines were not a distinct right from the right to the soil where they were under the land of the lord of the manor. 'In cases of copyholds' he went on, 'a lord may have a right under the soil of the copyholder: but where the soil is in the lord, all is resolvable into the ownership of the soil; and a grant of the soil will pass everything under it.... There is no doubt but that the mines might have been reserved. If it had been so intended, it would have been by express words; but there is no such reservation here.' The mines were part of the soil, and property in the soil passed to the grantees as freeholders. Everything that was intended to be reserved was expressed, and all those rights were incorporeal hereditaments and not corporeal hereditaments like mines. Thus the exception in the savings clause was not broad enough to save them.[29]

Townley v Gibson shows that mines under freehold land vested in the lord are part of the soil, and that if they are not to pass on transfer of the freehold then the savings provision[30] must be clearly expressed to extend to the soil containing the mines as a corporeal hereditament. The savings clause in the 1777 Inclosure Act extended only to incorporeal hereditaments by way of reservation and not to corporeal hereditaments by way of exception.

---

[29] See also the judgments of Ashurst J and Grose J.

[30] In the instrument concerned, whether act, award or deed.

The basic distinction between an exception and a reservation in a contract[31] for the transfer of land is that an exception must be a parcel of the thing granted whereas a reservation issues out of the thing granted.[32] When construing exceptions and reservations clauses in relation to mines and minerals, it is in every case a question of construing the contract as a whole; and the distinction referred to above applies whether the contract is for the grant of a freehold or leasehold interest. In 1871 in *Duke of Hamilton v Graham*, Lord Hatherley LC (with whom the majority agreed) explained the distinction and its legal consequences in this way: [33]

> The law of England, I apprehend, is this, – when you demise a property, saving and accepting out of the demise a certain part of that property – for instance, if you demise the surface, and save and except the minerals, then there is no demise of the minerals whatever to the lessee of the rest; the person who takes the interest in the surface has no ownership in the minerals. The general rule which prevails when a property is demised, that is demised in absolute right, that the whole property *usque ad coelum* in the one direction, and *ad inferos* in the other direction, belongs to the person who is the owner of the property, is at once intercepted when you find certain strata of the property reserved and excepted out of the demise, so that these strata remain in the lessor, and he has not parted with them, or transferred them to the lessee. The lessor has as full, complete, and perfect interest in them, and they are as much his own property as before the demise was made. The lessee takes no interest or right whatever in them. If on the other hand… you

31 Or Inclosure Act. As Lord Kenyon said, private legislation was to be construed according to the intention of the parties.

32 *The Durham and Sunderland Railway Company v Walker* (1842) 2 QB 940 at 967 (Court of Exchequer Chamber per Tindal CJ).

33 (1871) 9 M (HL) 98 at 102. The appeal was from Scotland, but on this point the House of Lords held that English law and Scottish law were the same.

> reserve certain rights and interests parting with the property, whether you use the word 'except' or not (there is no magic in words), the thing done is this – you have parted with the property, the right reserved cannot therefore be an exception out of what you granted, because you have not excepted any part of the property but the whole is disposed of, and when you reserve or except a right (whatever phrase you choose to use for that purpose), it is in effect a right which must enure to you by way of regrant from the person to whom you make the disposition of the whole property.

Thus if a lord upon a transfer of land wanted to retain an interest in mines and minerals beneath the surface he could do so in one of two ways. Either he could except the mines and minerals from the transfer, so that they were not conveyed at all and he retained an estate in fee simple in the mines and minerals. Or he could reserve an incorporeal right in the minerals by way of a *profit à prendre*, which would be a new right created at the time of the conveyance. The choice between exception or reservation was normally critical and has consequences which may determine the question of ownership today.

Where the reservation is not of minerals but of a mine or quarry, then a mine or quarry is properly the subject matter of an exception but not of a reservation because a reservation issues out of the thing granted. Where a mine or quarry purports to be reserved, it is in fact excepted, because it cannot be the subject-matter of a re-grant to the grantor.[34] Thus – confusingly – the clause containing the exception or reservation may begin with the words 'excepting and reserving', or with the word 'excepting' when it is a reservation, or with the word 'reserving' when it is an exception. The drafting is crucial. In *Duke of Sutherland v Heathcote*,[35] the Court of Appeal had to interpret a clause 'saving and reserving [to the Duke's predecessors-in-title] full and free liberty by all

---

[34] Robert Forster MacSwinney, *The Law of Mines, Quarries and Minerals* (2nd edn, 1897), pp. 216-17.

[35] [1892] 1 Ch 475.

necessary ways and means to search for, get, dig, drain, and carry away, the coal, ironstone, and minerals which may or shall be found within the several lands hereby granted'. It was held that the reservation did not operate as an exception of the minerals but only as a grant by Heathcote's predecessor-in-title of a right to work them; that there was nothing to show that this right was to be exclusive; and that it did not prevent Heathcote from working them so long as he did not disturb the Duke in any working which the Duke was carrying on. Heathcote had therefore not infringed the Duke's rights, and the Duke's claim for an injunction to restrain him from working the minerals failed. Lindley LJ explained: 'a *profit à prendre* is a right to take something off another person's land; such a right does not prevent the owner from taking the same sort of thing from off his own land; the first right may limit, but does not exclude, the second. An exclusive right to all the profit of a particular kind can, no doubt, be granted; but such a right cannot be inferred from language which is not clear and explicit.'[36]

A similar kind of problem to the Duke of Sutherland's arose a century and a half later in *ARC Aggregates Ltd v Branston Properties Ltd*, where the court followed Lord Hatherley LC's analysis of exceptions and reservations and applied it in a dispute about the drafting of a transfer of freehold property. ARC had excepted mines and minerals from the transfer and claimed that it retained a freehold estate in them; whereas the developer Branston argued that the transfer conveyed to itself the corporeal fee simple in the soil of the property and everything beneath the soil, so that there was reserved to ARC merely an incorporeal easement, right or privilege in respect of the mines and minerals. If so, Branston argued, any encroachment upon the mines and minerals while creating the foundations for building development would not constitute a trespass. The court rejected Branston's argument, making a declaration in ARC's favour that it was the freehold owner of the mines and minerals but leaving open the question whether ARC was entitled

36 At 484.

to an injunction to restrain Branston from encroaching on the minerals.[37]

Dates of mineral reservations

When courts today have to construe mineral reservations it often happens that the reservation in question appears in a document made decades or even centuries before. The meaning of words may change over time. In 1842 in *Shore v Wilson*, Coleridge J was one of ten judges asked by the House of Lords to consider the meaning of words in deeds from the early 1700s setting up a charity. He said:

> When, therefore, we are called on to construe deeds of the years 1704 and 1707, it seems to me that we are not only at liberty, but are bound, to inquire what at that time was the meaning of the phrases used in them; not taking for granted, because they bear a certain clear meaning now, that they did so then; and we are also, I conceive, bound to inquire whether at that time they bore any technical or scientific sense; and if so, we must judge from the context whether in the particular instance they were used in that sense.[38]

The phrases in issue concerned the theologies and contemporaneous language of different church denominations within the Christian faith, but where the words are terms used in mineral reservations in contracts drafted by lawyers, whether Inclosure Acts or Awards or land grants, it becomes necessary to interpret them in the context of the law at the time. In 1889 in *Consett Waterworks Company v Ritson*, the Court of Appeal had to construe an Inclosure Act of 1773. Lord Esher MR said: 'the Inclosure Act is passed and we have to construe it .... as we have so

37 [2020] EWHC 1976 (Ch), Zacaroli J.

38 9 Cl & Fin 355 at 528; 8 ER 450 at 519.

often said, as if we had to construe it a day after it was passed.'[39] In 1891 in *Duke of Sutherland v Heathcote*, another division of the Court of Appeal had to construe a mineral reservation in a deed of exchange of 1783. Delivering the judgment of the court, Lindley LJ said: 'In order to understand the effect of this deed, it is necessary to carry our minds back to 1783, and construe it as such instruments were construed at that date. We must not forget that in those days a grant did not pass lands, mines, or minerals, although it might confer a right to work them.'[40] Thus the exercise of construction involved analysing not just the words but the law at the date of the Inclosure Act or deed, together with the relevant background. In these respects, at least, the approach of the senior Victorian judiciary to contractual interpretation was not far removed from the modern approach which takes as its starting point Lord Hoffmann's speech in *Investors Compensation Scheme Ltd v West Bromwich Building Society*.[41] More recently, as explained in the Supreme Court in 2017 by Lord Hodge in *Wood v Capita Insurance Services*: text and context are used as tools to ascertain the objective meaning of language used in the contract. 'The extent to which each tool will assist the court in its task will vary according to the circumstances of the particular agreement or agreements.'[42] The further back in time the contract was made, the more likely it is that the background to the contract will have to be investigated. 'Since a contract must be interpreted according to its meaning at the date when it was made, it ought to follow that the relevant background is likewise to be

39 [1922] 2 Ch 187 at 188. Lord Esher MR was sitting with Lindley and Lopes LJJ.

40 [1892] 1 Ch 475 at 483.

41 [1998] 1 WLR 896 at 912-913.

42 *Wood v Capita Insurance Services Ltd* [2017] AC 1173 at [8] to [15] and per Lord Hodge at [13], considered and applied by the Court of Appeal in the manorial minerals case of *Wynne-Finch v Natural Resources Body for Wales* [2023] 3 All ER 162 at [29] per Henderson LJ giving the judgment of the court.

ascertained by reference to the date at which the contract became binding on the parties.'[43]

The implications of applying this guidance to text and context should not be underestimated when dealing with a manorial minerals reservation in a land grant or Inclosure Act made in the 19th century or before, when conveyancing law and practice as well as landholding arrangements were very different from today. It was not until the Real Property Act 1845 came into force that the freehold of corporeal tenements and hereditaments, which included open mines or quarries, could be transferred by grant.[44] Before that, a freehold conveyance took effect only on livery of seisin.[45] Thus while land containing mines or quarries, opened or unopened, could be transferred, it was not possible to transfer unopened mines or unopened quarries by themselves where, in the absence of knowledge about them, livery of seisin was impossible. Apart from conveyancing formalities, the transfer of land had to accommodate two difficulties largely unknown today. The first was that, where land was held in family settlements, the tenant for life could be liable for waste to those entitled in remainder or reversion. Diminution in value of the freehold could trigger an action for waste against a tenant for life; and such diminution would occur if land was sold at too low a price. Here lay the second difficulty. Fixing the correct price required accurate pre-sale valuation by the vendor's surveyor, but the problems of valuing land beneath the surface – in other words, the sub-strata which might (or might not) contain minerals – made the valuer's task more complex and increased the risk of inaccurate valuation. Valuation was required not only before selling land but also when it came to calculating the extent of areas of land to be exchanged or allotted under Inclosure Acts or Awards. The easiest and cheapest

---

[43] Sir Kim Lewison, *The Interpretation of Contracts* (8th edn, 2023) at 3-170; *BlueCo Ltd v BWAT Retail Nominee Ltd* [2014] EWCA Civ 154 at [75] per Briggs LJ.

[44] 8 & 9 Vic c.106, s 2. The Act came into force on 1 October 1845.

[45] MacSwinney, *The Law of Mines, Quarries and Minerals* (2nd edn, 1897), p.216, n.2.

way of conducting the valuation, or the calculation for an Inclosure Act or Award, was to avoid valuing the sub-surface by excepting it from the sale, exchange or allotment. The exception took the form of a minerals reservation so that if anything of value or use to the vendor or his successors in title was subsequently discovered beneath the surface, its benefit would remain in them, its financial value could be properly calculated, and there would be no risk to the tenant for life of liability for waste. So well established was this thinking that the mechanism for minerals reservations and subsequent valuation was incorporated in the extensive parliamentary legislation of the 1840s dealing not only with enclosure but with the discrete and different subjects of copyhold enfranchisement and compulsory purchase.

Soil

'Soil' in an Inclosure Act includes the surface and everything below it down to the centre of the earth. But this is only its *prima facie* meaning, and what it actually means will depend on the construction of a particular act.[46] 'Soil' could have a wide meaning and a narrow meaning, but lack of clarity in an Act led to courts being asked to determine which applied. In 1859 in *Pretty v Solly*,[47] Sir John Romilly MR sitting in the Court of Chancery had to construe an Inclosure Act of 1804 which contained a section reserving to the lord of the manor 'all manorial rights, except the right to the *soil*, and enacts that he may thenceforth hold and enjoy all rents… "and all *mines*, minerals, quarries" … incident to the Manor ("except clay and the right to the soil as aforesaid"), as if the Act had not been made.' [Emphasis in original] Noting that '[soil] *prima facie* … would include everything above or below it', he distinguished *Townley v Gibson*,[48] where the court had held that mines were part of the soil, on the basis that throughout the 1804

46 MacSwinney (2nd edn, 1897), p.31.

47 (1859) 26 Beav 605, 53 ER 1032

48 Where the court had held that mines were part of the soil, Grose J saying (100 ER 377 at 380): 'now what are the mines but part of the soil?'

Act the word 'soil' had been used differently from the word 'land' so that it was equivalent to 'surface'. The lord had therefore lost his right to the surface of the land, which had been allotted to commoners in severalty, but had not lost his right to the mines and minerals beneath it.

In *Master and Fellows of St Catharine's College Cambridge v Rosse*, the same, narrow meaning was attributed to 'soil' in the operative part of an Act where its recital stated that the lords were 'owners of the soil of the commons and wastes within the manor, and of the mines and minerals therein', with its operative provisions transferring some of the commons and wastelands to the lords and the residue to allottees in severalty – but otherwise remaining silent as to mines and minerals. The Court of Appeal held that the allottees of the commons and wastes took an estate in fee simple only in the surface of their allotments, the underlying mines and minerals being reserved to the lords.[49] While the Court of Appeal had based its decision on the content of the recitals, the House of Lords thought the recitals did no more than make clear that the lords' rights as owners of the soil included minerals; and so it overturned the Court of Appeal by finding that the meaning of 'soil' had not been cut down and that the minerals had passed to the allottees.[50]

Mines, minerals and quarries

The term 'mines and minerals' and the individual words 'mines' and 'minerals' have no standard definition in English law. As Lord Watson said in *Glasgow Corporation v Farie*, 'mines and minerals are not definite

49 [1916] 1 Ch 73 (Lord Cozens-Hardy MR, Bankes, Warrington LJJ), upholding Neville J (see Lord Cozens-Hardy at 86) at first instance where the case was reported as *Master and Fellows of St Catharine's College, Cambridge v Greensmith* [1912] 2 Ch 280.

50 [1919] AC 468. The HL affirmed the CA's decision on the second point, agreeing that the lords of the manor were not entitled to let down the surface of the land for the purpose of working minerals beneath.

terms: they are susceptible of limitation or expansion, according to the intention with which they are used.'[51] The term and words occur very widely in manorial documents and title documents, as well as in private and public statutes which may or may not relate to manorial minerals. Where the words 'mines and minerals' occur, sometimes with individual minerals identified and sometimes followed by words such as 'any other minerals', it is in every case a question of looking at the particular words used and deciding from the context their meaning and effect.[52]

The word 'quarry' also has no standard definition but it 'usually implies surface working of minerals, leaving no roof overhead.'[53] There is, however, imprecision depending on what is extracted. 'The word "quarry" is, no doubt, inapplicable to underground excavations; but the word "mining" may without impropriety be used to denote some quarries.'[54]

---

51 (1888) 13 App Cas 657 at 675.

52 This is explored at length in the next chapter.

53 *Halsbury's Laws* (2024), vol 76, para 4.

54 *Glasgow Corporation v Farie* (1888) 13 App Cas 657 at 677 (Lord Watson). The difficulties which courts have in distinguishing between mines and quarries is illustrated from the (dissenting) speech of Lord Herschell in the same case (at 683-684): 'What, then, is the interpretation to be put upon the word "mines"? I think the primary idea suggested to the popular mind by the use of the word is an underground working in which minerals are being or have been wrought. It is certainly often used in contrast to "quarry", as indicating an underground working as opposed to one open to the surface. But to limit it in the enactment we are construing [section 18 of the Waterworks Clauses Consolidation Act 1847] to an underground cavity, in which minerals are being or have been wrought, would be obviously inadmissible. The enactment was clearly intended to extend to minerals lying underground which had hitherto been undisturbed.'

Mineral reservations in public general statutes 1841-1922

Acts affecting copyhold

A century on from the abolition of copyhold tenure in 1926, the provisions about minerals in the Copyhold Acts 1841 to 1894 are little known. Yet they remain important. In relation to mineral reservations in favour of lords on enfranchisement of copyhold land, they preserved rights which may still be enforceable today. These rights are often unregistered, and the context of registration and non-registration is explained by HMLR Practice Guide 65 as follows:

> Rights in respect of mines and minerals reserved to the lord on enfranchisement (whether under section 48 of the Copyhold Act 1852, section 23 of the Copyhold Act 1894 or paragraph 5 of Schedule 12 of the Law of Property Act 1922) do not fall within section 1(1)(a) of the Law of Property Act 1925 but rather within section 1(2)(a) of the Law of Property Act 1925. Such rights cannot be registered with their own title under section 3(1)(a) of the Land Registration Act 2002. Where there was a custom of the manor that the lord was entitled to enter the copyhold land of the tenant and take the minerals, it may be possible to register the rights reserved to the lord on enfranchisement under those Acts under section 3(1)(d) of the Land Registration Act 2002, but only when the rights are profits à prendre in gross.[55]

For the content of the reserved rights it is necessary to go to the Copyhold Acts themselves. The 1841 Act, whose long title was 'An Act for the commutation of certain manorial rights in respect of lands of copyhold and customary tenure', provided that no commutation under it 'shall operate to affect any rights of lords of manors to … any rights in mines and minerals or quarries within or under the said lands and hereditaments, or any other manorial rights whatever, unless expressly

[55] HMLR PG 65: *Registration of mines and minerals* (updated 6 April 2018), para 1.

commuted under this Act.'[56] The decision to commute rested with the lord and not the copyholder,[57] and was therefore voluntary. Where there was such commutation, the lord's rights in mines and minerals remained unaffected unless lord and copyholder agreed otherwise.

Two further Copyhold Acts were passed in 1843 and 1844, the long title of each of them respectively stating that the purpose was to amend and explain the act or acts before. The 1843 Act provided that commutation or enfranchisement of copyhold lands could be made 'either wholly or in part for the consideration of a conveyance of lands parcel of the same manor as the lands commuted or enfranchised … or any right to mines or minerals in or under such lands, or any right to waste in lands belonging to such manor.'[58] The 1844 Act varied the scope of the 1843 Act by providing that consideration for commutation or enfranchisement could be extended to lands or to any right to mines and minerals outside the manor provided that, in the opinion of the Copyhold Commissioners, they could be conveniently held with the same manor.[59]

The 1852 Act contained much more significant changes. First, a power of compulsion was given to both parties, enabling lord or copyholder to compel enfranchisement (at their own cost) in the manner set out under the Act.[60] This required appointment of a valuer to calculate the sum to

56 Copyhold Act 1841 (4 & 5 Vict. c. 35), section 82. It was passed on 21 June 1841.

57 It was referred to as 'The Voluntary Enfranchisement Act': see *Kerr v Pawson* (1858) 25 Beav 394; 53 ER 687.

58 Copyhold Act 1843 (6 & 7 Vict. c. 23), s. 1. The Act became law on 27 June 1843.

59 Copyhold Act 1844 (7 & 8 Vict. c.55), s.5. The Act became law on 29 July 1844.

60 Copyhold Act 1852 (15 & 16 Vict. c.51), s.1. Its full title was 'An Act to extend the provisions of the acts for the commutation of manorial rights, and for the gradual enfranchisement of lands of Copyhold and Customary Tenure'. It became law on 30 June 1852.

be paid to the lord by the copyholder for enfranchisement.[61] The Act permitted both lord and copyholder to appoint valuers, and for the Copyhold Commissioners to determine any dispute between them as to the correct level of valuation.[62] The valuers were required under section 16 to take into account all relevant circumstances relating to the land, and lawyers advised lords to be cautious about reliance on valuers in relation to mines and minerals. Rolla Rouse, barrister and author of a leading practitioner text on copyhold enfranchisement and valuation, wrote in his commentary on section 16: 'On the part of lords of manors generally, it will be advisable not to include rights in mines, minerals, etc., which, under section 48, are not to be included without consent, unless a fixed sum is agreed on as the compensation in respect of such rights, as it may be imprudent to trust to the allowance of valuers.'[63] For those lords who were tenants-for-life under family settlements and impeachable for waste, there was a strong incentive to exclude minerals upon enfranchisement by means of a broad minerals reservation.

A second change introduced by the 1852 Act concerned the term defining mines, minerals and quarries. The term 'rights in mines and minerals or quarries' in the 1841 Act was abandoned at section 48 of the 1852 Act for 'rights to any mines, minerals, limestone, lime, clay, stone, gravel, pits, or quarries'. Whatever estate or rights a lord or copyholder had in these before enfranchisement were not to be affected by enfranchisement.[64] These words, and the substance of the provision,

---

61 Copyhold Act 1852, sections 3 to 9, and 16.

62 Copyhold Act 1852, ss 3 and 9.

63 Rolla Rouse, *The Copyhold Enfranchisement Manual* (2nd edn, 1858), p. 231. The book was published by Butterworths and went through a number of editions.

64 Copyhold Act 1852, s.48. In *Kerr v Pawson* (1858) 25 Beav 394; 53 ER 687, Sir John Romilly MR had to compare s.82 of the 1841 Copyhold Act with s.48 of the 1852 Copyhold Act. He said (at 407; 692): 'The difference between the two Acts being, that under the first Act the enfranchisement is not to affect those [mineral and other] rights of the lord "unless expressly commuted," and under the second they are not to

were repeated in section 23(1) of the Copyhold Act 1894 and then in the LPA 1922 at paragraph 5 of Schedule 12. The expansion of the wording in the 1852 Act, its retention in the 1894 and 1922 Acts, and the continuing applicability of the wording today is significant.[65] Copyhold land that only became freehold in 1926 will still be subject to the wording contained within the 1852 Act reservation. After 1852, when the legislature had decided to clarify by way of expansion the content of mineral rights which remained with the lord after enfranchisement, it became necessary to protect the position of the owner of the lands enfranchised by ensuring that the mineral rights reserved to the lord did not jeopardise the owner's ability to exploit and enjoy what had become his freehold. This protection came six years later and was conferred by section 14 of the Copyhold Act 1858:

> After enfranchisement, whether under the voluntary or compulsory proceedings of 'the Copyhold Acts', the owner of the lands so enfranchised shall, notwithstanding any reservation of mines and minerals in the said acts or in any instrument of enfranchisement contained, have full power and right to disturb or remove the soil so far as may be necessary or convenient for the purposes of making roads or drains or erecting buildings or obtaining water upon the said lands:[66] provided always, that this shall not prejudice the rights to any mines or minerals, or to

---

be made the subject of any commutation at all and are not affected in the slightest degree.'

65 LPA 1922 Schedule 12, at paragraphs 4 to 7, dealing with the effect of enfranchisement, is no longer in force, but its effects remain. See p.285 below.

66 In a commentary on the 1858 Act at p.264 of the 1858 edition of his *Copyhold Enfranchisement Manual*, Rolla Rouse noted at this point: 'The Copyhold Bill of 7th June contained also the words 'or for digging stone or brick or other earth to be used upon the land enfranchised, or for any other purpose necessary or convenient to the full enjoyment, improvement, or cultivation of the land enfranchised,' but these words were afterwards struck out, and the proviso as to mines, etc., introduced.'

work and carry away the same, which were reserved by section 48 of The Copyhold Act 1852.

This section was re-enacted as the proviso to section 23(1) of the Copyhold Act 1894 and later, in the LPA 1922, as the proviso to the Twelfth Schedule, paragraph 5.[67]

These changes made by the 1852 and 1858 Copyhold Acts, which still applied to land enfranchised when copyhold was abolished in 1926, suggest that the legislature was trying to strike a balance between the rights of lords as mineral owners and the rights of surface owners of lands enfranchised under the Acts. Where conveyances of enfranchised land contained broadly drafted mineral reservations in favour of a lord, the practical difficulties which such reservations created for the surface owner were considerable. Although he may have acquired the land more cheaply if the price paid left out of account the value of any minerals underneath, any disturbance of the surface and immediate sub-surface which the new owner needed for his buildings or cultivation of his land exposed him to an action from the lord for trespass and damages. Section 14 was intended to protect him from this by enabling him to disturb or remove soil for specified purposes, but the extent of that protection was strictly limited in order to leave the lord as far as possible with his mineral rights and their value intact.[68]

---

67 For paragraphs 4 to 7 of LPA 1922 Schedule 12, see p.287 below.

68 There is a valuable commentary on what had been section 14 of the Copyhold Act 1858 in its substantive re-enactment as the proviso at section 23(1) of the Copyhold Act 1894: see Archibald Brown, *The Law and Practice of Enfranchisements and Commutations* (3rd edn,1903), pp.226-27. The publisher of this practitioner text was Butterworths. Brown's commentary is set out below at pp.282.

The General Inclosure Act 1845[69]

The protection given by this Act to the lord's right to mines and minerals on inclosure was equal to if not greater than that given by the Copyhold Acts. Although an inclosure scheme had to be prepared and submitted by way of application to the inclosure commissioners appointed under the Act, who examined it and had the power to make changes, the lord nevertheless retained a power of absolute veto. The commissioners could not proceed to an inclosure on an application unless the lord gave his consent.[70] It would have been surprising in these circumstances if the legislature had limited the lord's rights to minerals beneath land that had been his waste prior to inclosure. Thus the breadth of the statutory mineral reservation was very widely drawn, and did nothing to cut down what lords had previously been able to do by means of a private Inclosure Act. The Act provided by section 98:[71]

> That in every Case in which the Right to all or any of the Mines, Minerals, Stone, and other Substrata under any Land inclosed under this Act shall exist as Property distinct and separate from the Property in the Surface, and shall not be compensated upon the Inclosure, the Right and Property in such Mines, Minerals, Stone, or other Substrata, and all Rights and Easements auxiliary to or connected with the Exercise or Enjoyment of the Right and Property in such Mines, Minerals, Stone, or other Substrata shall be in no wise affected by the Inclosure ...

This applied to the situation where, before the application for inclosure, the lord owned the minerals as part of his ownership of the land to be inclosed. The section left no doubt that there was a distinction between the surface and everything beneath it, described as the substrata, and

69 For a recent and helpful discussion of the general operation of the 1845 General Inclosure Act, see *Densham v Charity Commission for England and Wales* [2018] UKUT 402 (TCC).

70 Section 29; and *Musgrave v Forster* (1870-1871) LR 6 QB 590 at 594 (Cockburn CJ, Blackburn and Lush JJ).

71 Section 98 is set out in full below at p.271.

that if there was no compensation to the lord for his mines, minerals, stone and substrata, then everything beneath the surface remained vested in him. It is probably safe to assume that no lord gave his consent to an inclosure application made under the 1845 Act unless either he received adequate compensation for his property beneath the surface or that inclosure of his waste and its allotment to others was subject to the statutory minerals reservation. Moreover, the express conferral on the lord of all rights and easements associated with sub-surface extraction put his powers of working on a statutory basis.

The compulsory purchase legislation of 1845-1847

A third category of legislation affecting landowners' mineral rights in the 1840s came in a series of consolidating acts intended to facilitate the compulsory purchase of land where a private local act was obtained for its acquisition for public purposes, such as the construction of a railway, gasworks or reservoir. The first of these acts was the Lands Clauses Consolidation Act of 1845, and separate acts were passed for England and Wales, and for Scotland, to deal with railways whose routes passed through towns and countryside where landowners complained that their property was being invaded. The provisions of these consolidating acts, which of course were public general acts, had previously been inserted into private acts but involved considerable delay and expense. For the future they could be incorporated by reference when the private act giving Parliament's approval for the project was passed.[72] Unlike the Copyhold Acts 1841 to 1844 and the General Inclosure Act 1845, the

72 The 1845 Acts were prepared and passed by the second government of Sir Robert Peel, which ran from September 1841 to July 1846. This was, therefore, legislation passed by a Conservative government with a majority in the House of Commons and the House of Lords, and whose members were generally more sympathetic to the landed interest than to industrial interests. For the political and economic context of the 1845 Acts, see the passage on 'Parliament and the Railways' in Sir Llewellyn Woodward, *The Age of Reform, 1815-1870* (Oxford, 1962), pp.43-47.

consolidating acts were not confined to manorial mineral rights and reservations addressed mineral rights and reservations generally.

The consolidation acts provided statutory mineral reservations in favour of the landowner whose land was being acquired by the railway company or other undertaking. Using language to define minerals in similar though not identical terms to that used in the Copyhold Acts 1841-1844 and the Inclosure Act 1845, the mineral reservations were again widely drafted. Thus section 77 of the Railways Clauses Consolidation Act 1845 (1845 c. 20) provided:[73]

> The Company shall not be entitled to any Mines of Coal, Ironstone, Slate, or other Minerals under any Land purchased by them, except only such Parts thereof as shall be necessary to be dug or carried away or used in the Construction of the Works, unless the same shall have been expressly purchased; and all such Mines, excepting as aforesaid, shall be deemed to be excepted out of the Conveyance of such Lands, unless they shall have been expressly named therein and conveyed thereby.

The scheme of the English and Scottish Railways Clauses Consolidation Acts was explained by the House of Lords *in Great Western Railway Company v Bennett* (1867) LR 2 HL 27 and again in *North British Railway Company v Budhill Coal and Sandstone Company* [1910] AC 116, where Lord Loreburn LC said: 'it is an advantage to railway companies that on acquiring lands for their enterprise they are not compelled to purchase minerals lying thereunder, and may wait and enjoy the support until the mineral owner requires them either to purchase the minerals or to take the risk of forfeiting the support'.[74]

---

73 There was a corresponding provision at s 70 of the Railways Clauses Consolidation (Scotland) Act 1845. Sections 78 and 79 of the English Act and 71 and 72 of the Scottish Act provided a mechanism enabling the minerals owner to serve notice on the railway company with a request to work the minerals and for compensation to be paid to the owner if the request was refused.

74 At 126.

Lord Gorell said: 'The sections are to regulate the rights of railway companies who purchase land with the object of making a permanent line of railway with necessary works on the land, and the rights of owners of the land who sell to them. The object of the companies is to obtain such an interest as will enable their lines and works to be properly constructed and maintained. For this they do not require to take the benefit of mines of minerals and the exploiting thereof, and therefore an exception of these is made so that an owner thereof, who may not at the time his land is taken know whether it does or does not contain minerals, can either work the minerals, or, if a company does not wish him to do so for fear of injury to their line and works, they may prevent him from doing so by paying him adequate compensation'.[75]

Manorial minerals: ownership disputes

The ten-year deadline imposed by the LRA 2002 for the registration of manorial rights generated a great deal of activity by landowners to register manorial mineral rights. HMLR treats a seignorial right to minerals as one of the lord's rights preserved under the LPA 1922, and so the loss of priority given to that right (which could destroy its value) was a matter which individual owners and trustees of landed estates had to address before the expiration of the deadline on 12 October 2013. But there has never been, and is not now, any requirement for a minerals estate to be registered. The types of registration prompted by the LRA 2002 included a unilateral notice (registered by the minerals owner against the surface owner's title) and, in the case of unregistered land, a caution against first registration. The evidential requirements for the registration of a notice or caution are simpler than those for the registration of a freehold minerals estate, and where these types of registration have manorial origin the notice or caution may reflect a claim to minerals lying beneath manorial waste while the claim to register an estate is almost certainly based on a specific minerals reservation contained within a grant or Inclosure Act. The party

[75] At 129-130.

applying for registration will need to establish either that they are the lord of the manor or that they are the successor in title to the lordship of the lord who was party to the original grant.

The land in respect of which the application is made will usually be a freehold estate whose owner has hitherto believed that he is entitled to everything beneath the surface of his land. For the owner of a residential suburban plot who receives notification from HMLR of an application to register a notice or caution against that plot, there is probably little to worry about unless, perhaps, there was a custom of the manor that the lord retained a right to enter, win and work minerals on or underneath the land.[76] Even if the applicant claiming ownership of the minerals could establish title to them, the surface freehold owner has possession of the land in which they are contained, and they cannot be extracted without his consent. But for owners of larger plots who are developers or who intend to develop the land, the position may be much more serious. They may find themselves subject to a claim for trespass or damages or both, and their own title documents may expressly exclude the minerals or may be subject to an express reservation of the minerals in favour of a third party. There are companies as well as private individuals with a business model of acquiring lordships which carry the right to waste and any minerals lying beneath that waste, or of acquiring rights contained in minerals reservations in historic grants made by lords of the manor. Even if the award of an injunction or damages for such a company or individual is unlikely, there may still be financial advantage for them in pressing a claim because of its nuisance value.

The validity of claims to rights of this nature can be challenged in various ways, and whatever form of challenge is adopted will require extensive documentation from public sources and, perhaps, private archives. First, if the right is based on lordship title, the title should be investigated to confirm that it is genuine. Whether lordship titles are registered or unregistered they can be challenged, although where the

76 Although even this would be subject to a freeholder's right to support.

title is registered the burden of proof will clearly rest with the challenging party and may be difficult to discharge. If the lordship title is unregistered, then the burden of proof for establishing its validity rests with the party asserting title and again, depending on the circumstances, may be difficult to discharge. If the right is based on a mineral reservation within a grant or Inclosure Act, then it will be necessary to interpret the scope of the reservation to identify what minerals may be available to the applicant, and what powers of working to get them and what rights to compensation for the surface owner are involved. Any ambiguities in the reservation will be construed in favour of the surface owner, and a court will be reluctant to allow the surface to be damaged by the minerals owner. In 1919, referring to the Court of Appeal in Chancery decision of 1872 in *Hext v Gill*,[77] Lord Atkinson in *Thomson v Master and Fellows of Saint Catherine's College Cambridge*[78] said, 'I think it clearly establishes that … where no power to work the mines is expressly or impliedly conferred and the only power to work them is derived from the mere fact of ownership of them, the surface owner cannot be deprived of the support of the surface to which he is entitled as of natural right. Nor can that surface be destroyed, however necessary both may be for the commercial or other working of the mines.' In such a situation, neither the minerals owner nor the surface owner can exploit the minerals without the consent of the other.

Manorial mineral owners seeking an injunction or damages for trespass against surface owners for interference with minerals will need to do a good deal more than establish title. It will be necessary to establish the location, extent and value of the minerals, and each of these questions will require expert input. Value will be net value because of the need to subtract the cost of extracting the minerals, and a further discount may be required for such sum by way of profit as would have induced a third party to undertake the extraction.[79] The credibility of any mineral

77 (1872) LR 7 Ch 699.

78 [1919] AC 468 at 494.

79 *A-G v Tomline* (1877) 5 Ch 750 at 768 per Fry J; and (1880) 15 Ch 150, CA (James, Cotton, Thesiger LJJ).

owner's claim against a surface owner may also depend on the requirement for minerals planning permission from the relevant mineral planning authority.[80] Despite these difficulties facing a mineral owner advancing a claim, the mere existence of the claim creates a problem for developers who have started or intend to start commercial or residential development. Funders and prospective purchasers will need to be informed of the claim and reassured, while negotiations with the minerals owner could invalidate the developer's existing or proposed insurance even if the negotiations were designed to obtain a release of the mineral owner's rights.

Adverse possession of manorial minerals[81]

Minerals do not constitute a freehold estate separate from the surrounding soil unless they have been severed from it by reservation, whether on a conveyance by a lord of the manor to the purchaser of a freehold of land previously in the manor, or within an Inclosure Act, or on the enfranchisement of copyhold land either voluntarily or by statute. The impossibility of conveying minerals until 1845 except by livery of seisin, and a tenant for life's concern to avoid liability for waste on a claim by a reversioner, created a situation where grants or transfers of manorial land almost invariably contained mineral reservations in favour of the lord.[82] The effect of the reservation was to create two

[80] Either the County Council, the unitary authority, or the National Park authority. Government Guidance states: 'Minerals extraction may only take place if the operator has obtained both planning permission and any other permits and approvals. These include permits from bodies such as the Environment Agency, and licences from Natural England and, in relation to coal resources, the Coal authority.' See *gov.uk/guidance/minerals#minerals-overview* (published 17 October 2014; accessed 9 Sept 2024).

[81] On the subject of adverse possession of minerals, there is a valuable analysis in Stephen Jourdan KC and Oliver Radley-Gardner, *Adverse Possession* (2nd edn, 2011), p.254 et seq.

[82] *Townley v Gibson* (1788) 2 TR 701; 100 ER 377 was a notable exception to this because the draftsman of the 1777 Inclosure Act in that case failed

separate estates in and beneath the same area of land. The landowner owned the surface and everything beneath it that was not included within the minerals estate. Where a minerals estate had been created, the extent of it depended on the terms of the reservation. The consequence was, as Lord St Leonards explained in the 1862 edition of his book, *Real Property*, that 'the grantee of the land enjoyed the lands, but possession of the land is not possession of the mines which became a distinct inheritance on the severance of the two estates.'[83] Thus neither a surface owner nor a squatter who may acquire possession of surface land after the expiration of a limitation period will automatically acquire possession of the minerals beneath it if the land was subject to an earlier minerals reservation. However, he may acquire some of those minerals if the wording of the reservation was not sufficient to keep them with the lord.

Cases today of adverse possession of manorial minerals will normally require investigation of the relationship between the terms of the mineral reservation and the facts surrounding the surface owner's occupation of the land. The surface owner will own all those minerals beneath the land that are not included within the reservation. But where minerals are included in the reservation, he will not succeed in a claim for adverse possession of them unless (on normal adverse possession principles) he has both factual possession of them and the requisite intention to possess.[84] Factual possession in this context will involve exploitation of the minerals themselves. If only one or some of the minerals reserved have been exploited, there will be no adverse

---

to understand that at common law the right to mines and minerals was not distinct from the right to the soil: see Lord Kenyon CJ at 705, 379. Without express words in a minerals reservation clause, the right to mines and minerals could not be retained under a general reservation of seignorial (i.e. lordship) rights.

83 Lord St Leonards, *Real Property* (1862) p.33.

84 On the principles set out by the House of Lords in *J.A.Pye (Oxford) Ltd v Graham* [2002] UKHL 30 at [40]; [2003] 1 AC 419 at 435, 447.

possession of others which have been reserved but not exploited.[85] Similarly, although it may be a question of fact and degree, if the surface owner exploits a particular mineral in one area of his freehold but not the same mineral in a different area, there may be no adverse possession of the mineral concerned in that different area.[86]

Cases of high authority from the 19th century suggest that adverse possession must be open so that it is obvious to a reasonably careful owner. In the House of Lords in 1879, Lord Blackburn in *Lord Advocate v Lord Blantyre* discussed the principles for assessing evidence in adverse possession claims.[87] 'The weight of each act as evidence depends on the circumstances; one very important circumstance as to the weight being, whether the act was such and so done that those who were interested in disputing the ownership would be aware of it…. This is what is very clearly explained by Lord Wensleydale (then Baron Parke) in *Jones v Williams.*' In that latter case, Parke B had said that if acts relied on in support of adverse possession 'are done in the absence of all persons interested to dispute them, they are of less weight.'[88] The same view was taken in the minerals case of *Earl of Dartmouth v Spittle*, where Kelly CB held that trespass to mines 'committed underground' for over twenty years and 'without the knowledge of the then owner of the mines' did not amount to adverse possession; and Pigott B, agreeing, said that 'the trespasses committed by the defendant in the present case have not the same legal effect as an adverse possession of the surface.'[89] If disputing a claim to adverse possession of minerals, this line of authority may assist a lord or his successor in title who is the legitimate

---

85 *Curtis v Daniel* (1808) 10 East 275 at 276-77 per Lord Ellenborough CJ and Bayley J; 103 ER 779-780; *Wynne-Finch* [2020] EWHC 1924 at [194(i)] per Falk J.

86 See *Glyn v Howell* [1909] 1 Ch 666.

87 (1879) 4 HL 770 at 791-792. Although a Scottish appeal, Lord Blackburn made clear that the principles applied as much to English law as to Scottish.

88 (1837) 2 M & W 326 at 332; 150 ER 781 at 784 (Court of Exchequer).

89 (1871) WR 444 at 445 (Court of Exchequer).

owner of minerals beneath the surface of land that is or was manorial waste, but who is unaware of a trespasser (probably the surface owner) extracting the minerals because the extraction process is difficult or impossible to observe.[90]

Manorial minerals, mining and the Duchy of Cornwall

Manors in Cornwall often have particular characteristics which distinguish them from those in other parts of England and Wales. Mining and minerals working in Cornwall was historically for tin and, much later, china clay.

Issues affecting tin mining were regulated by the Stannaries Courts,[91] pursuant to royal charters of 1201 and 1305 granting special privileges to tin-miners in return for payment of dues. Stannary law recognised a right of tin-bounding – i.e. laying a claim to mining rights over land by cutting turf and laying stones to mark the area. The rights applied mainly to waste land but were sometimes exercisable over other land. From the 16th century, mining leases (or 'setts') were granted. Customary law allowed tin-miners to cut entrances to mines through land belonging to others, and to divert streams and foul water in the course of mining operations. Mining for other minerals did not fall under their specialist jurisdiction. After the abolition of the Stannaries Courts pursuant to the Stannaries Court (Abolition) Act 1896,[92] their specialist jurisdiction was transferred to the county courts. The customs, laws and practices of tin mining and tin-bounding formerly adjudicated in the Stannaries Courts will be taken account of and applied by the

90 This appears to have been part of the factual matrix in *Wynne-Finch v NRBW* but the remarks about adverse possession of both the first instance judge and the CA were *obiter* because the claimants' case failed on the ground that mudstone was not a mineral within the reservations of an Inclosure Act of 1816 or conveyances of 1919. Adverse possession, therefore, did not arise.

91 In Devon as well as in Cornwall.

92 59 & 60 Vict c.45.

civil courts (at County Court or High Court level depending on the value and complexity of the case).

Manors in Cornwall were more likely to be coastal, which today may raise questions about ownership of foreshore, but the presence of royal manors owned by the Duchy of Cornwall remains an important feature. The historic lands of the Duchy since its creation in 1337 were inalienable until the Duchy of Cornwall (No 2) Act 1844 (also known as the Assessionable Manors Act).[93] Its long title was 'An Act to confirm and enfranchise the Estates of the Conventionary Tenants of the ancient Assessionable Manors of the Duchy of Cornwall, and to quiet Titles within the County of Cornwall as against the Duchy; and for other Purposes.' The Act applied to the lands within the 17 assessionable manors where the Duke was the lord and where certain tenements, known as 'conventionary tenements', were held by way of lease perpetually renewable every seven years. Since the lands were held by lease and not by copyhold, the custom that possession of the minerals was in the tenant did not apply: hence the Duke of Cornwall and his licensees were entitled to get the minerals without the consent of the tenant. Six of the manors were sold for the redemption of land tax, reserving mines and metallic minerals to the Duke. The Act also laid down a code for the working of minerals. The code provides different rules for the sold manors (mines and metallic minerals) and the unsold ones (mines, minerals, stone and substrata). Commissioners were appointed to make awards under the Act; and their award is a record of title and establishes the extent of the Duchy mineral rights within those manors.[94] In further land sales over the next 80-90 years, most of the former leasehold land within the affected areas was bought from the

---

[93] 7 & 8 Vict c.105 (Royal Assent: 9 August 1844).

[94] The manors sold were Tewington, Tybesta, Moresk, Tywamhail, Helston-in-Kerrier and Calstock. The unsold manors were Helston-in-Trigg, Penmayne, Tintagel, Restormel, Penlyne, Penkneth, Talskedy, Liskeard, Rillaton, Stoke Climsland and Trematon.

Duchy by tenants at nominal sums, leaving the Duchy in possession only of the mines and minerals. That remains the position today.[95]

The Act further provided extensive powers to the Duke to exploit his right to minerals on the assessionable lands, whether sold or unsold.[96] Subject to certain restrictions, the Duke and all persons authorised by him, with their agents and workmen, may enter on all land comprised in any of the assessionable manors (whether sold or unsold) in which any mines, minerals, stone or substrata belong to the Duke. They may then search, dig for, open and work the mines and get, carry away and dispose of the minerals, stone or substrata, with ancillary powers connected to those purposes and 'making to the Persons entitled to the Surface of such Lands or Tenements, or to such Water, adequate Compensation for the Damage which shall have been done or occasioned by the Exercise of the Rights, Privileges, and Easements aforesaid, and making to the Persons entitled to the same adequate Compensation for the Materials so taken as aforesaid.'[97]

---

95 On the extent of the Duchy's mining rights in assessionable manors, see *Halsbury's Laws*, vol 29 (2024), para 144.

96 See sections 53 to 55. For the operation of the Act, see *A-G for the Prince of Wales v Collom* [1916] 2 KB 193 (Atkin J).

97 Section 55.

CHAPTER SIX

MANORIAL MINERALS RESERVATIONS IN THE COURTS

Introduction

For more than 200 years a good deal of judicial attention has been given to the task of interpreting manorial and non-manorial minerals reservations, and extensive case law now reflects a variety of approaches from which it is not easy to derive consistent principles.[1] The basic situation to which these principles apply is the vertical severance of estates in land, as described by Sir George Jessel MR in *Eardley v Granville*: [2]

> If a freeholder grants lands, excepting mines, he severs his estate vertically, i.e., he grants out his estate in parallel horizontal layers, and the grantee only gets the parallel layer granted to him, and does not get any underlying mineral layer or stratum. That underlying stratum remains in the grantor. The freeholder retains the mineral stratum as part of his ownership; and whether or not he takes the minerals or subsoil out of the

1 The subject of manorial minerals lies at the interface of manorial law and minerals law. For analysis of minerals cases generally, see "The Interpretation of Minerals" by Martin Dray, delivered as one of the Blundell Lectures in June 2018. Issues arising from mineral reservations are covered both there and by Mark West, "The Ownership of Surface Voids created by Mineral Extraction", *The Conveyancer* (2011), vol 75, pp.26-42.

2 (1876) 3 Ch D 826 at 834, approved by Lord Atkinson in *Thomson v St Catharine's College, Cambridge* [1919] AC 468 at 487. It is striking that although Jessel MR begins by referring to 'mines', he then goes on to speak of 'minerals' as if the terms are synonymous.

> stratum, the stratum still belongs to him as part of the vertical section of the land.

In the 19th and early 20th centuries, cases about mines and mineral reservations clauses were frequently litigated in the appellate courts by leading advocates because of the value of the minerals at stake, such as coal or china clay. In 1909, in *North British Railway v Budhill Coal and Sandstone*,[3] 'the House of Lords conclusively rejected the proposition that there was any ordinary or primary meaning to be attached to the word "minerals".'[4] That rejection was part of a process which had started in the House of Lords decision of 1888 in *Lord Provost and Magistrates of Glasgow v Farie* with criticism of a wide meaning of minerals, when Lord Macnaghten had said that the word 'minerals' in its widest signification 'probably means every inorganic substance forming part of the crust of the earth other than the layer of soil which sustains vegetable life'.[5] As described by Lawrence Collins LJ in *Coleman v Ibstock Brick Ltd*,[6] this process was one where the courts endeavoured to give the word 'minerals' a more restricted meaning 'so as to effectuate not only the intentions of the parties to instruments but, more importantly, to make effective the transfers of land to railway companies for the building of railways.'

Compulsory transfers of land for track for railways were subject to a statutory exception by s 77 of the Railways Clauses Consolidation Act 1845 (1845 c. 20). This provided:

> The Company shall not be entitled to any Mines of Coal, Ironstone, Slate, or other Minerals under any Land purchased by them, except only such Parts thereof as shall be necessary to

3 [1910] AC 116. The decision was made on appeal from the Court of Session.

4 The words quoted are those of Slade J in *Earl of Lonsdale v Attorney-General* [1982] 1 WLR 887 at 916C.

5 (1888) 13 App Cas 669 at 689.

6 [2008] EWCA Civ 73 at [9].

> be dug or carried away or used in the Construction of the Works, unless the same shall have been expressly purchased; and all such Mines, excepting as aforesaid, shall be deemed to be excepted out of the Conveyance of such Lands, unless they shall have been expressly named therein and conveyed thereby.

Section 77 had corresponding provisions in the Scottish Railway Clauses (Consolidation) Act 1845[7] and the Waterworks Clauses Act 1847.[8] (The Lands Clauses Consolidation Act 1845 apparently had no similar provision.[9] The wave of legislation generated by Parliament in the 1840s for facilitating railway construction and other public undertakings, which initiated compulsory purchase on an extensive scale, was to raise serious questions in the courts. Railway companies, public corporations and landowners with minerals found themselves in conflict over the meaning of 'minerals' in circumstances where the term had been tested and defined in earlier cases about mineral reservations in land grants or Inclosure Acts frequently, though not always, involving lords of the manor. That meaning had to be adapted to different circumstances, and the process of restricting it was carried forward primarily in the House of Lords by decisions in Scottish cases whose implications took English judges some time to appreciate. However, the abolition of copyhold and subsequent decline of manorial work in English courts after the 1922-1925 property legislation produced a situation where lawyers and judges can easily lose sight of the copyhold and manorial law questions associated with mineral reservations which would have been obvious to their predecessors.

The legislation of 1845-1847 contained definitions sections but did not define 'minerals' or 'mines and minerals'. But in 1910 Lord Loreburn LC, who gave the leading speech in *Budhill*, said that two Scottish common law decisions of 1818 and 1841 which had cut down the

---

7 Section 70.

8 Section 18.

9 Although sections 97 and 99 specified arrangements for compensating lords on compulsory purchase of copyhold, customary and common lands.

meaning of the word 'minerals' in private conveyances were of the greatest importance for interpreting the Scottish Act of 1845. The reason was that when 'When an Act of Parliament uses a word which has received a judicial construction it presumably uses it in the same sense.'[10] Whatever the position with the Scottish Act, the English Act of 1845, with an identically-worded provision, was passed only months before an important decision in the Court of Exchequer which, far from restricting the meaning of 'minerals', confirmed its broad extent. This decision, *Earl of Rosse v Wainman*, was upheld on appeal by seven judges of the Court of Exchequer Chamber in 1848, who said that they had fully considered the case, thought it attended with considerable difficulty, and considered that the judgment below must be affirmed.

At first instance, the Court of Exchequer in *Wainman* had to construe an Inclosure Act of 1815 containing a reservation of 'all mines and minerals, of what nature or kind so ever, lying and being within or under the said commons and waste grounds' of the lord of a manor. Parke B, sitting with Alderson B, held that

> The term 'minerals' here used, though more frequently applied to substances containing metals, in its proper sense includes all fossil bodies or matters dug out of mines... Beds of stone, which may be dug by winning or quarrying, are therefore properly minerals, and so we think they must be held to be in the clause in question, *bearing in mind that the object of the act was to give the surface for cultivation to the commoners, and to leave in the lord what it did not take away for that purpose*' [emphasis added]

The Court of Exchequer Chamber was until the transfer of its jurisdiction to the new Court of Appeal in 1875 the senior appellate court in civil matters below the House of Lords, so it is not surprising that its decision in *Wainman* carried weight with the judiciary and

10 [1911] AC 290 at 299. The two Scottish decisions were *Menzies v Earl of Breadalbane* (10 June 1818), 19 Fac Coll, 531, 1 Sh App. 225 (HL); and *Duke of Hamilton v Bentley* (1841) 3 D. 1121, Court of Session (29 June 1841). See further below at p.207.

authors of practitioner texts.[11] In *Micklethwait v Winter* the emphasised words of the extract cited above from Parke B's judgment in *Wainman* had identified a principle that proved to be a starting point for the construction of earlier Inclosure Acts. The badly drafted Act of 1759 in *Micklethwait* had omitted a minerals reservation clause in favour of the lord but at the time of its passing, the soil and freehold of the common allotted under the Act were vested in him, subject to certain rights of pasture. The coal and minerals and unopened stone quarries under the surface of the common also belonged to him as part of the freehold, and he was entitled to work the mines. The Act did not recite the particular rights of the lord but provided that certain allotments should be made to the commoners in lieu of their rights, and to him for his right as lord 'to and in the soil of the said common', and also to and for the damage he would sustain by having to make satisfaction to the proprietors of the lands enclosed for digging for any coals and minerals. The Act also provided that if the lord should enter upon any of the lands for the purpose of digging 'any coals or other minerals', he should make satisfaction to the proprietors of the lands for damage done. The

---

11 As Lord Esher MR put it in *Duke of Devonshire v O'Connor* (1890) 24 QBD 468 at 473, CA, the Court of Exchequer Chamber was 'a Court of co-ordinate jurisdiction with this Court', and the principles of its judgments were 'binding upon us'. The *Wainman* decision was, in effect, that of no less than nine judges, where the only substantive judgment of Parke B (later Lord Wensleydale) was agreed by eight others. Even Lord Halsbury, despite his repeated concerns about judicial interpretation giving a wide meaning to the term 'minerals', apparently regarded *Wainman* as correctly decided: see *Lord Provost and Magistrates of Glasgow v Farie* (1888) 13 App Cas 657 at 669 where in an intervention with counsel he said that '[*Wainman*] was a lord of the manor case, and the fact that the lord had a right to everything under the surface was the foundation of Lord Wensleydale's judgment.' The Court of Exchequer Chamber was a court of co-ordinate authority with the Court of Appeal in Chancery and then with the Court of Appeal which assumed the jurisdiction of both courts from 1875. See also *Tiverton Estates v Wearwell Ltd* [1975] Ch 146 at 151G and 157D; and J.H Baker, *An Introduction to English Legal History* (5th edn, 2019), p.211. On practitioner texts see below, pp.226-230.

defendant, as successor in title to one of the allottees, had opened up quarries to take stone for use as grindstones and flagstones and was sued by the lord in trover (i.e. conversion) for damages.[12] The lord argued that looking at the Act as a whole its object was clearly to preserve for him such rights in respect of minerals as he had at the time it was passed, and that the case was indistinguishable from *Wainman*. The court agreed, holding that although there was no clause in express terms excepting the mines and minerals, nevertheless, by necessary implication, the Act reserved to the lord his right to the mines and minerals under the lands inclosed, and that he was entitled to work them, paying compensation to the surface owners for any damage thereby caused.

Thus the decision in *Micklethwait* was that stone within an unopened quarry was a mineral reserved to the lord, but its real significance lay in its affirmation and application of the broader principle on which the *Wainman* judgement was based: that the normal purpose of an Inclosure Act promoted by a lord of the manor was to give the commoners only the pasture and to keep for the lord whatever remained. The unsuccessful defendant in *Micklethwait* had argued that the soil in which the freehold lay contained the minerals and had been transferred to the allottees; and so, because there was no express clause reserving the minerals, the case was indistinguishable from *Townley v Gibson*. That argument failed in *Micklethwait* primarily because of the presence in the 1759 Act of the compensation clause, which was not present in the 1771 Act in *Townley v Gibson*.[13]

The *Wainman* interpretation of 'minerals' was expanded in 1872 in another manorial minerals case, *Hext v Gill*.[14] This involved a private conveyance rather than an Inclosure Act, but on this occasion the scope of the meaning of minerals related to an issue that was becoming increasingly problematic in the courts: the right of a minerals owner to

---

12 Trover is now known as conversion.

13 See above chapter 2, p.42 for the common features of Inclosure Acts.

14 (1872) L.R. 7 Ch.App. 699.

win and get minerals in circumstances where the surface was in different ownership and where the surface would be damaged or destroyed by the process of extraction. *Hext v Gill* had its defenders and detractors and generated a significant divergence of judicial opinion. However, its definition of the meaning of minerals may, in a proper context, still be applicable today.[15]

The minerals definition rule in *Hext v Gill*

The decision in *Hext v Gill* requires both careful reading and an awareness of those features of 19th century property law that have long disappeared. The decision contains two rules, quite different in nature, and two judgments, which are often read as presenting rival tests for the first rule. However, the second judgment properly understood is not just supportive of the first test but offers further principled reasons for it. The first, minerals definition rule is a canon of construction, which gives no more than a *prima facie* meaning to the word 'minerals' and which recognizes that it must yield or bend to context. The second rule, which has been generally followed, concerns evidence and burden of proof in relation to the mineral owner's powers of working the minerals.[16] What complicates discussion of the decision is that there is

---

15 *Earl of Lonsdale v A-G* at 924C.

16 The court's understanding in *Hext v Gill* (at 713 and 718) was that if the express powers of working were insufficient to enable a particular mineral to be worked, it did not follow that the reservation did not include that mineral. Thus the provisions relating to powers of working were of little assistance in identifying whether a particular mineral was included within the reservation. Although *Hext v Gill* concerned the effect of a reservation in the grant of a freehold from what had been a copyhold tenement (i.e. there was an enfranchisement), there was no difference in principle between that situation and the typical one between lord and copyholder, where the lord as freeholder had an estate in the minerals beneath the land of the copyholder who as the surface owner had an estate in the soil. Possession of the soil and the minerals was in the copyholder, although property in them was in the lord. In the absence of agreement with the lord, the minerals had to remain unworked: see *Eardley v Granville* (1876)

a variant in the text at a crucial passage in the leading judgment by Mellish LJ. The variant, if correct, does much to neutralise subsequent criticism of the leading judgment and offers a more cogent rationale for the first rule; but it is not necessary to accept the variant as the definitive text for the first rule to be read with the nuance the variant clearly suggests. This was recognised by those appeal court judges who were contemporaries or near contemporaries of Mellish LJ,[17] but their affirmation and explanation of the rule was not enough to prevent criticism of it in the House of Lords. That criticism identified in the second judgment by James LJ an alternative test for defining a mineral. Over time, this test came to displace the *prima facie* meaning advanced by the first rule which Mellish LJ had proposed and which James LJ himself had enthusiastically endorsed. Ironically, the test attributed to James LJ has repeatedly been found in later cases to be not only inconclusive but also costly for the parties because of the extent of evidence it requires.

The first issue in *Hext v Gill* was the construction of a minerals reservation clause in a grant of 1799 made by the Duke of Cornwall as lord of a manor. The grant was of the freehold in a copyhold tenement to the copyholder, and it reserved to the Duke and his lessees 'all mines and minerals within and under the premises with full and free liberty of ingress, egress and regress to dig and search for, and to take, use, and work the said excepted mines and minerals', without provision for compensation. Beneath the tenement lay china clay, whose extraction would involve destruction or serious damage to the surface of the land. Neither party to the 1799 grant contemplated this. In 1869 the surface owner of the freehold sought an injunction to restrain the minerals owner from getting the china clay. This was refused at first instance on the basis that china clay fell within the meaning of 'mines and minerals'. The appellate court, comprising Mellish LJ and James LJ, upheld the

3 Ch D 826 at 832-33 and 835 per Jessel MR, which is consistent with *Hext v Gill* per Mellish LJ at 718.

17 See below, pp.200-203.

judge[18] by finding that china clay was included in the reservations but reversed the outcome by giving the surface owner his injunction. The court further held, in the words of the headnote, that 'when a landowner sells the surface, reserving to himself the minerals with power to get them, he must, if he intends to have power to get them in a way which will destroy the surface, frame the reservation in such a way as to show clearly that he is intended to have that power.'

Mellish LJ, who gave the leading judgment, said this about the meaning of 'mines' and 'mines and minerals' in reservations clauses:

> There was a great deal of discussion before us as to the meaning of the word 'mines', whether it is confined to underground working, or may possibly extend to open working, or whether it does not apply to the workings at all, but in this sort of reservation means the metal, the veins, and seams themselves, which are in a secondary sense called 'mines'. I think that it is not necessary here to go into these questions, for whatever may be the meaning of the word 'mines' when used alone, it is here combined with the more general word 'minerals.' And the authorities seem to show that where there is an exception of 'mines and minerals,' the putting the word 'mines' before 'minerals' does not restrict the meaning of the word 'minerals.' Many authorities, some at law and some in equity, have been brought before us to show what is the meaning of the word 'minerals.' But the result of the authorities,[19] without going

18 Wickens V-C.

19 At this point of the judgment, there is a variant of the text in 20 WR 957 at 960, 27 LT 291 at 295, and 41 LJ Ch 761 at 762-63 as follows: 'The result of the authorities appears to be this, that the word 'minerals' includes every fossil substance, every substance in fact of every kind which can be got from underneath the surface of the earth, and for a profitable purpose. A grant of minerals probably would not give a right to go and get them merely for the purpose of annoying your neighbour, and not for the purpose of profit. That would be an absurd construction to put upon it. The reasonable construction seems to be that the word 'minerals' includes everything which can be got from under the surface of the earth for the

through them, appears to be this: that *a reservation of 'minerals' includes every substance which can be got from underneath the surface of the earth for the purpose of profit, unless there is something in the context or in the nature of the transaction to induce the Court to give it a more limited meaning.* [emphasis added] Ought it to have a more limited meaning in the present case? The circumstances, as far as they are material to be stated, are these: The seller was the lord of the manor. What he sold was the freehold of a copyhold tenement. Now the lord of a manor is, beyond all question, entitled to the minerals, in the most general sense of the word, under a copyhold tenement. There is nothing to be got out of the soil and sold for a profit which the copyhold tenant, in the absence of some special custom, is entitled to get without the permission of the lord; the property of it is in the lord, although it is true that, in the absence of special custom, the lord cannot get it without the license of the tenant. The position of the parties, therefore, furnishes no reason for restricting the meaning of the word 'minerals,' and there being no special words before 'mines and minerals' which might furnish an argument for restricting them to things *ejusdem generis*, I am of opinion that the surface, and all profit that can be got from cultivating the surface, or building on it, or using the surface, is intended to be conveyed, but that the right to everything under the surface, and to all profit that can be got from digging anything out from under it, is intended to be

---

purpose of profit, unless there is something in the context or in the nature of the transaction which would induce the court to give it a more limited meaning.' There appears to be a reference to this variant of the text in the judgment of Bowen LJ in *Earl of Jersey v Guardians of Poor of Neath Poor Law Union* (1889) 22 QBD 555 at 562: 'Mellish LJ does not say, nor, I think, mean, that the test was whether the minerals could be worked at a market profit at the time, but whether they had a use and a value of their own independent of and separable from the soil.' Fry LJ (at 563) was of the same opinion. The view of Bowen and Fry LJJ is probably to be preferred because it is based on three of the contemporaneous reports.

> reserved. I am therefore of opinion that china clay is included in the reservation.[20]

So far as minerals reservations were concerned, this passage in the judgment was not new law but a statement of the law as it stood in 1872 and had been for many years. The authorities which Mellish LJ referred to he did not name, but it is clear from the case report[21] that they included a series of decisions by large number of experienced judges, including those from the senior appellate courts including the House of Lords. The decisions went back for a period of more than twenty-five years in which those courts were construing minerals reservations clauses in private acts and conveyances dating from 1759 to 1821.[22] Mellish

---

20 At 712-713.

21 Which sets out the first instance judgment of Wickens V-C (at 705-706) and, on appeal, the cases relied on by counsel in the Court of Chancery Appeals (at 708). The cases included *Earl of Rosse v Wainman* (1845) 14 M&W 858, 153 ER 724 (Parke B) and, on appeal (1848) 2 Ex 799, 154 ER 714 (Lord Denman CJ, Wilde CJ, Patteson, Coleridge, Maule, Cresswell and Williams JJ); *Micklethwait v Winter* (1851) 6 Ex 644, 155 ER 701 (Pollock CB, and Barons Alderson, Platt, and Martin); *Darvill v Roper* (1855) 3 Drew 294, 61 ER 915 (Kindersley V-C); *Rowbotham v Wilson* (1860) VIII HLC 348 (Lords Brougham, Wensleydale, Chelmsford, and Kingsdown. Lord Campbell LC did not hear the argument and gave no opinion but observed 'that the judgment now being given in accordance with that of the court over which I formerly presided, I entirely concur in it'); *Bell v Wilson* (1865-66) LR 1 Ch App 303 (Turner and Knight Bruce LJJ) , *Midland Railway Company v Checkley* (1867) LR Eq IV 19 (Lord Romilly MR); *Duke of Buccleuch v Wakefield* (1869-70) LR 4 HL 377 (Lords Hatherley LC, Chelmsford, Colonsay).

22 *Earl of Rosse v Wainman*: enclosure of manorial commons and wastes by Inclosure Act of 1814; *Micklethwait v Winter*: enclosure of lord's common by Inclosure Act of 1759; *Darvill v Roper*: deeds of partition and conveyance of 1798-1799 between tenants in common; *Rowbotham v Wilson*: enclosure of commons and commonable lands pursuant to an award made under an Inclosure Act of 1770; *Bell v Wilson*: conveyance of 1810; *Midland Railway Company v Checkley*: enclosure pursuant to Canal Act of 1793; *Duke of Buccleuch v Wakefield*: enclosure and allotment to customary tenants of manor of moors, commons and wastes to be held in

LJ's test for the *prima facie* meaning of minerals was plainly derived from those decisions. His reference to the position of lords generally and to the intention to reserve 'the right to everything under the surface, and to all profit that can be got from digging anything out from under it' is consistent with an understanding of 'profit' that was not market profit[23] but, as the variant text indicates,[24] usefulness to the lord. This understanding of profit runs directly counter to the idea of exceptionality in value as a requirement for or pointer towards the meaning of 'minerals' which has been influential since it was first articulated in Lawrence LJ's judgment in 1931 in *Waring v Foden*.[25]

The second issue concerned the effect of this finding on the land of the surface owner. Mellish LJ said this:

> The Vice-Chancellor in his judgment fully acknowledged the difficulty that, if the Defendants had the right to take china clay, the reservation might be absolutely destructive of the grant, but said he could not see where he was to fix the limit to the reservation if its words were not to be taken according to their full and strict meaning. I feel myself that it is very difficult to say where the limit is to be placed. It is very difficult to lay down exactly what the owner of the minerals may do for the purpose of getting them; but I do not think it would be right or just to the owner of the surface to say that his surface may be destroyed because there may be a difficulty in saying exactly what the owner of minerals may do and what he may not do in every case. In the present case I think the result is this, that the general reservation of minerals includes the china clay a mineral the existence of which apparently was not known to the parties at

free and common socage by Inclosure Act of 1821. As noted above, the grant in *Hext v Gill* itself was a conveyance of 1799.

23 As Lord Halsbury thought in *Lord Provost and Magistrates of Glasgow v Farie* (1888) 13 App Cas 657 at 670.

24 See above, p.187, n.19.

25 [1932] 1 Ch 276 at 294.

> the time when the instrument was executed, and which cannot be got without destroying the surface. It appears to me that the fair result of that state of things is that the lord of the manor is practically in the same position as he would have been in if this had remained a copyhold tenement, viz., that the right to the clay is in him; but inasmuch as he has not reserved the power to destroy the surface, and inasmuch as this clay cannot be got without destroying the surface, he cannot get the clay unless he can make some arrangement with the owner of the surface.[26]

On this second issue Mellish LJ was undoubtedly developing the law,[27] in effect suggesting as a corollary to his minerals definition rule a further rule or principle that the surface owner cannot be deprived of support to the surface by the minerals owner unless there was unambiguous agreement to that effect. This produced a just result between, on the one hand, the competing claims of a lord with the benefit of a minerals reservation and powers to extract them without compensation; and, on the other, a landowner at risk of having the surface of his property

---

26 At 718.

27 From the point where it stood after *Rowbotham v Wilson* (1860) 8 HLC 347. In the House of Lords' decision in *Thomson v Master and Fellows of St Catharine's College, Cambridge* [1919] AC 468 at 492-494, Lord Atkinson (dealing with the second question on that appeal and in the majority on that question) gave his full endorsement to that part of Mellish LJ's judgment dealing with the surface owner's right to support of the surface. 'This case of *Hext v Gill* has been very many times cited with approval. During the course of argument I asked Mr Talbot if he could refer to any case where it was disapproved of, or the soundness of the principle it lays down questioned, and his reply was in the negative. I think it clearly establishes that… where no power to work the mines is expressly or impliedly conferred, and the only power to work them is derived from the mere fact of ownership of them, the surface owner cannot be deprived of the support of the surface to which he is entitled as of natural right. Nor can that surface be destroyed, however necessary both may be for the commercial or other working of the mines.'

destroyed by china clay working.[28] Mellish LJ's solution was simple, effective and flexible. It accommodated the wide range of meaning that the courts had given to the word 'minerals' while protecting the surface owner from the substantive derogation from grant that would occur if the more destructive workings of minerals and damage they caused to the surface were allowed to the minerals owner.[29] It was a wide, primary meaning that could be narrowed depending on the circumstances. Provided the reservation in the grant was properly drafted, the property in the minerals remained in the lord while possession of the land remained in the surface owner so that, as far as the minerals were concerned, there was a stand-off. Neither could exploit the minerals without the consent and co-operation of the other.

The other judgment in *Hext v Gill* by James LJ consisted of two short paragraphs. The first, agreeing with Mellish LJ, was *ratio.*

> I entirely concur both with the conclusions and reasoning of the Lord Justice. The long and uniform series of authorities appear to me to have established a very convenient and consistent system, giving the mineral owner every reasonable profit out of the mineral treasures, and at the same time saving the landowner's practical enjoyment of his houses, gardens, fields,

---

28 In 1870, shortly before his appointment later that year to be a Lord Justice of Appeal in Chancery, Mr George Mellish QC had appeared in *Duke of Buccleuch v Wakefield* (1869-70) LR 4 HL 377 for the unsuccessful respondent, Mr Wakefield. He argued (at 385): 'the real question here amounts to this: whether a lord may work his mines, not only under the proper lands of the manor, but under those which have been sold and are freed from manorial rights, and work them without leaving any support whatever to the surface of the land; whether, in fact, he may so destroy the land that it will be unfit for building or for the feeding of cattle.' As Mellish LJ, his judgment on the second issue in *Hext v Gill* appears to have been his answer to that question.

29 As they were by the House of Lords in *Duke of Buccleuch v Wakefield,* albeit on payment of compensation for damage done.

and woods, without which the grant to him would have been illusory.[30]

The 'system' which James LJ referred to was something more than the courts giving every reasonable profit to the minerals owner and practical enjoyment of the surface grant to the landowner. The courts' intervention took place only when parties to grants (or, more likely, their successors-in-title years later) were in dispute. Whether the grants were made in a conveyance or pursuant to an Inclosure Act and Award, if they contained mineral reservations then the land transferred at the time was either, in the case of conveyance, the subject of consideration or, in the case of Act or Award, formed part of a broader exchange and allotment of lands whose quantities had to be calculated by surveyors. Whatever form the grant took, there was need for valuation; and an important part of the valuation process was valuation of what lay beneath the surface of land.[31] On the eve of any land transfer, sub-surface valuation was problematic because those responsible for it would have incomplete or no knowledge of the existence, extent and value of whatever lay beneath the surface.[32] Where the land was substantial in

30 At 719.

31 It is notable that while the Inclosure Consolidation Act of 1801 granted (by s.20) commissioners the power to allot 'Timber trees and other Trees' to go along with the allotted land on which they stood, and to determine the amount of compensation to be paid to the pre-allotment owners of that land, there was no such provision for mines and minerals. The Act was silent about them.

32 The problem of sub-surface minerals valuation was well known to practitioners and was central to the 19th century understanding of a minerals reservation as excluding everything beneath the surface. '*In the enfranchisements from rights in mines and minerals* a very great obstacle would, in practice, exist in the way of any general rule for computing the value, and those rights are excepted from the compulsory clauses of the Copyhold Acts.' [emphasis in original] See Rolla Rouse, *The Copyhold Enfranchisement Manual* (2nd edn, 1858), p.94. Rouse was a barrister of the Inner Temple and his book was published by the leading law publishers, Butterworths. The flavour of its content and the complexity of the subject are conveyed by its full title: *The Copyhold Enfranchisement*

extent and the lord wanted to protect his interest in it and avoid potential liability for waste,[33] the solution to the problem was to leave sub-surface valuation out of account by reserving the minerals to the vendor in the transfer document so that any questions about value or workings could be dealt with later (and through the courts if necessary) if and when valuable sub-strata material came to light.[34] This was done

---

Manual giving the Law, Practice and Forms in enfranchisements at Common Law and under Statute; and in Commutations; with the Values of Enfranchisement from the Lord's various rights; the Principles of Calculation, being clearly explained, and made practical, by numerous Rules, Tables, and Examples.

33 If the lord was a tenant for life of an entailed estate (as many 18th and 19th century lords were), he was under an obligation to the reversioners not to commit waste by damaging the value of the freehold interest. A reversioner could claim that a tenant for life disposing of a freehold interest had failed to obtain the value properly due for it if that value did not include a proper sum for minerals beneath the land. If their existence and extent were unknown at the time of sale, it was more convenient to deal with valuation later, as and when any minerals were discovered.

34 This analysis is informed by the judgment of Kindersley V-C in *Darvill v Roper* (1855) 3 Drew 294 at 302-303, 61 ER 915 at 919. 'The language of the reservation is "mines of lead [etc] and other mines or minerals." Having directed these surveyors to make their survey and valuation, and these surveyors having made their reports, then the language of one of the deeds for carrying this into effect [...] provided that the profits of the mines excepted out of the valuation should be taken between the parties according to their several estates, rights, [etc], in the premises. [....] It is to be observed that the whole scope and object of the transaction was this – tenants in common wishing to hold in severalty. Their object was partition, with as little exception as possible; to divide so much as it was possible to divide without great difficulty. Thus, if there were on the land stones, or rocks, even masses of clay which were apparent on the surface, or apparent to the eye, that is, apparent to persons going over the land for the purpose of surveying it, their intention was to make partition of all that. But with regard to those [etc] which were or might be of value, but which were deep in the earth, and the valuation of which could not be easily or at all made, except by subterraneous [sic] digging or boring, it is

by conveyancers and surveyors who, together with the courts, dealt with the transfer and improvement of land and made up what James LJ called the 'very convenient and consistent system'. The Copyhold Acts 1841-1894 provided the statutory framework for this system in relation to enfranchisement of copyhold land, which had been the transaction which triggered the dispute in *Hext v Gill*.[35]

The second paragraph of James LJ's judgment was *obiter* but advanced a suggestion which became influential and remains so today.

> But for these authorities I should have thought that what was meant by 'mines and minerals' in such a grant was a question of fact what these words meant in the vernacular of the mining world and commercial world and landowners at the end of the last [18th] century; upon which I am satisfied that no one at that

---

natural to suppose that those were to be excepted. That is, their object would be to except only such things as could not be valued'.

35 Section 23(1) of the Copyhold Act 1894, which consolidated the provisions of the previous Copyhold Acts since 1841, imported a statutory exception in favour of both lord and tenant for mines, minerals and other rights, while allowing the surface owner 'full power to disturb or remove the soil so far as is necessary or convenient for the purpose of making roads or drains or erecting buildings or obtaining water on the land.' The first paragraph of section 23(1) repeated the similar provisions of section 48 of the Copyhold Act 1852. See *Kerr v Pawson* (1858) 25 Beav 394; and *Pretty v Solly* (1859) 26 Beav 606. The proviso at the end of section 23(1), from which the above quotation is taken, re-enacted the provisions of section 14 of the Copyhold Act 1858. The proviso at the end of section 23(1) was itself re-enacted in substantially the same form in the proviso at the end of paragraph 5 of Sch 12 of the LPA 1922. Sch 12, though not in force today, and is regarded by HMLR as identifying those mineral rights that remained in the lord following statutory enfranchisement of copyhold land as from 1 January 1926. There is an illuminating commentary on the proviso in Archibald Brown, *The Law and Practice on Enfranchisements and Commutations, as well by the common law as under the Copyhold Act, 1894, and other acts* (3rd edn, 1903), pp.226-227. The commentary is set out below at p.282.

> time would have thought have thought of classing clay of any kind as mineral.

Later courts have interpreted these words as showing that James LJ accepted that he was constrained by authority but was suggesting that a better way of construing 'mines and minerals' was by reference to what the term meant in the vernacular of the mining and commercial worlds and landowners at the time of the grant. Yet his words do not have to be read that way. His judgment expressed neither veiled dissent nor regret at being constrained by authority,[36] and his whole-hearted endorsement of Mellish LJ's judgment must have included a recognition that the application of the vernacular test could have led to an unjust result because china clay was not, in 1799, classed as a mineral.[37] Since

---

[36] Note the words used by Lord Greene MR in *Young v Bristol Aeroplane Co Ltd* [1944] 1 KB 718 at 723: 'Cases in which this court has expressed its regret at finding itself bound by previous decisions of its own and has stated in the clearest terms that the only remedy of the unsuccessful party is to appeal to the House of Lords are within the recollection of all of us and numerous examples are to be found in the reports.'

[37] In argument before him in *Hext v Gill*, James LJ was referred to *Darvill v Roper* (1855) 3 Drew 294, 61 ER 915, where the parties had provided Kindersley V-C with evidence of scientists, mineralogists, engineers, solicitors and people local to the site of the minerals as to the vernacular meaning of 'minerals' in Denbigh and Flint in 1799. The V-C found the evidence so conflicting that it was of no use to him in his decision: see 3 Drew 294 at 296, 299, 301 and 61 ER 915 at 917-918. James LJ would have been aware of the cost of such evidence and its limited assistance when the grant to be construed was so distant in the past. In a recent minerals reservations case in the Chancery Division, *Cleveland Potash Limited v Drummond and others* [2024] EWHC 1292 (Ch D), the deputy judge observed at [14]: 'there have been relatively few cases where the direct evidence is conclusive as to a vernacular usage or meaning (for example it was not found in *Darvill v Roper* and *Wynne-Finch v Natural Resources Body for Wales* [2022] 3 All ER 162, CA'. The deputy judge, Clare Ambrose, was presented with a great deal of evidence about vernacular usage and meaning but found it of little use in the case before her: see [96], [99] and [109]. The grant containing the reservation was made in 1946 and did not concern manorial minerals. In *Earl of Lonsdale*

a construction of 'mines and minerals' on the vernacular test alone would have excluded china clay from the reservation, it would also have meant that the consideration for the 1799 grant assumed the willingness of a lord to accept the risk of foregoing profits on lucrative sub-strata that lay, unknown to him, beneath his land at the time of sale.[38] The 'convenient and consistent system' referred to by James LJ, and the rule of construction derived from previous authority proposed by Mellish LJ with James LJ's enthusiastic support, avoided that assumption and the uncertainty to which it gave rise.[39]

The minerals definition rule after *Hext v Gill*: impact of non-manorial minerals cases

The subsequent judicial treatment of *Hext v Gill* highlights its continuing importance as a leading case on the construction of manorial minerals reservations in land grants. But that importance has been obscured by later decisions in the House of Lords which, while not overruling the outcome of *Hext v Gill* itself, expressed the gravest doubts about Mellish LJ's finding about the ordinary or primary meaning of

---

v A-G [1982] 1 WLR 887 at 928C, Slade J found the evidence as to vernacular usage concerning Crown grants of mining and mineral leases in 1880 and 1935 'quite inconclusive' on the question of whether the terms 'minerals' or 'mineral substances' at either of those dates were meant to include oil or natural gas.

38 Had the lord in *Hext v Gill* not been the Duke of Cornwall but someone who was tenant-for-life under a family settlement, he would also have been risking a potential action for waste from those in reversion or remainder. See Megarry and Wade, *The Law of Real Property* (10th edn, 2024), 3-066 et seq, and cases there referred to.

39 Since *Earl of Lonsdale v A-G* and *Wynne-Finch v NRBW*, the parties to disputes about the meaning of minerals in mineral reservation clauses may need to address both a vernacular test and an exceptionality test. As noted in *Coleman v Ibstock Brick Limited* [2008] EWCA Civ 73 by Lawrence Collins LJ at [49]: 'the question of construction in cases such as the present may require a sophisticated factual inquiry into the background, the minerals in question, and the district.'

the word 'minerals' in a mineral reservations clause. These doubts were expressed in cases not about manorial minerals reservations but about compulsory purchase agreements made by statutory undertakers which incorporated minerals reservation clauses from codes enacted in section 77 of the Railways Clauses Consolidation Act 1845, section 70 of the Railways Clauses Consolidation (Scotland) Act 1845 and section 18 of the Waterworks Clauses Act of 1847.[40] These acts were used by the promoters of undertakings, themselves authorised by statute, to import standard terms into compulsory purchase agreements of private land needed for the undertaking. The purpose of these provisions[41] was to enable minerals valuation in a compulsory purchase context to be dealt with in the same way as it had been for years by minerals reservation clauses in private grants and private Inclosure Acts: issues about valuation were not to delay the transfer of land but instead would be dealt with after transfer – perhaps many years later – once the nature and extent of the minerals, and their owner's willingness and ability to exploit them, had become known.

<u>Lord Halsbury and the *Farie* case</u>

In *Lord Provost and Magistrates of Glasgow v Farie*,[42] the minerals reservation from s 18 of the Waterworks Clauses Act 1847 was incorporated in a conveyance by which the Glasgow Corporation purchased land from Mr Farie which, as both parties knew, contained a valuable seam of clay lying two feet beneath the surface across the ground on which the Corporation proposed to build reservoirs. The

40 For the wording, substantively the same in each Act, see p.180 above.

41 See s 77 of the Railways Clauses Consolidation Act 1845 (8 & 9 Vict c.20); and the corresponding provision at s 70 of the Railways Clauses Consolidation (Scotland) Act 1845. Sections 78 and 79 of the English Act and sections 71 and 72 of the Scottish Act provided a mechanism enabling the minerals owner to serve notice on the railway company with a request to work the minerals and for compensation to be paid to the owner if the request was refused.

42 (1888) 13 App Cas 657 (Lords Halsbury LC, Watson, Herschell (dissenting) and Macnaghten.

conveyance made no reference to the clay; and Mr Farie, relying on the statutory minerals reservation, claimed it was excepted from the sale and demanded a sum almost equivalent to the original purchase price. In the Court of Session which found for Mr Farie, Mellish LJ's test in *Hext v Gill* was applied; but the House of Lords, faced with the question of whether clay was included in the minerals reservation, reversed the Court of Session.[43] Lord Halsbury LC, expressly confining his opinion to Scottish law,[44] said he preferred what he described as the test suggested by James LJ, and that he could not assent to the 'definition' of minerals in a minerals reservation given by Mellish LJ.[45] 'In the first place it introduces as one element the circumstance that the substance can be got at a profit. It is obvious to see that if that is an essential part of the definition the question whether a particular substance is or is not a mineral may depend on the state of the market, and it may be that a mineral one year is not a mineral the next'.[46] Agreeing with the first instance judge's view that to allow Mr Farie to work 'the common clay which constitutes the subsoil of the greater part of the land of this country' would entitle him to destroy the surface of the land conveyed to the Corporation, Lord Halsbury concluded by saying that he 'hesitate[d] very much to adopt the reasoning of [*Hext v Gill*] notwithstanding the high authority by which it was decided.'[47] Lord Watson, by contrast, thought *Hext v Gill* of little relevance to the facts of *Farie* because the context was so different; yet he apparently affirmed it, noting that the contract had been 'between the lord of the manor and the purchaser of the freehold of a copyhold tenement within the manor… which excepted "all mines and minerals," and in these

43 That clay was included had been decided in two English cases: *Midland Railway Company v Haunchwood Brick and Tile Co* (1882) 20 Ch D 552; *Loosemore v Tiverton and North Devon Railway Co* (1882) 22 Ch D 25.

44 At 669.

45 At 669-670, 673.

46 At 670.

47 At 669-670, 673.

circumstances it was sufficiently clear that the copyholder had only right to the surface, and had no right to minerals of any kind.'[48]

Jersey v Neath: the Court of Appeal's explanation of the minerals definition rule

The impact of Lord Halsbury's words in *Farie* became apparent just over six months later in the Court of Appeal's decision in *Earl of Jersey v Neath Poor Law Union*.[49] The case concerned an ordinary freehold conveyance of 1829 reserving 'all mines of coal culm iron and all other mines and minerals whatsoever except stone quarries'.[50] Nearly sixty years later, the minerals owner claimed compensation for damage caused to a seam of brick earth and clay through which the defendants had built a sewer. An arbitrator awarded him £30 and the owner brought an action to enforce the award, the defendants relying on *Farie* to argue that *Hext v Gill* had been overruled so that the accuracy of its definition was now in doubt. The court, finding nothing in the context to show the reservation should have a more limited meaning, applied the minerals definition rule in *Hext v Gill* and held that the reservation included the brick earth and clay.

Although the outcome of *Jersey v Neath* is of limited interest, the decision is remarkable for the way in which three very experienced judges, giving reserved judgments, went to extraordinary lengths to defend and explain the minerals definition rule in *Hext v Gill*, to distinguish *Farie*, and to say, as politely as they could, that Lord Halsbury was wrong. Their judgments put the full authority of the Court of Appeal behind *Hext v Gill* and can be read as a concerted

48 At 674-675. In *Earl of Jersey v Guardians of the Poor of the Neath Poor Law Union* (1889) 22 QBD 555, CA, Fry LJ said at 564: 'The speeches of Lord Watson and Lord Macnaghten appear to me to leave the case of *Hext v Gill* untouched; whereas the speech of Lord Herschell clearly adopts it as the principle of his decision.'

49 The full name of the case was *Earl of Jersey v Guardians of the Poor of the Neath Poor Law Union* (1889) 22 QBD 555.

50 The word 'ordinary' is that of Lord Esher MR at 557.

exercise to protect it from future attack from any angle. Lord Esher MR said that *Farie* could have been determined within the rule because the rule extended to context; and the context of *Farie*, which was the making of a reservoir, showed that 'the clay was to be used in carrying out the purpose of the Waterworks Clauses Act or the conveyance, and could not have been intended to be reserved.'[51] He stated the rule in terms,[52] adding that it was 'absolutely right', 'an excellent rule of construction, founded on a long series of cases' and, in the absence of a decision of the House of Lords overruling it, was binding on the Court of Appeal.

Bowen LJ echoed Lord Esher, making the same points and adding new ones. He too said the rule was 'absolutely right' as one for ordinary reservations in ordinary grants which applied unless there was something in the context to throw light upon and alter it.[53] It was the result of a long extent of authorities and was propounded by both Mellish LJ and James LJ 'than whom no greater authorities, I venture to say, have sat in our time in courts of law.' Thereby, any notion that James LJ preferred or was even suggesting a different rule based on the vernacular test was apparently rejected. Bowen LJ made three further observations. First, 'that the rule has been in existence for seventeen years and has produced a very great effect upon business transactions during that time, and I do not suppose it will be lightly disturbed or without grave consideration.'[54] Second, that 'Mellish LJ does not say, nor, I think, mean, that the test was whether the minerals could be worked at a market profit at the time, but whether they had a use and a

---

51 At 560.

52 At 559, quoting from the report of *Hext v Gill* at (1872) LR Ch App 699 at 712.

53 At 560-62.

54 At 561. Bowen LJ had practised at the commercial bar. He was appointed a judge of the Queens' Bench division in 1879, a Lord Justice of Appeal in 1888, and a Lord of Appeal in Ordinary in 1893. In 1889 he had significantly more judicial experience as well as experience of commercial law than Lord Halsbury.

value of their own independent of and separable from the rest of the soil.'[55] This explanation of what Mellish LJ was saying is supported by the variant text of the report of *Hext v Gill* which may indicate that Lord Halsbury was referring to a less complete version of the text of Mellish LJ's judgment than was available to Bowen LJ and the Court of Appeal.[56] Third, after analysing the opinions of the other three judges in *Farie* sitting with Lord Halsbury, Bowen LJ said that 'Lord Watson and Lord McNaughton do not seem to me to reject *Hext v Gill*, though I do not know how far either of them or both of them would in the first instance have come to the same conclusion. Lord Herschell, on the contrary, distinctly recognises *Hext v Gill*, and uses over again the exact language of Mellish LJ, for I think it is obvious that the three lines which were cited in the argument from Lord Herschell's judgement are really an abbreviation of Lord Justice Mellish's words.'

Fry LJ said he was 'entirely of the same opinion' and then focussed on the vernacular test referred to in James LJ's judgment, which he said was 'pointed out … and deliberately rejected by the Lord Justice, as one to which he could not give effect, although he preferred it.' Remarking that Lord Halsbury suggested the test 'would remove all difficulties', Fry LJ thought its effect would be to introduce a very considerable difficulty of its own 'requiring the consideration of the meaning of the words, not only in the English language as commonly used, but in the vernacular of three classes of persons.' Like Bowen LJ, he then referred to the speeches of the other lords in *Farie*, saying that those of Lords Watson and Macnaghten left *Hext v Gill* untouched, whereas Lord Herschell 'clearly adopts it as the principle of his decision'. The real question in *Farie*, Fry LJ thought, was whether there was something in the nature of the transaction[57] which prevented the application of the *prima facie* meaning of the mineral reservation's words. His answer was in the affirmative, because it was reasonable to anticipate that the purchasers

---

55 At 562.

56 See the textual variant above at p.187, n.19.

57 The compulsory purchase of land pursuant to statute for the construction of a reservoir.

relying on the statute would acquire such an interest in the surface as would enable the reservoir works to be constructed and then maintained by them.[58] So Fry LJ accepted that the circumstances of a particular transaction could modify the operation of the *prima facie* rule in *Hext v Gill*; but what it did not do, he thought. was to displace the rule altogether because the rule itself recognised that a standard definition of mines and minerals was not always applicable and would have to yield in a particular context.

Within months of the *Jersey v Neath* decision by the Court of Appeal, *Hext v Gill* received further affirmation of a less conclusive but still important kind from the House of Lords itself in *Midland Railway Company v Robinson*.[59] Lords Herschell, Watson and Macnaghten who heard the appeal, this time on the interpretation of the word 'mines' in s 77 of the Railway Clauses Consolidation Act 1845, had all sat in *Farie*, and all of them said that the opinions they had expressed in *Farie* remained unchanged.[60] Lord Herschell in *Farie* had given the sole dissenting opinion where he had referred to *Hext v Gill* and at two passages had respectively interpreted the word 'minerals' and the scope of the s 77 minerals reservation in terms that showed he accepted the definition of 'minerals' in Mellish LJ's judgment and that he thought that definition applicable in the context of s 77.[61] Now, in *Robinson*,

---

58 Fry LJ's judgment is at 563-66.

59 (1889) 15 App Cas 19.

60 Lord Herschell at 26; Lord Watson at 34; and Lord Macnaghten at 34.

61 See Lord Herschell in *Farie* (1888) 13 App Cas 657 at 683: 'I think that the word "minerals" imports, *prima facie*, and apart from any context, all substances other than the vegetable matters forming the ordinary surface of the ground. In this widest sense clay is unquestionably a mineral. But we have to look to the context to see whether the word is here used in a more limited sense.' Having looked at the context, he concluded at 685: 'I think the reservation must be taken to extend to all such bodies of mineral substances, lying together in seams, beds or strata, as are commonly worked for profit, and have a value independent of the surface of the land.' These passages suggest that Fry LJ was correct in *Jersey v Neath*

he gave the longest and most detailed opinion which in effect qualified and explained his earlier reference in *Farie* to profit and value.[62] He said: 'when I stated in my opinion the reservation extended "to all such bodies of mineral substances lying together in seams, beds or strata as are commonly worked for profit and have a value independent of the surface of the land," I did not intend by these latter words to suggest that the value of the mineral substances at the time of the reservation was the test whether they were reserved or not. I used them in order to emphasise the fact that it was not every scattered piece of mineral lying under the land that could be called a mine but only mineral substances lying in seams, or beds, or strata.' He doubted that much assistance could be obtained from cases where a construction had been put upon the word 'mines' in agreements between parties unaffected by any statutory enactment – in other words, context was relevant because the same words in private agreements and agreements made pursuant to statutes for statutory purposes could not be construed in the same way. And he added, referring to Lord Chelmsford's words in *Great Western Railway Company v Bennett*,[63] 'that [s 77] reserves to the mine owner all the minerals however near they may be to the surface,' that the other lords who took part in the judgment shared that view, and that 'it is impossible to say how many transactions in the last twenty years may have been carried through on this view of the law. There has been no judicial expression of a contrary opinion that I am aware of until quite recently in *Farie's Case*.'[64] This was the same point – reliance by parties to business transactions on decided case law over many years – as had been made by Bowen LJ in *Jersey v Neath* about *Hext v Gill*.

---

when he said (at 564) that, in *Farie*, Lord Herschell had 'clearly adopt[ed]' it [i.e. *Hext v Gill*] as the principle of his decision'.

62 *Midland Railway Company v Robinson* (1889) 15 HL 19 at 26-27.

63 (1867) LR 2 HL 27 at 38. Mr Bennett, the successful respondent, was represented by Mr George Mellish QC. As Mellish LJ five years later in *Hext v Gill*, he was fully aware of the problems posed by the construction of minerals reservations under sections 77-79 of the 1845 Act.

64 Ibid, at 31.

Preference for the vernacular test

Between 1892 and 1911, there were a number of reported cases in the High Court where the rule in *Hext v Gill* was applied or distinguished, and an even greater number of reported cases in the appellate courts dealing with the rule mostly in the context of statutory minerals reservation clauses found in s 77 of the Railway Clauses Consolidation Act 1845 and the corresponding s 70 of the Railway Clauses Consolidation Act (Scotland) 1845. As the law evolved through these cases, there was no overruling of *Hext v Gill* (as fortified by *Jersey v Neath* and *Midland Railway Co v Robinson*), but there was an increasing tendency to distinguish Mellish LJ's rule of construction within it and to prefer the vernacular test referred to by James LJ, and then to identify a further test of exceptionality. The purpose of the 1845 Act was to enable a railway company to acquire land to construct and maintain the railway; and the land beneath the line, which supported the line, was needed for that purpose. The s 77 reservation[65] excepted from the railway company's purchase 'mines of coal, ironstone, slate, or other minerals' so that they were retained by the landowner. If, after purchase, the landowner wanted to get the minerals, he first had to serve notice on the company, and if the company did not agree to pay him compensation then the landowner had the right to work and get the minerals even if by doing so he let down and destroyed the surface, whether by subterranean working or open working from the surface itself. Because the conveyance was statutory, the purchaser did not enjoy rights of adjacent and subjacent support under the Act whereas he would have done so under the common law had the land acquisition been the result of contract.[66] And there was a risk, that the courts had

---

[65] Or s 70 in the act applicable to Scotland.

[66] *GWR v Bennett* (1867) LR 2 HL 27, referred to by Buckley J in *GWR v Blades* ([1901] 2 Ch 624 at 630. In 1867, counsel for Mr Bennett, the landowner and successful respondent, had been Mr George Mellish QC, who as Mellish LJ in 1872 was aware of the issue about support created by the statutory minerals reservation. He was also aware of how the Law Lords viewed the meaning of minerals in the context of the s 77 reservation. Lord Chelmsford had said: 'That this section reserves to the mine-owner all the

to guard against, that a landowner could bring a claim for compensation against the railway company even if he had no intention of working the minerals across some or all of the area for which the claim was made.[67] If, as in *GWR v Blades* in 1901,[68] clay lay on or just below the surface and was a mineral, the landowner could extract a very high price from the railway company, which was in a situation analogous to the plaintiff in *Midland Railway Co v Robinson* or to Glasgow Corporation in *Farie.* Faced with the question of whether the clay was excepted by the s 77 reservation or not, Buckley J held that a rule different from *Hext v Gill* applied because of the nature and price of the transaction, the object of the contracting parties, and the fact that clay was the soil of the district.

This was a sensible outcome consistent with both *Farie* and *Hext v Gill,* but it did not address Lord Halsbury's point in *Farie* that a statutory reservation of minerals should not mean anything different from a reservation of minerals in a private deed.[69] In 1903, Lord Halsbury chose to make his point again and with greater force. He presided as Lord Chancellor in the Court of Appeal in *Todd, Birleston v North Eastern Railway,*[70] and took the opportunity to criticise *Jersey v Neath*

---

minerals, however near they may be to the surface … appears very clearly from the exception of "the parts necessary to be dug or carried away or used in the construction of the company's works," as these will, of course, be the minerals lying nearest to the surface.'

67 The plaintiff railway company in *Midland v Robinson* argued (at 23) that the legislature could not have intended to give an owner the power by notice to compel a railway company to purchase the minerals when there was no real intention of working them.

68 [1901] 2 Ch 624.

69 *Lord Provost and Magistrates of Glasgow v Farie* (1888) 13 App Cas 657 at 672. In *GWR v Carpalla China Clay* [1910] AC 83, Lord Macnaghten took the same view at 85 (Lords Atkinson, Collins, Shaw of Dunfermline and Loreburn LC concurring).

70 [1903] 1 KB 603 at 607-608. Although the Lord Chancellor was entitled to preside in the Court of Appeal, the pressure of his other duties meant that he rarely did so. It seems too great a coincidence to think that Lord Halsbury had not deliberately chosen to sit on a case where he could

during exchanges with counsel and then to give the briefest of judgments saying that the decision in *Farie* 'must be binding on all courts'.[71] However, it was not until four House of Lords cases decided in 1909 and 1911 that the tide turned conclusively against the rule of construction advanced by Mellish LJ in *Hext v Gill*.[72]

Limits on the minerals definition rule: the House of Lords and the railway cases

The first of these was *North British Railway v Budhill Coal and Sandstone Company*,[73] where the question was whether sandstone was a mineral within the meaning of s 70 of the Railways Clauses Consolidation (Scotland) Act 1845, which reserved from the company buying land 'any mines of coal, ironstone, slate, *or other minerals*.' [emphasis added] The influence of Scottish common law is striking in the House's approach to interpreting s 70. Two cases of 1818 and 1841, *Menzies v*

intervene further on the subject of mineral reservations. Judgment was given on 9 Feb 1903.

71 By which he meant English as well as Scottish. This was apparently the opposite of what he had said at the outset of his speech in *Farie* (at 669).

72 In 1908, in *GWR v Carpalla China Clay* [1909] 1 Ch 218, Farwell LJ (at 237-238) addressed Lord Halsbury's observation in *Farie* about profit, saying that 'without desiring to criticise Lord Halsbury, I venture to think that he was a little hard on Mellish LJ. I do not think the Lord Justice intended to say that the definition of 'mineral' can depend on the fluctuation of the market. What I understand him to mean is that china clay might be regarded as a mineral because it is one of those things which are usually worked with the object of making a profit, not because a profit is made, but because the object is to make a profit, and the substance is extracted from the soil for the purpose of making a profit out of it when gotten. It is not taking the soil itself but extracting a mineral substance from the soil.' The House of Lords affirmed the Court of Appeal's judgment: [1910] AC 83 at 86.

73 [1910] AC 116

Earl of Breadalbane[74] and *Duke of Hamilton v Bentley*,[75] had established the proposition that in Scotland 'freestone' was not included within an exception or reservation in a private conveyance of mines and minerals.[76] The 1845 Act, Lord Shaw noted in *Budhill*, was passed within four years of *Hamilton v Bentley* and he did not see how it could be suggested 'that Parliament then and thus using the language 'mines', 'minerals' etc ... did so in a sense different from that authoritatively accepted as the common law of the land.'[77] This way of thinking was strongly at variance with what the House of Lords had said in 1867 about the minerals provisions in the 1845 Act in *Great Western Railway Company v Bennett*: that 'it was obviously the intention of the legislature, in making these provisions, to create a new code as to the relation between mine owners and railway companies, where lands were compulsorily taken for the purpose of making a railway. The object of the statute evidently was to get rid of all the ordinary law on the subject.'[78] Now, however, Lord Loreburn LC said that 'the decisions in 1818 and 1841 as to the meaning of the word "minerals" in private conveyances are of the greatest importance in interpreting this statute. When an Act of Parliament uses a word which has received a judicial construction it presumably uses it in the same sense ... it would be very strange if a court, having before it two conveyances with a reservation of minerals in both, were obliged to treat the reservation as meaning one thing in the first and a quite different thing in the second, merely because the one was a voluntary conveyance by agreement and the other

---

74 (10 June 1818), 19 Fac. Coll. 531, 1 Sh. App. 225. The decision was of the House of Lords.

75 (1841) 3 D. 1121, Court of Session (29 June 1841).

76 See Lord Shaw of Dunfermline at 135. 'Freestone' can refer to any fine-grained rock, such as sand stirred or limestone, that can be easily quarried and worked without breaking or splitting.

77 At 136.

78 (1867) LR 2 HL 27 at 40 per Lord Cranworth. *GWR v Bennett* was relied on in argument by counsel for the unsuccessful respondent in *Budhill* ([1910] AC 116 at 123) but no express reference to it appears in the decision.

was compulsory under the Act.'[79] Lord Gorell thought that the foundation of the judgments in the two Scottish cases was the proposition that the words mines and minerals 'are used in the ordinary sense in which they are understood and used by land owners and those engaged in mining and commerce.'[80] This was a reference to the test suggested by James LJ in *Hext v Gill* which Lord Gorell thought appropriate to apply to s 70, thereby rejecting Mellish LJ's test, which he thought gave insufficient effect to the context of s 70.[81] The House favoured this test because, as Lord Loreburn explained, no solution could be derived by piecing together even the most eminent authorities, which were contradictory and put the matter at large.[82] Sandstone was the common substratum of the soil in many parts of England and Scotland, and if it were a mineral then what the railway company bought was liable to be destroyed altogether unless the company chose on notice to buy the ordinary rock lying beneath it.[83] 'I think it is clear,' Lord Loreburn added, 'that by the words "or other minerals" exceptional substances are designated, not the ordinary rock of the district.'[84]

---

79 At 127.

80 At 130 and 133.

81 Lord Gorell at 130 characterized Mellish LJ's test as being that the term 'minerals' 'includes every substance which can be got from underneath the surface of the earth for the purpose of profit.' He thought this gave insufficient effect to the context of s 70, explaining (at 132-133) that 'if it had been intended in framing [section 70] to adopt [either it or Lord Herschell's test in *Farie*], it would have been unnecessary to specify particularly coal, ironstone, and slate. Moreover, they would make the decision depend on the cost of production and labour and the state of the market, and render uncertain that which those framing the section must have contemplated as reasonably certain.' Lord Gorell's opinion on these matters was agreed with by the whole House.

82 At 125.

83 At 126.

84 At 127.

The second case was *GWR v Carpalla China Clay*, where a conveyance of 1881 contained a minerals reservation clause pursuant to s 77 of the English Act of 1845. The question before the House was whether, on the facts, china clay (the same substance as in *Hext v Gill*) was a mineral. Lord Macnaghten, who gave the only reasoned opinion, held that china clay was a mineral because it was not part of the ordinary composition of the soil in the district and its presence was rare and exceptional.[85]

The third, Scottish, case was *Caledonian Railway Company v Glenboig Union Fireclay Company*.[86] There the question, once again, was the meaning of 'minerals' in reservation clauses of conveyances of 1856, 1881 and 1883 made pursuant to s 70 of the Scottish Act of 1845.[87] Lord Loreburn LC, again presiding, said that the principle of the *Budhill* and *Carpalla* decisions was that the court had to find what the party must be taken to have bought and sold, that no definition of minerals was attainable because it had a variety of meanings, and that what the railway company intended to get and the landowner had intended to give was the land beneath the railway line for support. However, where 'anything exceptional in use, character, or value was thereunder, that was reserved, provided it could be included under the word "minerals" as understood in the vernacular of the mining world, and the commercial world, and the landowner.' If evidence was given of the common meaning at the time the matter came to court, it should be assumed that it was the same at the time of the sale, unless sufficient ground was given for coming to a country conclusion.[88] Thus fireclay, a substance valuable for the manufacture of bricks capable of resisting high temperatures, was of an 'exceptional character as to its properties

---

85 [1910] AC 83 at 86. Lords Loreburn LC, Atkinson, Collins, and Shaw of Dunfermline all agreed.

86 [1911] AC 290.

87 The conveyance dates appear from the Court of Session judgment at [1910] SC 951 at 952.

88 [1911] AC 290 at 299 per Lord Loreburn LC, with whom the whole House comprising Lords Macnaghten, Shaw of Dunfermline and Robson agreed.

and value', and therefore was a mineral within the meaning of the reservation. Lord Loreburn concluded his opinion with these words: 'It is impossible in my view to give further assistance in ascertaining when a substance is to be treated as a mineral within the Act of Parliament than we have endeavoured to give in the cases already cited.' The only cases cited in the opinion were *Budhill* and *Carpalla*.

The fourth case, again from Scotland, *was Symington v Caledonian Railway Company* which concerned another s 70 minerals reservation in a conveyance of 1852.[89] The House had to decide whether 'freestone' was a mineral within the meaning of the term in the reservation. In a brief opinion, Lord Loreburn explained that while *Budhill*, *Carpalla* and *Glenboig* set out the relevant law, in every case 'it is always a question of fact'. Thus freestone, which in *Budhill* had been held not to be a mineral, could be a mineral in another case on different facts if it was exceptional in use, value and character and was not the common rock of the district so that it did not swallow up the grant.[90]

The minerals definition rule doubted

In 1931, in *Waring v Foden*,[91] the Court of Appeal had to determine whether a reservation of 'mines minerals and mineral substances' in a private conveyance of 1926 operated to reserve the sand and gravel lying within or under the land granted. The vendor had reserved the power to 'work and get the same by underground workings only.' Counsel for the appellant vendor, sought to distinguish between the five House of Lords decisions between 1888 and 1912 on the basis that they were 'code cases' dealt with under statutory procedure, arguing that non-code cases were more reliable guides in private contracts and conveyances dealing with the surface, mines and minerals.[92] Lord Hanworth MR

---

89 [1912] AC 87.

90 At 92-93. Lords Atkinson and Gorell concurred in Lord Loreburn's opinion, and Lord Shaw agreed with the result.

91 [1932] 1 Ch 276.

92 At 290.

said that view was definitely rejected by Lord Loreburn in *Budhill*, and that in private conveyances regard must be had to cases relating to the construction of the words 'mines and minerals' in statutory provisions.[93] It is clear from reading the judgments, which all refer at some length to *Hext v Gill*, that the court was asked by counsel to make a clear choice between the tests for defining 'minerals' advanced by Mellish LJ and James LJ. Lord Hanworth MR did not go as far as this, but Lawrence LJ did, saying:

> The decision in *Hext v Gill* was followed by a sharp difference of judicial opinion on the question whether the true principle was that laid down by Mellish LJ or that suggested by James LJ. This difference of opinion was finally settled by the *Budhill* and *Glenboig* cases, in which the House of Lords definitely decided that the view suggested by James LJ was the right view.[94]

Lawrence LJ then summarised the two main principles to be gathered from *Budhill* and *Glenboig*:

> … first, that the word 'minerals' when found in a reservation out of a grant of land means substance is exceptional in use, in value and in character … and does not mean the ordinary soil of the district which if reserved would practically swallow up the grant …; and, secondly, that in deciding whether or not in a particular case exceptional substances are 'minerals' the true test is what that word means in the vernacular of the mining world, the commercial world and land owners at the time of the grant, and whether the particular substance was say regarded as a mineral.'

He then said, on the question of profit:

93 At 288-290. Counsel for the respondents (who were successful) had conceded that such a distinction had existed until the HL decision in *Budhill* (15 Nov 1909).

94 At 294.

> Further, it is to be noted that the fact that certain substances can be worked for the purpose of profit may have a bearing upon the question whether they have been recognised as included in the term 'minerals', but does not necessarily determine that they have been ordinarily understood to be so included.

Thus the question 'whether a given substance is or is not a 'mineral' within the meaning of the instrument in which it is mentioned is a question of fact to be decided according to the circumstances of the particular case.'[95]

Romer LJ, who gave the third judgment, referred to but declined to rule on the argument by counsel for the respondent that Mellish LJ's definition of minerals could not now be relied on and that James LJ's should be used instead as 'the one that now holds the field'. Lawrence LJ's judgment shows that he agreed, but Romer LJ did not. Whichever of the two definitions applied, he said, both the context of the deed of conveyance[96] and the vernacular meaning to be attributed to minerals in 1926 excluded sand and gravel from the reservation.[97]

The minerals definition rule in mining leases

A willingness to adopt Mellish LJ's definition of minerals was exhibited by the Court of Appeal in 1965 in *O'Callaghan v Elliott*.[98] The question for the court was whether a lease of 1948 was or was not a mining lease. If it was, the tenant had no right to a new lease under the Landlord and Tenant Act 1954 because the act did not apply to a tenancy created by

---

95 At 294-295.

96 Which was the sale of surface property in an area where there were nearby, at the time of the conveyance, a number of gravel pits which were being worked from the surface, as well as others which had been worked from the surface until shortly before. The reservation gave power to the vendor to work and get 'mines minerals and mineral substances .... by underground workings only'. See 277 and 286.

97 At 299-300.

98 [1965] 1 QB 601.

a mining lease. For the purpose of the LTA 1954, the definition of mining lease was contained in section 25 of the Landlord and Tenant Act 1927 which said that 'the expression 'mining lease' means a lease for any mining purpose or purposes connected therewith, and 'mining purposes' include the [...winning, working, getting etc] of mines and minerals, in or under land.' The lease in question contained a term requiring the tenant to work and get sand and gravel from the land. Lord Denning MR, with whose reasoning Davies LJ agreed, said this:[99]

> In this particular statute, I think that the words 'mines and minerals' are used in the wide sense which was given to them by Lord Romilly MR in *Midland Railway Co v Checkley* and by Mellish LJ in *Hext v Gill.* The words 'mines and minerals' include every substance which can be got from underneath the surface of the earth for the purpose of profit.
>
> In many cases the wide meaning of 'mines and minerals' is cut down by the context. It often does not include the ordinary rock or subsoil of the district. For instance, if a railway company acquires land on which to build a railway, it does not require the mines or minerals under the land. They are reserved to the previous owner. In such a case the previous owner can claim exceptional substances, but he cannot claim the ordinary rock of the district, see *North British Railway Co v Budhill Coal and Sandstone Co*. Similarly when a man sold a piece of land where the subsoil was sand and gravel, but reserved to himself the 'minerals', it was held that he did not reserve to himself all the sand and gravel; for the purchaser could not even build a house without cutting into the sand and gravel, see *Waring v Foden.*
>
> In this statute, there are no such circumstances to cut down the meaning of the words 'mines and minerals'. I think they include all substances capable of being worked for profit below the top surface of the land. They include sand and gravel...

99 At 608C-F.

What the Court of Appeal did in *O'Callaghan v Elliott* was to approach the exercise of construing the term 'minerals' in a statute in a significantly different way from how the same court, in *Waring v Foden*, had previously construed it in a reservation. Davies LJ said he found it 'a little difficult to follow' Lawrence's LJ's observation in *Waring* that value might be a criterion in in deciding whether a substance was a mineral.[100] Russell LJ thought the cases on exceptions and reservations from a grant did not help at all, were related to the circumstances of a particular case, and that 'the inquiry under the [Landlord and Tenant] Act of 1954 is necessarily a totally different inquiry from that under an exception and reservation.'[101] Thus although the court in both *O'Callaghan v Elliott* and *Waring v Foden* was dealing with sand and gravel, the question of whether they were minerals depended on the facts and on the relationship of instrument, context and statute, and this determined whether the exceptionality and vernacular tests were relevant. The court found them of no relevance in *O'Callaghan v Elliott*, and instead adopted Mellish LJ's definition of 'minerals' while seeing no need to address Lawrence LJ's view that the House of Lords had decided that it was wrong and that James LJ's test was right.

The minerals definition rule acknowledged again

O'Callaghan v Elliott marked a partial but important rehabilitation of Mellish LJ's test. This was clarified, with its limit being more clearly stated, in *Earl of Lonsdale v Attorney-General*, where Slade J rejected a submission that 'in the absence of a contrary context, there is a normal primary meaning which attaches to the word 'minerals', that is to say every substance which can be got from underneath the surface of the earth for the purpose of profit.'[102] Slade J had to consider whether the meaning of 'mines and minerals' in a conveyance of 1880 as varied by a deed of exchange of 1935 extended to oil and natural gas. He concluded it did not, holding that the phrase 'mines and minerals' was not a

[100] At 609B.

[101] At 610E-G.

[102] [1982] 1 WLR 887 at 923H-924B.

definite term; and that the court had to consider, *inter alia*, what the phrase meant in the vernacular of the mining world, landowners and commercial men at the time of the grant, and in doing so had to have regard to all the terms of the conveyance and the circumstances in which the phrase was used.[103] This decision was reached after a thirteen day trial which enabled the judge to review a large number of the relevant authorities and to summarize his conclusions from them in a series of propositions, of which the first seven were as follows:

> (1) Though the wide sense given to the phrase 'mines and minerals' by Lord Romilly MR in *Midland Railway v Checkley*, LR 4 Eq 19 and by Mellish LJ in *Hext v Gill*, LR 7 Ch App 699 is a sense which the phrase is capable of bearing and can still be attributed to it in a proper context see, for example, *O'Callaghan v Elliott* [1966] 1 QB 601, it cannot now properly be regarded as a primary or literal sense which is always to be applied in the absence of a sufficiently clear contrary context: see, for example, the *Budhill* case [1910] AC 116 and *Waring v Foden* [1932] 1 Ch 276.
>
> (2) The phrase 'mines and minerals' is not a definite term, but is one that is capable of bearing a wide variety of meanings: see, for example, the *Budhill* case [1910] AC 116, 130 per Lord Gorell and the *Glenboig* case [1911] AC 290, 299 per Lord Loreburn LC. One possible meaning that had been attributed to the word 'minerals' in *Darvill v Roper*, 3 Drew 294 and other pre 1880 authorities was 'all such substances as are dug out of the earth by means of a mine.' This remains a possible meaning in a proper context.
>
> (3) Unless the meaning is clear from the four corners of the relevant instrument itself, the first duty of the court in construing a grant of mines and minerals is to try to ascertain what the phrase meant in the vernacular of 'the mining world,

[103] At 924D-925B.

the commercial world and land owners at the time of the grant,' in accordance with the test suggested by James LJ in *Hext v Gill*, LR 7 Ch App 699, 719 And approved by the House of Lords in the *Budhill* case [1910] AC 116. The common link between the three categories of persons referred to by James LJ is, I think, that they are all persons who may ordinarily be expected to have both some knowledge of mines and minerals and also some experience of dealing with them in the course of commerce in this country.

(4) The meaning of the phrase in this vernacular sense may be derived either from direct evidence as to the vernacular meaning at the relevant time or by inference drawn by the court, as in *Barnard-Argue-Roth-Stearns Oil and Gas Co Ltd v Farquharson* [1912] AC 864. If there is clear evidence as to the vernacular meaning at the date of the trial then, in the absence of evidence to the contrary, the court may be justified in assuming that there was a similar vernacular usage at the date of the grant: see the *Glenboig* case [911] AC 290, 299 per Lord Loreburn LC.

(5) Where it is clearly established that, at the date of the grant, a particular vernacular meaning was attributed to the phrase 'mines and minerals' by 'the mining world, the commercial world and landowners', the court will be predisposed to adopt that meaning. The vernacular test, however, is not a rigid test to be applied without regard to all the other terms of the instrument in question and the circumstances in which it is used: see *Borys v Canadian Pacific Railway Co* [1953] AC 217, 223 per Lord Porter. The court must never overlook the commercial background and apparent commercial purpose of the transaction.

(6) One pointer to the parties' intentions may be to consider whether or not these substances in question are exceptional in use, in value and in character: see for example *Waring v Foden* [1932] 1 Ch 276, 294 per Lawrence LJ. Another

pointer is the evidence as to the general state of knowledge of the relevant substance at the date of the grant and the way in which it was then regarded and treated as a commercial matter: see, for example, *Barnard v Farquharson* [1912] AC 864, 869 per Lord Atkinson. A third, significant pointer may be derived from any express powers of working that are conferred by the instrument in question: see for example the same case at p.869 per Lord Atkinson.

(7) In considering whether a grant or reservation of mines and minerals includes a specified substance, it is irrelevant that the parties did not actually have that substance in mind. The test of their intention is an objective one: see for example the *Reardon-Smith* case [1976] 1 WLR 989, 996 per Lord Wilberforce.[104]

Slade J's review of the construction of mines and minerals reservations was described as 'extensive and valuable' in 2021 in the Court of Appeal decision in *Wynne-Finch v Natural Resources Body for Wales*, where it occupied a prominent place in the judgment, with propositions (3) and (6) being singled out for their relevance in construing minerals reservations of 1816 and 1919.[105] What is striking about Slade J's review is that it began with his acknowledgement that Mellish LJ's definition in *Hext v Gill* was a sense that can still be attributed to the words 'mines and minerals' 'in a proper context'. While he considered the circumstances of the mining lease in *O'Callaghan v Elliott* as one example of it, he did not elaborate much on what he thought 'a proper context' might involve before moving on to the vernacular test suggested by James LJ and the exceptionality test suggested by Lawrence LJ in *Waring v Foden*. In particular (and because he did not need to in the case before him), he gave no specific consideration to the question of whether there should be any distinction between mineral reservations made by lords of the manor in respect of grants of copyhold or freehold

[104] *Reardon-Smith Line Ltd v Hansen-Tangen* [1976] 1 WLR 989

[105] [2022] 3 All ER 162 at [30]-[32].

lands and mineral reservations made in other circumstances, whether compulsory purchase with statutory reservations or where the context was of a freehold grant from 1 January 1926 by which time copyhold tenure was abolished. The issue of proper context is dealt with further below,[106] after consideration of recent manorial case law in the Court of Appeal after Slade J's decision.

Wynne-Finch: the rule superseded?

In *Wynne-Finch v Natural Resources Body for Wales*,[107] the claimants were trustees of a family settlement and legal owners of the lordships of the manors of Arwystli and Cyfeiliog. These extended over large areas of mid-Wales before the disposal of much of the manorial lands by the family after the First World War.[108] NRBW were the lessees of 40 freehold or long-leasehold titles owned by the National Assembly for Wales, who were successors in title to those who had purchased the lands from the family. For over 40 years, on its own admission, NRBW had been using mudstone extracted from quarries across the area to build and maintain forest roads and tracks, as well as a wind turbine and telecommunications mast. The trustees claimed *inter alia* that NRBW's land was held subject either to common form mineral reservations in the 1919 conveyances or to the statutory reservation in the Arwystli Inclosure Act of 1816.

The 1919 conveyances reserved 'all mines beds and quarries of coal and ironstone and all other metals stone and minerals within and under the hereditaments and premises conveyed'. The 1816 reservation reserved to the lord of the manor rights to 'delve, search for, get up, make merchantable, and take and carry away' 'any Mines, Ores, Coals, Metals

---

106 At p.226.

107 [2021] EWCA 1473; [2022] 3 All ER 162

108 When the property within the settlement existing at that date remained entailed. The entail was barred only in the 1980s: see the first instance judgment [2020] EWHC 1924 (Ch) at [6], Falk J.

or Minerals whatsoever' in or under the former waste of the manor. These reservations, the trustees argued, covered mudstone;[109] and they sued for an account, trespass and conversion, claiming ownership of everything under the topsoil and seeking damages for the mudstone's value.[110]

The first instance judge, Falk J, dismissed the claim in what Henderson LJ described, when the case reached the Court of Appeal, as 'a careful, comprehensive and scholarly judgment'.[111] So far as the 1919 conveyances were concerned, Henderson LJ (giving the judgment of the court) identified five strands in the judge's reasoning and agreed with all of them.[112] First was her finding that mudstone was the common rock of the district and did not satisfy any test of exceptionality, so that it would not have been viewed as a material that was worthwhile quarrying and selling commercially, whether in 1816 or 1919. Second, she found no direct evidence of the vernacular meaning of the words used at the time of the relevant grants but concluded that, in the context of the locality, none of the mineral world, commercial world or landowners would have had in mind mudstone – an evaluative finding of fact which she was entitled to reach on the evidence before her. Third, the judge regarded the powers of 'searching for mining working [and] getting' contained in the 1919 reservation as an important part of the context, finding that they obviously contemplated the destruction and removal of the surface.[113] Fourth, the judge referred to the 'purpose of profit' test, described by Lord Esher MR in *Jersey v Neath* as 'an excellent rule of construction' and held that the test imported 'that the material

---

109 The claimant trustees relied on *Hext v Gill* and *Midland Railway Co v Checkley* in respect of the 1919 reservations and, in addition, on *Wainman v Earl of Rosse*, *Micklethwait v Winter* and *Consett Waterworks Company v Rittson* in respect of the 1816 reservation: see judgment of Falk J at [84] to [93].

110 At [122(i)].

111 [2022] 3 All ER 162 at [7].

112 [2022] 3 All ER 162 at [40] to [46].

113 See Falk J's judgment at [112].

has some value that makes commercialisation possible'. In 1816 and 1919, mudstone would not have been in that category. Fifth and finally, the judge laid weight on 'important issues of practicality' which included cogent further reasons for concluding that the trustees' claim to ownership of everything under the topsoil made no practical sense. Given the shallowness of the topsoil, it would be impossible for the allottees having the freehold to erect any form of permanent farm or building or even put in fencing without trespassing on the lord's property. The parties to the 1919 conveyances or the awards pursuant to the 1816 Inclosure Act would not have contemplated that compensation be paid to the lord of the manor for those sorts of disturbance to the mudstone; and even if a term were implied that the grants extended both to subsoil and to whatever layer of stone was necessary for those uses of the surface land that would have been contemplated at the time of the grant, it was wholly unclear, if the trustees' case were correct, where any 'literal boundary line' could be drawn if not immediately below the topsoil.

Turning to the minerals reservation in the 1816 Inclosure Act, Henderson LJ doubted that much assistance was provided from Lord Esher MR's statement in *Consett Waterworks Company v Ritson* that, in relation to Inclosure Acts which were in a common form[114] which had existed over many years, 'the Courts would be doing wrong if after a canon of construction has been laid down with regard to such documents it should not be followed.' He preferred instead Lindley LJ's guidance in the same case: 'the cardinal principle is to put the true construction on the Act with which you have to deal … these Inclosure Acts have been examined and discussed so often that there may be said to be now some subordinate rules to assist one in arriving at a true construction.'[115] Henderson LJ next considered the submission that

[114] The words 'common form' used by Lindley LJ to describe Inclosure Acts are not to be understood in the same way as the words 'standard form' now applied to modern contracts, particularly those used widely across the building and civil engineering industry and issued by the JCT or ICE.

[115] *Wynne-Finch* at [54] to [55]; *Consett Waterworks Company v Ritson* [1922] 2 Ch 135 at 188-189, 194. These two formulations, by Lord Esher MR

Wainman was the leading case on the meaning of 'minerals' in Inclosure Acts. But he did not think it directly in point on the construction of the reservation in the 1816 Arwystli Inclosure Act for three reasons. First, it was 'a decision on the particular wording of a different Inclosure Act which is not in this respect based on any standard form'. Second, the stone in question in *Wainman* was 'a valuable building stone which could never be said of the mudstone in the present case.' And third, the *Wainman* Act contained a final clause, not present in the Arwystli Act, that the first layer or stratum of earth 'be kept separate' without mixing with the lower strata'. *Micklethwait,* Henderson LJ thought, added nothing of significance to *Wainman*, but like *Wainman* concerned 'stone with real commercial value, which could be quarried and sold at a profit' and therefore was wholly different in character from 'commercially valueless mudstone'.[116]

Against that background, Henderson LJ turned to the judge's reasoning about the powers of working provisions in the Reservation of Mines clause in the Arwystli Act. After deciding that mudstone, because of its ubiquity in the area of the allotments, did not satisfy any test of exceptionality, and that it would not have been viewed as a material that was worthwhile quarrying and selling commercially in 1816 (or indeed 1919), and that there was no direct evidence of the vernacular meaning of the words used at the time of the relevant grants but that nobody would have had mudstone in mind as a mineral, the judge then said:[117]

> The powers of working are important in this context. There are three particular points that can clearly be derived from the

---

and by Lindley LJ respectively, appear to indicate agreement on the fundamental point that at the time of the *Consett* decision in 1889 there were in existence rules of construction about common form Inclosure Acts that could be used to determine the true construction of any particular Inclosure Act before the court.

116 *Wynne-Finch* at [55] to [64]

117 See [107] to [111] of Falk J's first instance judgment; and [65] to [67] of the CA judgment.

> wording of the 1816 Act. First, the right is expressed as a right to 'make merchantable and take and carry away'. Mudstone would neither have been regarded as merchantable, nor worth carrying away. Secondly, there is an express right to 'erect and use' roads and other infrastructure. In my view it would clearly have been in the contemplation of the parties that rock in the vicinity could be used for these purposes, as it always had been and as was practically necessary. It had a value in that sense, but that was not what the reservation was getting at. The value in question was an aspect of the powers of working. Thirdly, the express power to 'delve, search for, get up …' must be taken to extend to the destruction and removal of mudstone that would inevitably surround the veins or seams of minerals that were being sought.'

Henderson LJ agreed,[118] adding that 'the critical point … is that the reservation of mines and minerals in the 1816 Act is not apt to include mudstone, both because of its ubiquity and because of its lack of commercial value. This conclusion is then supported by all the relevant issues of practicality which the judge discussed.'[119]

Manorial minerals reservations after *Wynne-Finch*

The *Wynne-Finch* litigation produced the first Court of Appeal decision in over a hundred years on the meaning of 'minerals' in a manorial minerals reservation clause. The extent to which that decision contains principles of general application that will be applied in future disputes remains to be seen. But in an approach which may well be repeated, the courts in *Wynne-Finch* chose to construe manorial minerals reservations by following *Waring v Foden* and relying on cases dealing with statutory undertakers in preference to earlier cases dealing with manorial grants contained in private agreements or pursuant to Inclosure Acts and

---

118 At [72].

119 For those issues of practicality see [122] of the first instance judgment.

awards. The existence of these two classes of case, and the relevance of any distinction between them, is easily overlooked because of the divergence of judicial opinion about the definition of minerals which was apparently resolved by the House of Lords in its decisions between 1909 and 1911, followed by the abolition of copyhold tenure in 1926 and the Court of Appeal's decision in *Waring v Foden* in 1931. The successive editions of practitioner textbooks on manorial law had come to an end, and subsequent understanding of the subject declined. Yet the 'issues of practicality' in *Wynne-Finch*, identified by Falk J in her judgment and which weighed heavily with her and with the Court of Appeal, were well-known to lawyers and taken full account of in the legal system in the hundred years before 1926. Legislators recognised and made allowance for them in the Copyhold Acts 1841-1894 and in the Law of Property Act 1922;[120] and judges confronted them in ruling that owners of surface freeholds should not have their grants swallowed up by the destructive workings of minerals owners claiming rights under reservations made decades before.[121]

The solution offered by the minerals definition rule in *Hext v Gill* was, in essence, to take the position between lord and copyholder, where the lord owned the surface and everything beneath it useful to him but where possession was in the copyholder, and to extend it to the position between the lord, or his successor in title, and the freeholder of what had formerly been a copyhold tenement. The solution required the rejection of the proposition, hitherto accepted in the courts, that

---

120 See chapter 2 above on Copyhold Acts and the LPA 1922.

121 See *Hext v Gill* itself rule 2; and *Butterknowle Colliery Company Ltd v Bishop Auckland Industrial Co-operative Company Ltd* [1906] AC 305. 'It was there stated, that, instruments inter partes or Inclosure Acts, if the introduction of a provision to the effect, that the surface must not be let down, would not be inconsistent with the actual provisions, the instrument or Act must be read as if such a provision had been introduced .... It is an amazing departure from the usual mode of construing documents.' See Robert MacSwinney, *The law of mines quarries and minerals* (3rd edn, 1907), p. viii. (MacSwinney appeared in the HL as junior counsel for the unsuccessful appellant.)

ownership of minerals conferred on the owner an implied right to do whatever was necessary to exploit them.[122] Without unambiguous agreement to that effect, Mellish and James LJJ held, the surface owner could not be deprived of support by the minerals owner. Thus the position created by the rule and its corollary was one of stand-off: neither the lord as mineral owner nor the freeholder as occupier of the land could extract the minerals without the consent of the other, and dispute about what constituted a mineral was discouraged if not avoided. The court could, if necessary, limit the meaning; but the stand-off encouraged negotiation and agreement, while protecting the legal rights of the parties; or, as James LJ put it in the first paragraph of his judgment, 'giving the mineral owner every reasonable profit out of the mineral treasures, and at the same time saving the landowner's practical enjoyment of his houses, gardens, fields, and woods, without which the grant to him would have been illusory.'[123]

None of the judges in *Wynne-Finch* appears to have considered this solution or Slade J's first conclusion from the authorities in *Earl of Lonsdale v A-G* that 'the wide sense given to the phrase 'mines and minerals' by Lord Romilly MR in *Midland Railway v Checkley* and by Mellish LJ in *Hext v Gill* is a sense which the phrase is capable of bearing and can still be attributed to it in a proper context'.[124] The question of what might constitute a proper context was not specifically considered in *Wynne-Finch*, although it is clear that none of the judges thought that the necessary constituents were present.

---

[122] Which was the House of Lords' conclusion in *Rowbotham v Wilson* (1860) 8 HLC 347, dealing with an Inclosure Act of 1770.

[123] *Hext v Gill* at 719. In *New Sharlston Collieries Company Ltd v Earl of Westmorland* (3 April 1900) the HL unanimously held that 'The mere fact of giving a right to sink pits and to work or get coal does not of itself establish a right to get rid of the common law right of the surface owner to have his surface undisturbed.' See report of the decision noted at *Bishop Auckland Industrial Co-operative Society Limited v Butterknowle Colliery Company Limited* [1904] 2 Ch 419 at 443, 445 (per Lord Halsbury LC).

[124] [1982] 1 WLR 887 at 924C-D.

The minerals definition rule: proper context

Contextual points when interpreting a minerals reservation include the nature of the transaction, the relative position of the parties, and what the words used in the agreement meant according to the law as it stood at the time.[125] The focus on legal understanding at the time of the agreement differs from the vernacular test, which is confined to the contemporaneous language and understanding of the mining and commercial world and landowners. An early example appeared in 1855 in *Darvill v Roper*, where solicitors gave evidence as to the meaning of 'minerals' in the local interpretation of the term in Denbigh and Flint in 1799, but this was not apparently directed to any accepted legal understanding.[126] However, with the development of case law, the restructuring of the higher and appellate courts, improvements in law reporting, and the wider circulation of legal literature amongst practitioners that gathered pace through the 19th century, it is possible to investigate whether there was any accepted legal understanding of the meaning of the word 'minerals' in mineral reservations by looking at the leading textbooks used by practitioners in the period. The same books also provide insight into which decisions of the courts were considered relevant and how they were understood, and how that understanding developed over time.

Foremost among these for manorial law were the two works most often relied on by counsel in argument in court and quoted by senior judges in their decisions: *Scriven on Copyholds*, and *Elton & Mackay on*

125 Note Lindley LJ's words in *Duke of Sutherland v Heathcote* [1892] 1 Ch 475 at 483, 'In order to understand the effect of this deed, it is necessary to carry our minds back to 1783, and construe it as such instruments were construed at that date. We must not forget that in those days a grant did not pass lands, mines, or minerals, although it might confer a right to work them.'

126 Perhaps because there was none. See (1855) 3 Drew 294 at 296, 299 and 301; 61 ER 915 at 917-918.

Copyholds and Customary Tenures.[127] Published by the leading legal publishers of the day,[128] it seems reasonable to assume they would have found their way into counsels' chambers and solicitors' offices. The issues that both works dealt with included copyholds, enfranchisements, manors, and manorial minerals reservations in the context of private agreements and Inclosure Acts. The seventh and final edition of *Scriven*, published in 1896, contained this illuminating passage about 'minerals', with reference to the authorities on which the text was based:

> In an action by the Lord of the Manor against his copyholder, for removing from the land loose stones which had been thrown upon it by the shivering of certain neighbouring rocks, there being no evidence to show that the stones, the subject of the action, had come down upon the land during the tenancy of the copyholder, the court held that they must be taken, *prima facie*, to form part of the soil of the copyhold, and that the copyholder could not remove them for his own profit: *Dearden v Evans* (1839) 5 M&W 11; 2 H&H 7; 3 Jur 703.[129]

---

127 The full title of *Scriven on Copyholds* was *A treatise on the Law of Copyholds and the other Tenures (Customary and Freehold) of Lands within Manors: with the Law of Manors and of Manorial Customs generally, and the rules of evidence applicable thereto; including the Law of Commons or Waste Lands; and also the jurisdiction of the various manorial courts* (7th edition, 1896), edited by Archibald Brown. Charles Elton QC and Herbert Mackay, *A Treatise on the Law of Copyholds and Customary Tenures of Land* (2nd edition, 1893). A supplement appeared in 1898 with annotations on the Copyhold Act 1894.

128 The 1896 edition of *Scriven* was published by Butterworth & Co and Shaw & Sons. The 1893 edition of *Elton & Mackay* was published by Wildy & Sons.

129 The principle which *Scriven* said that *Dearden v Evans* illustrated was that even loose stones lying on the surface of the land may be minerals which belong to the lord. Although the facts appeared to represent an extreme case, the decision was handed down in 1839 by the Court of Exchequer (Lord Abinger CB, Parke B and Alderson B) and in 1896 was still regarded as reliable authority.

> For it is to be remembered that the word minerals is a word of very wide significance, and extends to include, e.g., stone: *Bell v Wilson* LR 1 Ch App 307, and also brickearth, and clay: *Hext v Gill* LR 7 Ch App 699; *Earl of Jersey v Neath Union* 22 QBD 555; *Ruabon Company v Great Western Railway Company* [1893] 1 Ch 427; but see *Lord Provost of Glasgow v Farie*, 13 App Ca 657.

The editor of *Scriven*,[130] who had an advisory and litigation practice in copyhold, clearly did not think that *Farie* had displaced *Hext v Gill* and *Jersey v Neath*. The authors of *Elton & Mackay*,[131] whose second edition appeared in 1892 with a supplement in 1898 to take account of the Copyhold Act 1894, did not refer to *Farie* at all. Against the marginal note 'What are minerals', their text ran:

> 'Every substance which can be got from underneath the substance of the copyhold tenement for the purpose of profit is included in the term 'minerals': *Hext v Gill* LR 7 Ch 699; and it has been held that coprolites beneath the surface and china clay are minerals, and that the property in them is in the lord: *A-G v Tomline* 5 Ch Div 750; SC 15 Ch Div 150 (CA).'[132]

Both works, in their successive editions, would have been available to counsel and solicitors to guide them in their understanding of what the term 'minerals' meant in agreements or statutes dealing with mineral reservations. It is hard to believe that their treatment of the term, founded squarely on Mellish LJ's definition in *Hext v Gill*, did not contribute significantly to the state of affairs described in Bowen LJ's

130 Archibald Brown of 8 New Square, Lincoln's Inn. He had also edited the previous edition of 1881, and Bainbridge's *Mines and Minerals* (4th edition, 1878).

131 Charles Elton QC and Herbert Mackay, of Lincoln's Inn and the Middle Temple respectively. The first edition, by Elton alone (of 2 New Square, Lincoln's Inn), appeared in 1874. Its preface acknowledged that 'the first place must be given to the great work of Serjeant Scriven'.

132 Ibid, p.234,

observation of 1889 in *Jersey v Neath*: that 'the rule [in *Hext v Gill*] has been in existence for seventeen years and has produced a very great effect upon business transactions during that time, and I do not suppose that it will be lightly disturbed or without grave consideration.'[133]

A third leading text for practitioners, again often cited in the courts, was Robert Forster MacSwinney's *The law of Mines, Quarries and Minerals*. MacSwinney's focus was obviously different from that of the authors of Scriven and of Elton and Mackay, and he had a deeper knowledge of manorial minerals cases.[134] Unlike them, he attached great importance to *Farie*, where Lords Halsbury and Macnaghten had objected to Mellish LJ's definition of minerals in *Hext v Gill*. Drawing particular attention to this at the outset of the preface to the second edition of his book in 1897, he said the result was 'unsettling' and suggested that because the substantive language of the English and Scottish railway acts of 1845 was identical, the decision in *Farie* was binding in England.[135] Continuing this theme in the preface to the book's third edition in 1907, he had now to deal with Lord Halsbury's very pointed intervention presiding in the Court of Appeal in *Todd, Birleston* in 1903.[136] This, MacSwinney thought, meant that the earlier Court of Appeal decision in *Jersey v Neath*, which had explained Mellish LJ's definition, could not be relied on 'and meanwhile no further definition has been attempted. It is hardly too much to say, that … it is now impossible to tell for certain what the word 'mineral', in its legal sense

133 (1889) 22 QBD 555 at 561.

134 This clear from the authorities he cites in the successive editions of his book, published by Sweet and Maxwell. MacSwinney was not just an author but a very successful chancery practitioner who appeared in a many reported cases in the Chancery Division, Court of Appeal and House of Lords between the late 1870s and the mid-1920s. Although he never took silk, he was a leading junior and often led by the foremost silks of his day. His book was clearly well regarded and frequently cited with approval by judges in the superior courts.

135 Robert Forster MacSwinney, *The Law of Mines, Quarries and Minerals* (2nd edn, 1897), pp. v-vi.

136 See above, p.206.

... really means.'[137] After the House of Lords railway cases decided in 1909 to 1911, which were consistent in rejecting 'the proposition that there was any ordinary or primary meaning to be attached to the word "minerals"',[138] MacSwinney produced his fourth edition in 1912. Having reviewed the House of Lords cases, he concluded: 'a reservation to a lord in an Inclosure Act is construed more liberally than a similar reservation in an ordinary grant. There is nothing in *North British Railway Co. v Budhill & Co.* which throws doubt on [*Rosse v Wainman* and *Micklethwait v Winter*]'[139] This conclusion was based on careful reading of the *Budhill* decision, which showed that, for all their concerns about Mellish LJ's minerals definition having wide application, the law lords did not question its application to manorial mineral reservations in favour of the lord of a manor.[140]

The future of historic manorial minerals reservations

Reported cases about mineral reservations generally, and manorial mineral reservations in particular, are notoriously fact specific. It is therefore unlikely that *Wynne-Finch* will be the last word on the subject. The importance of Slade J's review of the authorities in *Lonsdale* as the starting-point for construing mineral reservations is well established and was again confirmed in *Wynne-Finch*. In relation to manorial mineral reservations, Slade J acknowledged that the wide sense given to the

137 Robert Forster MacSwinney, *The Law of Mines, Quarries and Minerals* (3rd edn, 1907), pp. v-vi.

138 The words quoted are those of Slade J in *Earl of Lonsdale v Attorney-General* [1982] 1 WLR 887 at 916C. The four cases were *North British Railway v Budhill* [1910] AC 116; *GWR v Carpalla China Clay* [1910] AC 83; *Caledonian Railway Co v Glenboig* [1911] AC 290; and *Symington v Caledonian Railway* [1911] AC 290.

139 Robert Forster MacSwinney, *The Law of Mines, Quarries and Minerals* (4th edn, 1912), pp. 26-28.

140 In support of his conclusion, MacSwinney referred (at p.28, n.5) to the speeches in *Budhill* of Lord Gorell at pp.133-134 and Lord Shaw at p.138. Lord Atkinson (at 138) agreed with Lord Gorell.

phrase 'mines and minerals' in *Hext v Gill* 'is a sense which the phrase is capable of bearing and can still be attributed to it in a proper context.' The particular context which Slade J identified what was that of a mining lease; but that, he said, was only an example. This means that there were other circumstances where the wide sense could apply.

It is notable that in *Farie* Lord Halsbury did not question the correctness of the decision in *Rosse v Wainman*,[141] and that Lord Watson did not question the correctness of the decision in *Hext v Gill*. Indeed Lord Watson said in words often quoted, and which were echoed later by Slade J: '"Mines" and "minerals" are not definite terms: they are susceptible of limitation or expansion, according to the intention with which they are used.'[142] But what has received no attention after MacSwinney's spotlight on them in his 1912 edition[143] are the passages from the speeches of Lord Gorell and Lord Shaw in *Budhill*, which acknowledge that *Rosse v Wainman* and *Micklethwait v Winter* were decided 'on the special terms of Inclosure Acts'.[144] Again, there was no questioning of the correctness of these decisions, and the effect of these passages appears to be that the House of Lords was recognising that in a lord of the manor case the wide sense of mines and minerals given to the term in *Rosse v Wainman* could apply. Since an Inclosure Act is no

---

141 He said to counsel during argument: '[*Rosse v Wainman*] was a lord of the manor case, and the fact that the lord had a right to everything under the surface was the foundation of Lord Wensleydale's judgment.' See (1883) 13 HL 657 at 667.

142 (1883) 13 HL 657 at 675.

143 At p.28.

144 Referring to the Scottish case of *Jamieson v North British Railway Co* (6 SLR 188), Lord Gorell said (at 133): 'the decision in that case appears to have been influenced by two English cases, *Earl of Rosse v Wainman* and *Micklethwait v Winter*, but these cases seem to have been decided on the special terms of Inclosure Acts.' Lord Shaw said (at 138): 'I agree with Lord Gorell that [the decision in *Jamieson v North British Railway Co*] may have preceded to some extent upon a misapprehension of the two English cases interpreting Inclosure Acts to which my noble and learned friend refers.'

more than statutory conveyance, there seems to be no reason in principle why the wide sense of the term could not be applied to a manorial minerals reservation whether under an act or in a private conveyance made by a lord.[145]

It remains to be seen what will happen when a court is next asked to examine the question of proper context where the wide sense of mines and minerals used in *Hext v Gill* might be appropriate. A likely trigger for such examination would be the nature and extent of a mineral interest preserved in former copyhold land by an enfranchisement agreement pursuant to one of the Copyhold Acts or by the compulsory statutory enfranchisement under the LPA 1922.[146] The intention of the Copyhold Acts in relation to the lord's mines and minerals was that the lord should own what he did before the agreement; and, when the time came for abolition of copyhold, the legislature's final word on the subject – in the automatic reservation at paragraph 5 of Schedule 12 in the LPA 1922 – reflected exactly this: an enfranchisement 'shall not affect' any of the lord's or the tenant's rights to mines and minerals as they stood before the Act commenced. The facts that would give rise to such a question are by no means unlikely because compensation awards made to lords pursuant to the LPA 1922 frequently left the automatic reservation in Schedule 12 unchanged.[147] Thus property in the minerals remained vested in the lord while possession was now in the former tenant: the same factual matrix as in *Hext v Gill.* The implications of any finding that there are contexts where the wide sense of mines and

[145] MacSwinney's reference at p.28 to an 'ordinary grant' could be to either a non-statutory grant or, perhaps more likely, to a non-manorial grant.

[146] Or, depending on its wording, an enfranchisement agreement made pursuant to common law (as in *Hext v Gill* itself) rather than one of the Copyhold Acts.

[147] For the location of evidence concerning post 1925 compensation awards, see chapter 7 below at p.252.

minerals is appropriate would illustrate the point powerfully made [148] that 'there are many more cases of superior and inferior freehold estates in England and Wales than is generally recognised' and that, by not dealing with 'some of the commonest instances of subinfeudation, including those created as a result of the enfranchisement of copyhold land', the LRA 2002 does not deal adequately with manorial rights.

[148] By Edward Nugee QC in his important article, "The Feudal System and the Land Registration Acts" (2008) 124 *Law Quarterly Review* 586-607. See Preface above for further discussion of the article.

CHAPTER SEVEN

EVIDENCE

The courts' approach to evidence in manorial cases

Evidence in manorial cases is unusual because it will usually include not only manorial documents but a substantial amount of historical material in addition to such ancient or contemporaneous documents, witness and expert evidence as the parties think relevant. As far as admissibility is concerned, there is no difficulty about referring to historical works, but they need to be reputable and reliable. In 1891 in *Read v the Bishop of Lincoln*,[1] the Privy Council held that where it is important to ascertain ancient facts of a public nature, the law does permit historical works to be referred to. Lord Halsbury LC said:[2]

> The House of Lords upon the impeachment of Warren Hastings, having first determined that it would only proceed upon judicial evidence, such as would be receivable in a court of law, received in evidence (being advised, it will be remembered, by the judges) Cantemir's History of the Turkish Empire. In the case of St. Katharine's Hospital, Lord Hale admitted Speed's Chronicles to be evidence of a particular point of history in Edward III's time, and Pemberton CJ received the same evidence to prove the death of Isabel, queen dowager of Edward II, and said he knew not what better proof could be given.

When it looks at historical works, the exercise the court is carrying out was explained by Lewison J in *Crown Estates Commissioners v Roberts*:[3]

---

1 [1892] AC 644.

2 At 653.

3 [2008] EWHC 1302 (Ch) at [2].

> .... Although this judgment contains a good deal of historical material, I am not resolving controversies between historians and scholars but deciding the issues in this case on the basis of the evidence before the court.

The court does not have the historian's luxury of making nuanced or qualified judgements. It has to make findings of fact of a binary nature[4] in accordance with the civil standard of proof according to the balance of probabilities on the evidence before it.

As far as ancient documents are concerned, they will be admissible together with evidence from historical or other works to explain the meaning of the words in them.[5]

Research

It is of particular importance in any case involving points on manorial law to assemble as much as possible of the relevant evidence at the earliest possible stage. While the same might be said about cases on any subject, in manorial cases much if not all of the evidence will consist of primary and secondary historical sources which it will be necessary to identify, understand and analyse. This will take time. It will also require input from those who are not legal advisers and who may be unable or unwilling to work to timescales required by lawyers or courts. Not only are those historical sources likely to be scattered amongst different locations, but the speed of their production and analysis will depend on the investigative skills of historical researchers and the ability of libraries, archives and their staff to respond to informed enquiry. Where relevant records are in Latin, they must be translated. Where they comprise lengthy manuscript indentures, the most important parts (at least) must be put into readable transcript form and, where possible, agreed with

---

4 In other words, that something either happened or did not happen.

5 *Halsbury's Laws of England*, vol 32 (2023), para 402; and see *Shore v Wilson* (1842) 8 ER 450 at 509; 9 Cl & Fin 355 at 501–502, HL, per Maule J.

other parties. Where they comprise maps and plans of the same locality at different periods, it will probably be necessary to instruct a surveyor to compare them in order to trace the evolution of physical features such as field or manorial boundaries. Readiness to incur research costs early on will pay dividends later. With facts and issues more clearly established before further expense is incurred, particularly in litigation, the problem or dispute should be quicker or easier to resolve.

Since every manor dates from before 1290, the potential extent of relevant documentation dates from the medieval period to the present. Rarely, however, are manorial records preserved in such quantities that major historical investigation is required. Crown manors, ecclesiastical manors and manors owned by corporations are likely to have more and better records than private manors because institutional ownership over centuries had both the ability and the need to spend money on the classification and preservation of records. Even so, the availability of documentation is invariably patchy because lords who were owners of manorial documents were unlikely to keep them if there was no compelling need to do so; and all documents, before they were kept and curated in secure archives, were subject to the ravages of fire, damp, and other kinds of accidental damage. The result is that where manorial records continue to exist, they are incomplete and may do little more than provide snapshots of particular periods. If a manor continued to exist until 1925 as a working manor or even, in the absence of a court baron, as a reputed manor, there is a good chance that central government records are available which will cast at least some light on the manor's operation in the 19th and early 20th centuries. Central government records were generated as a result of the Copyhold Acts 1841 to 1894 and the Law of Property Act 1922, and they document the enfranchisement of copyhold land and the extinguishment of manorial incidents.

Manorial records

Manorial records come in two kinds. The first are known as manorial documents, a statutory term deriving from the Law of Property Act 1922. The second are documents establishing devolution and title. Both types of record are important, and any case involving issues about manors or manorial law is likely to require examination of both. The difference between them is that manorial documents, although private records, are subject to statutory regulation and public supervision. The reason for this is that copyhold tenure, until its abolition on 1 January 1926, acted as a parallel registration system with records of copyhold transactions held on the books or court rolls of individual manors by their lords and, from 1841, by government. The abolition of copyhold tenure meant the end of the last significant role of manorial courts. Enfranchisement of copyhold land allowed the newly enfranchised freeholders to sell on, but purchasers from them and subsequently still needed assurance that the vendor had good title and to know what third party rights, if any, the land was subject to. The need for that assurance and knowledge was recognised by Parliament in the Law of Property Act 1922, which provided for the retention of manorial court rolls which recorded the devolution of title of copyhold land before 1926 as well as rights affecting the land.

Manorial court rolls and documents

Section 144 of the LPA 1922 granted a power to inspect court rolls.

> Any person interested in enfranchised land may on payment of the fee prescribed by the Lord Chancellor, inspect at any reasonable hour any Court Rolls of the manor of which the land was held; and Court Rolls shall (whether before or after the manorial incidents have been extinguished), for the purposes of section fourteen of the Evidence Act, 1851, be deemed to be documents of such a public nature as to be admissible in evidence on their mere production from the proper custody.

However, before copyhold was abolished, this part of the LPA 1922 was overtaken by the decision in *Beaumont v Jeffery* given on 8 July 1924.[6] Lawrence J, sitting in the Chancery Division, held that it was lawful to sell manorial documents including court rolls, and this threatened to make the operation of s 144 impossible. Parliament therefore amended the LPA 1922,[7] by adding to it a new s 144A which set in place a comprehensive scheme presided over by the Master of the Rolls for the preservation and future use of manorial documents. Such documents now received statutory definition,[8] and that definition expressly excluded documents evidencing title. The key features of the scheme were fourfold: first, that lords or anyone else entitled to possession of manorial documents must not destroy or wilfully damage them; second, that if in the archives of public institutions or learned societies, they were to be kept and preserved safely; third, that the Master of the Rolls could direct they were to be publicly available, and lords were entitled to production of manorial records free of cost; and fourth, that the Master of the Rolls could from time to time make rules by way of secondary legislation for implementing the scheme. Section 144A was in these terms:

> (1) All manorial documents shall be under the charge and superintendence of the Master of the Rolls.
>
> (2) Save as hereinafter provided, manorial documents shall remain in the possession or under the control of the lord for the time being of the manor to which the same relate and he shall not be entitled to destroy or damage wilfully such documents.
>
> (3) The Master of the Rolls may from time to time make such enquiries as he shall think fit for the purpose of ascertaining that any manorial documents are in the proper custody, and

---

6 [1925] 1 Ch 1.

7 By the Law of Property (Amendment) Act 1924.

8 See s 144A(6).

are being properly preserved, and the lord of the manor to which such documents relate, or the governing body of any public library, or museum or historical or antiquarian society, to which the same may have been transferred, as hereinafter provided, shall furnish the Master of the Rolls with all such information with respect thereto as he may require.

(4) The Master of the Rolls may direct that any manorial documents which, in his opinion, are not being properly preserved, or which he is requested by the lord of a manor to deal with under this subsection, shall be transferred to the Public Record Office, or to any public library, or museum or historical or antiquarian society, which may be willing to receive the same, and if the same shall be transferred to any public library, or museum or historical or antiquarian society, the governing body thereof shall thereafter have the custody thereof and shall be responsible for the proper preservation and indexing thereof.

(5) Nothing contained in this section shall prejudice or affect the right of any person to the production and delivery of copies of any manorial documents or to have the same kept in a proper state of preservation; in particular the lord of the manor shall remain entitled to require the same to be produced to him, or in accordance with his directions, free of any cost.

(6) In this section "manorial documents" mean court rolls, surveys, maps, terriers, documents and books of every description relating to the boundaries, franchises, wastes, customs or courts of a manor, but do not include the deeds and other instruments required for evidencing the title to a manor; "manor" includes a lordship and a reputed lordship; and "lord of the manor" includes any person entitled to manorial documents.

(7) The Master of the Rolls may make rules for giving effect to this section, and may revoke or vary any such rules.

Section 144A remains in force.

The Manorial Documents Register and the Manorial Documents Rules

In 1926 the Master of the Rolls ordered that the Manorial Documents Register (MDR) be kept as the official index to manorial records in England and Wales. The MDR provides brief descriptions of manorial documents[9] and their locations in public and private hands. It is maintained by the National Archives on behalf of the Master of the Rolls, and is now available online as a record of the whereabouts of manorial documents. Its importance as a research tool is much enhanced because the online version provides more detailed information than the paper index it replaced. As the National Archives website points out, 'For the purposes of the MDR the definitive proof of the existence of a manor is the survival of records produced by the manorial court.'[10]

Rules pursuant to the 1922 LPA were made by successive Masters of the Rolls in 1926 (now wholly repealed), 1959, 1963 and 1967. The relevant rules today are primarily to be found in The Manorial Documents Rules 1959,[11] which are striking for the obligations imposed on a lord of the manor[12] to preserve records and to provide information to the Historical Manuscripts Commission. The most important provisions of the 1959 Rules are these:

---

9 As defined by s 144A(6).

10 https://www.nationalarchives.gov.uk/help-with-your-research/research-guides/manorial-documents-lordships-how-to-use-manorial-document-register/

11 SI 1959/1399.

12 Or person otherwise entitled to manorial documents: see s 144A(6).

- The lord of the manor shall cause all manorial documents in his possession or under his control to be kept and used under conditions suitable for their safe and proper preservation and shall upon request furnish to the Master of the Rolls particulars of all such documents: paragraph 2.

- The lord of the manor shall inform the secretary of the Historical Manuscripts Commission whether any manorial documents in his possession or under his control are damaged or decayed, or whether he is unable to preserve them under proper conditions, in order that proposals may be made for the repair or better preservation of the documents; and the lord of the manor shall, so far as he is able, give effect to any such proposals: paragraph 3.

- Every change in the ownership of manorial documents shall be notified by the new owner to the secretary of the Historical Manuscripts Commission: paragraph 4.

- Whenever requested by the lord of the manor or the Master of the Rolls, the controlling authority of a record repository [i.e. the National Archives, public library, museum or historical or antiquarian society] shall produce manorial documents to him or in accordance with his directions: paragraph 9.

- The controlling authority of a record repository shall on payment of the prescribed fees permit manorial documents to be inspected at all reasonable times by any person interested in land enfranchised by or under the Copyhold Act, 1894 (57 & 58 Vict c. 46), or the Law of Property Act, 1922, and shall permit the taking of copies of such documents; and shall also, with the consent of the lord of the manor, permit the inspection of manorial documents, and the taking of copies thereof, for the purpose of historical research: paragraph 10.

- No manorial documents may be removed outside England and Wales without the consent of the Master of the Rolls: paragraph 11.

The 1963 and 1967 Rules made only minor amendments to the above. The 1963 Rules added local authorities to the category of record repository,[13] while the 1967 Rules required an owner of manorial documents who intends to remove them from a record repository to notify his intention to the secretary of the Historical Manuscripts Commission at least three months before the documents are removed.[14]

Evidence of contemporaneous law

The law as it applies at any particular date is derived from statutes in force, decided authorities and published textbooks. Where the meaning and effect of a historic document or transaction is in question, it will be necessary to understand the law as it stood at the time. Modern works of legal history may help but where they do not provide sufficient detail it is necessary to go to the textbooks that contemporaneous practitioners and judges consulted. Analysis of manorial law was a task which often faced 19th century judges, and they imparted clear guidance about the textbooks they preferred and the weight to be attached to them. In *Ecclesiastical Commissioners for England v Parr*, Lord Esher MR said:

> Text-books are, of course, not binding authorities on the Court, but there are some of them which have been by general consent treated as what I may call guiding authorities and, among these, *Gilbert on Tenures*, *Watkins on Copyholds*, and *Scriven on Copyhold*, have been so treated by all lawyers from the time they

13 See The Manorial Documents (Amendment) Rules 1963, SI 1963/976.

14 See The Manorial Documents (Amendment) Rules 1967, SI 1967/963. The lord must also state the place to which it is intended to remove them. It would seem to follow from this that, pursuant to s 144A(4), the Master of the Rolls, acting through the secretary of the HMC, could nevertheless require the manorial documents to remain in a record repository.

> were written, and it would be insensible for a Court dealing with copyhold law not to be guided by those authorities.[15]

In 1897 Lord Esher added to that list, for its passages on copyhold law, *Williams' Notes to Saunders*.[16] As far as manorial minerals were concerned, judges of the late 19th and early 20th centuries placed considerable reliance on successive editions of Robert Forster MacSwinney's *The Law of Mines, Quarries and Minerals*.[17]

Expert evidence

Permission to adduce expert evidence can be applied for and such evidence will be admissible in accordance with the rules relating to expert evidence under CPR 35. The contribution that an expert can make to the resolution of a manorial case will obviously depend on the nature of the case and what is at issue. Where old maps or plans need to be interpreted or transposed onto modern maps or plans, then a surveyor familiar with digital Geographic Information Systems techniques may have a role. Historians may also have a role so long as the issues they are concerned with lie within their particular field of expertise, and they restrict themselves to history. Instructions to expert historians in manorial disputes should be carefully drafted because the issues to be addressed in the case will probably involve both fact and law, and a court is likely to be sceptical about the evidence of a historian which trespasses into matters of law unless the historian has qualifications and experience in legal history.

15 [1894] 2 QB 420 at 428 (Kay and A.L. Smith LJJ agreeing at 432, 435).

16 *Western v Bailey* [1897] QB 86 at 89-90.

17 See pp. 229, 283.

Documents of title

Documents of manorial title are fewer than manorial documents and, particularly for the period from the late 19th century onwards, can be more elusive. They are not subject to statutory regulation, and there is not and never has been any requirement for enrolment or registration of lordship title. The MDR is not a register of title documents, and the MDR need only be informed of a transfer of manorial title if manorial documents are included in the conveyance. HM Land Registry keeps an index containing verbal descriptions of registered manors.[18] However, since registration of lordship title was only voluntary before 13 October 2003, the index is necessarily incomplete. According to the relevant HMLR Practice Guide, the registered manors that appear in HMLR's index are for lordship titles and give no indication of the extent of rights or land, if any, attached to the title. The entries do not have title plans, and there is no definitive record of the extent of the original manor.[19] The position is not helped by the fact that after 12 October 2003 registration of lordship titles was no longer possible.

Documents of title are more often found in family archives. These will typically include wills, settlements and sometimes conveyances, and they may or may not be deposited with a local record office. For legal practitioners, research into primary sources is likely to be a slower and more expensive task than consultation of secondary sources which may be available online.

18 Land Registration Rules 2003, rule 10(1)(b)(iv).

19 HMLR Practice Guide 13: Official searches of the index of relating franchises and manors (last updated 24 May 2021), section 5. To obtain information held in the index, it is necessary to use the prescribed form SIF to apply for an official search.

Inclosure award maps

It was not until around 1790 that a general practice developed of recording inclosure awards on maps. The location of those maps for the period before the General Inclosure Act 1845 is likely to be the county record office of the county in which the inclosure took place. The 1845 Act introduced central government to the inclosure process, so that awards and maps from that date became the responsibility of the Copyhold, Tithe and Inclosure Commissioners and, if they cannot be found at the county record office, should be available from the National Archives.[20]

Tithe Maps

The Tithe Commutation Act 1836 produced not only apportionments but surveys and maps with numbered plots identifying owners and occupiers. Using cartographic information alongside *The Victoria County History* and the volumes of *Kelly's Directory*, it should be possible to build up a picture of land use within manors for the period around 1840 which can serve as a guide for tracing devolution of title to particular plots of land. Tithe documentation may be found at local record offices and also at the National Archives.[21]

20 Roger Kain, John Chapman and Richard Oliver, *The Enclosure Maps of England and Wales 1595-1918* (Cambridge, 2004), pp.45-46. For Inclosure Awards and Maps from 1847 onwards see the National Archives catalogue entry MAF 1.

21 See National Archives document classes IR 29 and IR 30; and Roger Kain and Richard Oliver, *The Tithe Maps of England and Wales* (Cambridge 1995; and first paperback edn, 2011).

Printed sources: The Victoria County History and Kelly's Directory

Two sources of value, available online as well as in hardback, are *The Victoria History of the Counties of England* (the VCH) and *Kelly's Directory*, which covers England and Wales. Work on the VCH began in the late 19th century, initially under the supervision of a committee chaired by the Lord Chancellor, Lord Halsbury, to provide authoritative histories by independent scholars of every county of England. The topographical volumes usually contain detailed manorial histories which describe the descent of a manorial lordship from the manor's recorded origin to its extinction or, if the manor still survived, down to the date of publication. Those VCH volumes published in the early 20th century frequently identify contemporaneous holders of lordship titles.[22] Heavily footnoted, the VCH is soundly based on historic documents and, in the absence of better or later evidence, judges will normally regard it as authoritative. After the energy and extensive output of its early years, the VCH proceeded in fits and starts during the 20th century, and the project is not yet complete.

Kelly's Directory is a significant printed primary source dating from the Victorian period.[23] At first, volumes were issued every few years and then later as yearbooks providing the names of tradesmen, office-holders and leading figures in cities, towns and villages across every county of England, together with Monmouthshire and Wales. From the outset, the directories usually included not only the names but often the addresses of local landowners, landed gentry and lords of the manor with some indication of the extent of land owned. The directories were compiled by local editors using questionnaires sent to local government,

---

22 Apparently the result of written or oral investigation by the author of the VCH volume concerned.

23 Earlier versions of the directories, under different names but whose work was later absorbed within Kelly, date from at least the 1830s.

landowners and tradesmen, and the level of detail was often remarkable.[24]

Evidence of enfranchisement of copyhold land before 1925

The Enfranchisement of Copyholds Act 1841[25] and subsequent copyhold acts allowed permissive and ultimately compulsory enfranchisement at the request of lords or tenants. Where enfranchisement was by way of voluntary arrangement it was recorded by deed; where compulsory enfranchisement took place it was recorded in an award that fixed the level of compensation payable to the lord. Copyhold Commissioners were responsible for administration of the enfranchisement process and for keeping the records, but in 1889 their role passed to the Board (later Ministry) of Agriculture. For the period 1841 to 1925 the deeds and awards are held at the National Archives.[26] As the National Archives Reader's Guide points out,[27] they are arranged 'by county, manor, date and tenant's name and include evidences of

---

24 The first three villages in the 1913 edition of Kelly's Directory for Lincolnshire (at p.29) were Aby, Addlethorpe and Aisthorpe. Amongst a great deal of other information, (1) the entry for Aby says: 'The Earl of Ancaster, who is lord of the manor, Willoughby Wood esq. and Mr C.D. Stovin are the principal landowners'; (2) the entry for Addlethorpe says: 'Charles Francis Massingberd-Mundy esq. of South Ormsby Hall, is lord of the manor, and Charles Lucas esq. of Boston, and Miss Mackinder are the principal landowners'; (3) the entry for Aisthorpe says: 'Aisthorpe House is the residence of Joseph Clifton Ward esq. and Joseph William Ward esq. of Withcall House, near Louth, is lord of the manor and owns the whole of the land in the parish, with the exception of 40 acres.... The area [of the parish] is 828 acres...'

25 4 & 5 Vict. c. 35.

26 See class MAF 9.

27 Mary Ellis, *Using Manorial Records* (Revised Edition, 1997), p.66.

title supplied by manorial lords from 1900. Evidences of title supplied from 1840 to 1900 [are] … listed alphabetically by manor.'[28]

The Valuation Office Survey of 1910-1915

The Finance (1909-10) Act 1910 provided for the levy and collection of a duty on land based on any increased value of the land resulting from public money spent on communal infrastructure.[29] The levy was called an increment value duty, and its calculation and collection required a government survey nationwide. Section 26 of the Act was headed 'Valuation of land for purposes of Act' and in relevant part provided as follows:

> (1) The Commissioners [of Inland Revenue] shall … cause a valuation to be made of all land in the United Kingdom, showing separately the total value and the site value respectively of the land, and in the case of agricultural land the value of the land for agricultural purposes where that value is different from the site value. Each piece of land which is under separate occupation, and, if the owner so requires, any part of any land which is under separate occupation, shall be separately valued, and the value shall be estimated as on the thirtieth day of April nineteen hundred and nine.
>
> (2) Any owner of land and any person receiving rent in respect of any land shall, on being required by notice from the Commissioners, furnish to the Commissioners a return containing such particulars as the Commissioners may require as to the rent received by him, and as to the ownership, tenure, area, character, and use of the land, and the consideration given on any previous sale or lease of the land, and any other

---

28 See class MAF 20.

29 The Act (10 Edw. VII, c.8) also applied to Scotland.

> matters which may properly be required for the purpose of the valuation of the land...

The intention of the survey was to create a datum line set at 13 April 1909 against which any increase in value on subsequent sale of the property could be calculated. So that the duty could be calculated and collected, the survey provided information not only about the value but about the ownership, extent, tenure and use of identified property or plots of land throughout England and Wales. Details of this nature and on this scale are of particular importance for identifying the existence of manors (whether legal or reputed), the lands owned by their lords, the extent of copyhold land, and the location of manorial boundaries at a time shortly before the property legislation of 1922-25 abolished copyhold land and ended one of the last remaining pillars of the manorial system. The increment value duty was applied until repealed by the Finance Act 1920.[30]

The records generated by the survey came from the 118 valuation districts that were established, each in the charge of a district valuer and comprising a number of income tax parishes. It was through these valuation districts and income tax parishes that the work of the survey was organised and carried out. The records were of three main types. First were plans. These consisted of Ordnance Survey maps with manuscript annotations made by Valuation Office surveyors. Second were the accompanying field books which held information gathered about properties during the survey. The plans work as an index to the field books, and the plot numbers made on the plans were referred to in the field books. Two sets of plans were created. First were those used as working documents in the course of the original valuation: if extant, these are held at local archives. Second are the plans created after the valuation was completed: if extant, these are held at The National Archives.[31]

---

30 10 and 11 Geo. V, c.18.

31 Completed records do not survive for all areas, mostly because of damage suffered by Valuation Offices during the Second World War. Areas

The field books were bound and printed. They contained information from landowners and surveyors and usually included the names of owner and occupier; the owner's interest (freehold, copyhold); details of tenancy (term and rent); the area covered by the property; and figures entered for the purpose of valuation (i.e. market value). They sometimes include other details such as the date of erection of buildings; liability for rates, insurance and repairs;[32] date(s) of previous sale(s); and a sketch-plan of the property.

The third type of record was a survey form. Some were completed by landowners; some were completed by government departments who provided information about the land they occupied. Landowners' survey forms may be among estate records, solicitors' records, or at local archives. Government department survey forms will be at the National Archives.

---

affected included Basildon, Chelmsford, Liverpool, Birkenhead and most of the Wirral, Coventry, Portsmouth, Southampton and Winchester. Where plans did not survive, the relevant local record office may still have working plans.

32 Liability for repairs of works on copyhold land enfranchised in 1926 was retained under the Law of Property Act 1922: see Sch 12, para 6. If an issue arose as to the identity of who is liable for such repairs today, the field book could identify whether a lord was liable at a time shortly before enfranchisement. If so, that could be strong evidence that the current lord had ongoing liability. The liability could be substantial because para 6 defined it as being 'for the construction maintenance cleansing or repair of any dykes, ditches, canals, sea or river walls, piles, bridges, levels, ways and other works required for the protection or general benefit of any land within a manor or for abating nuisances therein'.

Manors and manorial title holders in 1925

The work done by the Copyhold Commissioners, their successors at the Board of Agriculture, and by the Inland Revenue Valuation Office together provide a documentary basis for lists of known manors and their owners in 1925. The National Archives holds these lists.[33]

Manorial records produced after 1925 and held by central government

Although the LPA 1922 abolished copyhold tenure as from 1 January 1926, it preserved for a limited period a number of defined manorial incidents: quit rents, chief rents and other similar rents or payments; fines, reliefs, heriots and dues (including fees payable to stewards); some forfeitures, and rights to timber.[34] Those remaining incidents were to be and were extinguished on 1 January 1936.[35] However, in the intervening ten-year period lords and their newly enfranchised tenants could agree amounts of compensation to be paid to the lord for the extinguishment of those incidents. Thereafter, until 31 December 1940, the lord or the tenant could apply to the Minister of Agriculture and Fisheries for determination of the amount of compensation under the Copyhold Act 1894. If no application for compensation had been made by 31 December 1940, then none was to be payable.[36] Delays caused to the statutory process by the Second World War gave rise to a subsequent Order in Council to deal with outstanding cases: this allowed further applications to be made in the twelve-month period from 1 November 1949 to 31 October 1950.

---

33 See classes HMC 5/6 (from the Ministry of Agriculture) and HMC 5/7 and HMC 5/8 (from the Inland Revenue). The same HMC 5 class contains subsequent correspondence with manorial owners.

34 See s 128(1) and (2).

35 See s 140.

36 S 140(c).

The consequence of these provisions was that the National Archives holds central government records of correspondence, awards and agreements relating to the extinguishment of manorial incidents covering the years after 1925 and into the 1950s. It is therefore possible from these records to identify holders of manorial title, the identity of tenants as pre-1926 copyholders or post-1925 freeholders, the location of pre-1926 copyhold land and the manorial incidents affecting that land.[37]

Welsh manors

For historical and linguistic reasons the development of manors in Wales gave rise to customs, procedures and terminology that were often different from those found in England. A unique printed source relating to Welsh manors is to be found in the report of *The Royal Commission on Land in Wales and Monmouthshire*, signed and delivered on 26 August 1896 as Parliamentary Paper (1896) C – 8221. The Commission was appointed by the government on 27 March 1893 to look at and report on land ownership across Wales and Monmouthshire and the relations between landowners, including the Crown and the Church, and their tenants. It spent three years taking oral and documentary evidence from them, and the minutes of that evidence were contained in five Parliamentary Papers published between 1894 and 1896. An Appendix to the report was also published in 1896. The evidence contained within the report is detailed and of high value.

Many manors in Wales were ecclesiastical manors, and following the disestablishment of the Church of Wales by the Welsh Church Act 1914 the property in those manors was transferred to the Commissioners of Church Temporalities in Wales, who transferred it

---

37 See National Archives classes MAF 13 (Certificates and Awards of compensation); MAF 27 (Certificates of determination of extinguishment 1936-1939 and 1949-1950); MAF 76 (Manorial registers containing references to certificates and awards); MAF 48 and MAF 233 (Registered files dealing with manorial incidents).

to the University of Wales in 1946. Manorial records and other documentation relating to Welsh manors are now available from the National Library of Wales at Aberystwyth.

CHAPTER EIGHT

LEGISLATION AND OTHER MATERIALS

The purpose of this chapter is to serve as a brief guide to legislation affecting manorial law. Most of it remains applicable today or, if not, continues to be relevant in providing context for the interpretation of manorial records which practitioners may encounter. There is also reference to contemporaneous commentary on the legislation.

Quia Emptores Terrarum 1290

Quia Emptores, enacted in 1290 by the Parliament of Edward I, is a conveyancing act still in force today.[1] There is no likelihood of it being repealed for as long as it remains a foundational support of the property law of England and Wales. While the Act is perhaps best known for preventing the creation of new manors, what else it did or did not do is important for understanding the context of any subsequent manorial record that practitioners may have to construe and apply.

The trigger for the Act and the mischief it was intended to address were set out on its face. This was the loss to 'Chief Lords' of the financial value of three incidents attaching to feudal tenure – escheats, marriages and wardships – as a result of steps taken by their (free) tenants when selling land they held of those same Chief Lords. The sale of land by a tenant (T) who held it on mesne tenure did not alienate it from a particular Chief Lord or any lord. T kept the money, but the lord (L) was still entitled to the annual services previously owed him by T if T had substituted another, S, in his place. L could proceed against S for those services if S did not provide them. However, instead of substitution, T could also pursue a different route by making himself

1 1290 18 Edw 1 c.1

lord of S while continuing as tenant of L. This mesne tenure of S was the outcome of the process known as sub-infeudation. It too allowed T to receive not only the original capital sum paid by S, but also services and the incidents due from him, which could either be nominal or else of greater but limited value because of the capital payment made by S. The problem arose for L when T died after his sale of the land. If T died with an infant heir, L was denied the substantial profits that could come from the lord's rights of wardship and marriage. If T died without an heir, all that could escheat to L was the seignory over S which was now of limited or no value.[2] Sub-infeudation was reducing the lord's income. The scope of the Act was limited to the remedy of this particular mischief.

It achieved this by prohibiting sub-infeudation by a tenant, whether in respect of the entirety of his tenement or part of it.[3] It applied only to freeholds and not to leaseholds, which became increasingly common as time passed and lords needed regular money. Leases 'had some of the advantages of sub-infeudation but were not caught by the feudal rules.'[4] It did not apply to the Crown, which could continue to grant manors if it wished to do so although it rarely did. Nor did it prevent the Crown from exercising the right of licensing subjects to create manors to be held of themselves notwithstanding the Act.[5] Thus manors could be and later were divided into several independent manors, which might take a name that had not been known before 1290.

The greatest yet unintended consequence of the Act was to undermine the whole manorial structure by replacing the nexus of feudal relationships based on sub-infeudation and personal service with

---

2 T.F.T. Plucknett, *Legislation of Edward I* (Oxford, 1949); J.H. Baker, op cit, pp.263-64. Escheat is a chief lord's right to take back property without an owner. The leading recent case on escheat is *Scmmla Properties Ltd v Gesso Properties Ltd* [1995] BCC 793.

3 See the first and second provisions of the statute set out below.

4 J.H. Baker, p.264.

5 Plucknett, p. 107.

transactional relationships based on money. As Plucknett put it, 'the lord could no longer grant demesne to be held in fee of the manor (i.e. of himself). If the freehold land of a tenant escheated to the lord of a manor for felony or for failure of heirs, it could, therefore, not be granted out to a new tenant to be held of the manor.'[6] The result over the following centuries was that the number of free tenants on manors declined. When it fell below two, the manor ceased to be a legal manor and a key element of manorial jurisdiction, the court baron, failed. At that point the manor became a reputed manor.[7] This had implications for conveyancing and devolution of title to manorial lands.

The text of those sections of *Quia Emptores* that remain in force is set out below.

1290 CHAPTER 1 18 Edw 1

A STATUTE of our LORD THE KING, concerning the Selling and Buying of Land. The Title Statute d'ni R. de t'ris vendend' emend' is in the Margin of the Roll, and of the *Vetus Codex* at the Tower, *fo.* 20: On the Close Roll 18 *Edw. I. m. 6. d,* this Statute is entered with the following Title in the Margin, 'Statute qd null emat tras de aliis tenend qa de capitalibz dnis, &c.' In the Printed Copies and Translations it is intituled, 'Statutum Westm. iij. The Statute of Westminster the Third, *viz.* of Quia Emptores Terrarum.'

I Freeholders may sell their Lands; so that the Feoffee do hold of the Chief Lord.

FORASMUCH as Purchasers of Lands and Tenements of the Fees of great men and other Lords have many times heretofore entered into their Fees, to the prejudice of the Lords, to whom the Freeholders of such great men have sold their Lands and Tenements to be holden in Fee of their Feoffors, and not of the

6 Ibid.

7 For the legal consequences of this, see chapter 2.

Chief Lords of the Fees, whereby the same Chief Lords have many times lost their Escheats, Marriages, and Wardships of Lands and Tenements belonging to their Fees; which thing seemed very hard and extream unto those Lords and other great men and moreover in this case manifest Disheritance: Our Lord the King, in his Parliament at Westminster after Easter, the eighteenth year of his Reign, that is to wit, in the Quinzime of Saint John Baptist, at the instance of the great Men of the Realm, granted, provided, and ordained, That from henceforth it shall be lawful to every Freeman to sell at his own pleasure his Lands and Tenements, or part of them; so that the Feoffee shall hold the same Lands or Tenements of the Chief Lord of the same Fee, by such Service and Customs as his Feoffor held before.

II Sale of Part Apportionment of Services.

AND if he sell any part of such Lands or Tenements to any, the Feoffee shall immediately hold it of the Chief Lord, and shall be forthwith charged with the Services, for so much as pertaineth, or ought to pertain to the said Chief Lord for the same parcel, according to the Quantity of the Land or Tenement [so] sold: And so in this case the same part of the Service shall remain to the Lord, to be taken by the hands of the Feoffee, for the which he ought] to be attendant and answerable to the same Chief Lord, according to the Quantity of the Land or Tenement sold, for the parcel of the Service so due.

The Tenures Abolition Act 1660[8]

After Henry VIII's creation of the Court of Wards and Liveries in 1540, fiscal feudalism had been exploited by the Crown to maintain its income from the aristocracy and gentry who held Crown land. Feudal tenures had survived but became widely unpopular with the landed classes and shortly after the accession of Charles II in 1660 the Convention

---

8 12 Car 2 c 24.

Parliament passed an act whose purpose is explained by its long title: 'An Act taking away the Court of Wards and Liveries and Tenures in Capite and by Knights Service and Purveyance, and for settling a Revenue upon his Majesty in Lieu thereof.' The abolition of the Court was accompanied by the conversion of the tenures *in capite* and by knight service into tenures held in free and common socage, with the practical effect that the rents normally due under socage were not payable to the Crown. At the same time, the future creation of tenures by the Crown was limited to free and common socage. Section 4, which is still in force, provided:

> And that all tenures hereafter to be created by the Kings Majestie his Heires or Successors upon any gifts or grants of any Mannours Lands Tenements or Hereditaments of any Estate of Inheritance at the common Law shall be in free and common Soccage, and shall be adjudged to be in free and common Soccage onely, and not by Knight service or in Capite, and shall be discharged of all Wardship value and forfeiture of Marriage Livery Primer-Seizin Ouster le main Aide pur faier fitz Chivalier & pur file marrier, Any Law Statute or reservation to the contrary thereof any wise notwithstanding.

Inclosure Acts[9]

Inclosure Acts begin with the Statute of Merton of 1235.[10] In the thirteenth century, legislative intervention was taken to prevent lords from achieving 'approvement' (i.e. enclosure) of waste on their manors to the extent that their tenants and neighbours with customary rights of common over that waste were effectively dispossessed of pasture. Lords were not stopped from enclosing land within their manors, which was freehold land in their ownership, but were limited in the quantity they could enclose so that tenants had sufficient for their needs. Lords could

[9] For further discussion of Inclosure Acts see chapter 2.

[10] 20 Hen 3 c.4.

and did continue to enclose both common arable fields as well as common pasture. From the seventeenth century they did so by informal agreement with those affected, then by formal agreement under contract enrolled in chancery, and then by private act of parliament which had become established as the preferred method of enclosure by around 1750.

The Inclosure Act 1773

Public legislation to address the continuing tide of enclosure began with the Inclosure Act 1773 (which remains in force). Its long title describes its purpose: 'An Act for the better Cultivation, Improvement, and Regulation of the Common Arable Fields, Wastes, and Commons of Pasture in this Kingdom.' The Preamble describes the reasons for the Act, which were located squarely in the desire of landowners for increased agricultural production and profit.

> Whereas there are in several parishes and places in this kingdom several wastes and commons, and several open and common fields, which, by reason of the different interests the several land owners and occupiers, or persons having right of common, have in such wastes, commons and fields, cannot be improved, cultivated or enjoyed to such great advantage for the owners and occupiers thereof, and persons having right of common, as they might be and are capable of if an improved course of husbandry was to be pursued respecting such open and common fields in each parish respectively, and such wastes or commons of pasture were to be properly drained or otherwise amended…

A number of the provisions of the Act are concerned with types of land of which there are now few examples and which, where they do exist, may fall outside manorial lordship: open arable fields and common grass fields. Section 15, however, may be of more relevance to a modern lord or lady of the manor because it enables him or her, with the consent of three-fourths of those with rights of common on the commons or wastes of the manor, to lease a twelfth part of the waste, with the net rent to be applied for improving the unlet part of the waste.

> And it shall and may be lawful to and for the lord or lords, lady or ladies of any manor, with the consent of three-fourths of the persons having right of common upon the wastes and commons within his, her or their manor, at a meeting to be held after fourteen days notice, such notice to be given in manner herein-before directed by the lord or lords, lady or ladies of the manor, or their agent respectively, at any time or times to demise or lease for any term or number of years not exceeding four years any part of such wastes and commons, not exceeding a twelfth part thereof, for the best and most improved yearly rent that can by publick auction be got for the same; and the clear net rents reserved to the lord or lords, lady or ladies, his, her or their heirs, executors, administrators or assigns, by any lease or leases to be granted as aforesaid, shall be by him, her or them, and the major part of his, her or their tenants, applied in the draining, fencing or otherwise improving of the residue of such wastes and commons.

Drainage, fencing and other improvements can be made over a four-year period following agreement between the lord and the commoners, and further agreements afterwards could extend the arrangements indefinitely. Section 18, again on the basis of co-operation between lord and commoners, enables two-thirds of the commoners, with the consent of the lord of the manor, to direct the opening and shutting of stinted commons or pastures.

> And whereas there are in many places common pastures, with stinted or limited rights of common therein, which are open the whole year, and it would be attended with great advantages to the commoners to shut up and unstock the same at particular seasons: It shall and may be lawful to and for two-thirds in number and value of such commoners, at a meeting to be holden after fourteen days' notice given in manner herein-before

> directed,[11] with the consent of the lord or lords, lady or ladies of the manor or manors in which such commons are situated, his, her, or their steward or stewards, agent or agents, to direct, order and fix the time when such common pastures shall be broke or depastured, and when the same shall be shut up and unstocked, such orders to continue in force for one whole year, and no longer.

The Inclosure Consolidation Act 1801

The long title of this act was 'An Act for consolidating in one Act certain provisions usually inserted in Acts of Inclosure; and for facilitating the Mode of proving the several Facts usually required on the passing of such Acts.' It became law on 2 July 1801.[12] Despite its long title it was not a consolidating act, but it standardised the extra-parliamentary processes for obtaining future private Inclosure Acts and for the implementation of those acts through the Award. Powers and duties were given to Inclosure Commissioners, who at this date were not government officials but professional men who had been and continued to be specially appointed for each enclosure. After the passage of the Act and completion of the Award, the commissioners were required to enrol the Award 'in one of His Majesty's Courts of Record at Westminster, or with the Clerk of the Peace for the County in which such Lands [subject to the Award] shall be situated.'[13] Section 20 of the Act provided that 'timber trees and other trees' standing upon allotted land were to be allotted and go along with those lands. Section 40 of the Act was a savings provision for the rights of lords of manors.[14]

> And be it further enacted and declared, that nothing in such Act shall lessen, prejudice, or defeat the Right, Title, or Interest of

---

11 See s.15 (set out above).

12 41 Geo III c. 109

13 Section 35.

14 Section 40.

> any Lord or Lady of any Manor or Lordship, or reputed Manor or Lordship, within the Jurisdiction or Limits whereof the Lands and Grounds thereby directed to be divided and allotted are situate, lying, and being, of, in, or to the Seigniories, Rights, and Royalties incident or belonging to such Manor or Lordship, or reputed Manor or Lordship, or to the Lord or Lady thereof, or to any Person or Persons claiming under him or her, but the same (other than and except the Interest and other Property as is or are meant or intended to be barred by such Act) shall remain, in as full, ample, and beneficial Manner, to all Intents and Purpose, as he or she might or ought to have held or enjoyed such Rights before the passing of such Act, or in case the same had never been made.

Section 44 of the Act disapplied any of its provisions that were in conflict with those set out in a particular private Inclosure Act.

> Provided always, and be it enacted, That all and every the Powers, Authorities, Directions, and Provisions in this Act contained, shall be only so far effective and binding in each particular Case, as they or any of them shall not be otherwise provided and enacted in any such Act hereafter to be passed as aforesaid.

The Act was silent as to mines and minerals.

The Arwystli Inclosure Act 1816

This was the private Inclosure Act before the courts in *Wynne-Finch v Natural Resources Body for Wales*.[15] Inclosure Acts were local but lengthy and this one ran to 38 printed pages, exclusive of the Award. Typical in purpose, form and structure though of course unique in wording, the

---

[15] 56 Geo 3, c.37. The first instance judgment is reported at [2020] EWHC 1924 (Ch) (Falk J); and the CA judgment upholding it at [2022] 3 All ER 162. Chapter 6 considers aspects of both judgments.

extract below sets out the preamble, recitals identifying the lord and the proprietors of freehold and copyhold lands within the manor, and the provisions relating to allotments and to the reservation of mines. As a conveyance made with the authority of Parliament, the Act was able in the allotments clause to alter the tenurial status of lands within the manor from copyhold to freehold and vice versa. The reservation of mines and minerals clause also kept in the lord all powers of working necessary for him and his successors to extract the minerals on payment of compensation to the allottees. Before the General Inclosure Act 1845, all Inclosure Acts were private acts in the form of a statutory conveyance. Different rules of construction apply to a statutory conveyance in a private act from those applicable to a public general statute. An Inclosure Act was a contract and to be construed as such.

> Whereas there are in the Manor of Arustley, in the several parishes of Lanidloes, Trefeglwys, Llanwnog, Llandinam, Penffrowed, and in the Township of Llyfin in the Parish of Carno, certain Tracts of Common and Waste Lands:
>
> And whereas Sir Watkin Williams Wynn, Baronet, is Lord of the Manor of Arustley aforesaid, and as such is or claims to be entitled to the Soil of all these said Commons and Waste Lands, and is also seised of or entitled to several Messuages, Lands, Tenements and Hereditaments within the said Manor; and in respect thereof is entitled to the Rights of Common and other Interests in, to, and upon the said Commons and Waste Lands:
>
> And whereas the Master and Fellows of University College, Oxford, Sir Edward Pryce Lloyd, Baronet, Sir Arthur Davies Owen, Knight, Charles Hanbury Tracy, John Edwards, Joseph Hayes Lyon, John Hunter, George Arthur Herbert, Thomas Marsh, William Howell Marsh, Bowen Woofnam, Charles Cole, and Edward Davies, Esquires, Evan Jones, and John Davies, Clerks, and others, are Proprietors of the residue of such of the Messuages, Lands, Tenements and Hereditaments within the said Manor as are not situate in the parish of Llangerig; and

in respect thereof have severally a Right of Common or other Rights in, over, and upon the said Commons and Waste Lands:

And whereas an Act was passed in the Forty-first year of the reign of His present Majesty, intituled, 'An Act for consolidating in one Act certain Provisions usually inserted in Acts of Inclosure, and for facilitating the mode of proving the several Facts usually required on the passing of such Acts:'

And whereas the said Commons and Waste Lands are of little value in their present state, and it would be a very great benefit to the several Persons interested in the said Commons and Waste Lands, except such parts there of as are situated in the said parish of Llangerrig, if their respective Rights were ascertained, and the same were divided and allotted unto and among them respectively in manner hereinafter mentioned; but as the same cannot be effected or otherwise apportioned without the Aid and Authority of Parliament;

May it therefore please Your Majesty, that it may be enacted… (etc)

[….]

And be it further enacted, That all and singular the Lands and other Premises which shall be allotted under or by virtue of this and the said recited Act, shall immediately after such Allotments are made be held under and subject to the same Tenures, Customs, Heriots, Rents and Services, as the several and respective Messuages, Buildings, Lands Tenements and Hereditaments, in respect whereof such allotted Lands shall be made, are now subject, or such of them as are applicable thereto.

[….]

Provided always, and be it enacted, That nothing herein contained shall prejudice, lessen or defeat any Right, Title or Interest which the Person who shall or may hereafter be entitled

> as Lord or Lords of the said Manor now have or hath, or shall hereafter have in or to any Mines, Ores, Coals, Metals or Minerals whatsoever, in or under the said Waste Lands within the said Manor of Arustley, or any part or parcel thereof; but that it shall be lawful to and for the said Lord or Lords, in and upon the said wastelands within the said manor, and the future Lord or Lords of the said Manor, in and upon the said Waste Lands, at any time or times hereafter, according to their respective Rights therein, to delve, search for, get up, make merchantable, and take and carry away, with all or any manner of Carriages, to their own respective uses, the said Mines, Ores, Coals, Metals and Minerals, or any part thereof; and to make, erect and use any Roads, Ways Sumps, Levels, Warehouses, Smithies, Engines, Machines, and other Conveniences and Erections, and to do any other acts which shall be necessary or proper for all or any of those purposes, and the same Warehouses, Smithies, Engines, Machines and other Conveniences or Erections, or any of them, at any time or times to alter, take down, remove, re-erect and take and carry away at their respective pleasures, the Lord of the said Manor, and the future Lord or Lords thereof respectively, making full Satisfaction from time to time to the respective Owners and Occupiers of the said Allotments of the said Waste Lands, for the Spoil and Damage which shall be done or occasioned thereon by the exercise of all or any of the said powers...

The Copyhold Act 1841[16]

Enfranchisement and commutation in respect of copyhold land had always been possible by agreement at common law, but Parliament's first intervention to facilitate them came in the Copyhold Act 1841.[17] The Act did not affect the common law position, but if the lord and

16 4 & 5 Vict. c.35; repealed by the Copyhold Act 1894.

17 4 & 5 Vict. c.35.

tenant agreed then enfranchisement or commutation could take place pursuant to the Act. The Act allowed for enfranchisement to be made by way of single payment or annual rentcharge. It legislated across a range of issues connected with enfranchisement such as definition, commutation of manorial incidents, compensation and its calculation, and the status of mines and minerals (with ownership assumed to be reserved to the lord in the absence of agreement to the contrary).[18]

The tenant's rights of common over the lord's wastes were to remain once the enfranchisement had been effected and the land had acquired freehold status. Other rights of the lord were not to be affected. Section 82 provided:

> … that no commutation under this Act shall operate to affect any rights of lords of manors to escheats, fairs, markets, appointments, franchises, royalties, rights, liberties, and privileges of chase and free warren, hunting, hawking, fowling, and of chasing and killing game, and beast of chase and free warren, and all ancient piscaries, fisheries, and rights of fishing, or any rights in mines and minerals or quarries within or under the said lands and hereditaments, or any other manorial rights whatever, unless expressly commuted under this Act…

Further protection to the lord's position was given by section 84, which provided that tenants should have power to grant rights of way and other easements over enfranchised land should the lord need them for mining purposes.

The Duchy of Cornwall (No 2) Act 1844[19]

Section 53 is headed and provides that 'All Mines and metallic Minerals under Conventionary Lands, and all Mines, Minerals, Stone, and Substrata and other Profits under and of other Lands in the unsold

18 See ss 14, 52, 82 and 84.

19 7 & 8 Vict c.105. Sections 53 to 55 remain in force.

Manors, to belong to the Duke of Cornwall.' It shows the extent of the Duke's ownership of minerals beneath the assessionable manors still in his ownership. Section 54 makes similar provision as to the mines and metallic minerals beneath those manors which the Duke had sold. Section 55 sets out very extensive powers of working which remain in the Duke in relation to all the assessionable manors, whether sold or unsold.

> All Mines and metallic Minerals in and under all and singular the Tenements now or at any Time within One hundred Years before the said First Day of May One thousand eight hundred and forty-four held as Conventionary Tenements of the said Manors mentioned in the said First Schedule hereunto annexed respectively, and all Mines, Minerals, Stone, Substrata, and all other Profits whatsoever in, upon, under, and of all Waste and other Demesne Lands of the same Manors respectively, and all Mines, Minerals, Stone, and Substrata in, upon, under, and of all other Lands lying within or Parcel of the same Manors respectively, and which said last-mentioned Mines, Minerals, Stones, or Substrata shall by such Award be determined to belong to the Duke of Cornwall, do and shall belong absolutely to the Duke of Cornwall as Possessions by the herein-before recited Charter granted, and thereby annexed to the Duchy of Cornwall as aforesaid, but without Prejudice to the Estates or Rights (if any) of any of the present Lessees of the Duke of Cornwall therein.

The Real Property Act 1845

This was an amending act which received the royal assent on 4 August 1845. Section 2 provided:

> After the first day of October 1845 all corporeal tenements and hereditaments shall, as regards the conveyance of the immediate freehold thereof, be deemed to lie in grant as well as in livery.'

Corporeal tenements and hereditaments included freehold estates in land, which in turn included land *ad inferos* – i.e. the sub-surface going down to the depths of the earth – and, therefore, whatever minerals lay beneath the surface. Until the section came into force, no land transaction could be completed without livery of seisin. This involved the vendor handing physical possession, or an acceptable symbol of it, to the purchaser. A frequent problem for vendors when calculating a sale price for the land was that they did not know of the existence or value of any minerals underneath the surface. Where a vendor was not simply a landowner but held the land as tenant for life under a family settlement, he was potentially liable for waste to those entitled in remainder or reversion if he failed to secure a reasonable price for the property he was selling. A common solution to the problem of potential liability was to reserve the minerals from the sale. This was one of the reasons why government legislation affecting land sales or transactions – whether by way of copyhold enfranchisement or enclosure or compulsory purchase – steered away from intervening on the subject of minerals and left matters to the parties themselves.

The Railway Clauses Consolidation Act 1845[20]

This was one of three acts passed in 1845 to facilitate the compulsory purchase of land for undertakings of a public nature authorised by private acts. The others were the Railway Clauses Consolidation (Scotland) Act[21] and the Land Clauses Consolidation Act.[22] When purchasing land for the construction of a railway, the railway company was not to be entitled to minerals unless expressly purchased. Section 77 provided:

> The company shall not be entitled to any mines of coal, ironstone, slate, or other minerals under any land purchased by

[20] 8 & 9 Vic. c. 20 (royal assent granted 8 May 1845).

[21] 8 & 9 Vic. c.33 (royal assent granted 21 July 1845).

[22] 8 & 9 Vic. c.18 (royal assent granted 8 May 1845).

> them, except only such parts thereof as shall be necessary to be dug or carried away or used in the construction of the works, unless the same shall have been expressly purchased: and all such mines, excepting as aforesaid, shall be deemed to be excepted out of the conveyance of such lands, unless they shall have been expressly named therein and conveyed thereby.

The wording of this section was repeated in identical terms in the Scottish Act of 1845,[23] and substantively also in the Waterworks Act 1847.[24] The statutory formula used for expressing the scope of the minerals excepted from any conveyance made under the Act was different from and apparently somewhat narrower than the formula used in the Inclosure Act 1845, passed three months later. For cases discussing the operation of the section in the English and Scottish acts, see chapter 6.

The Inclosure Act 1845

The Act received Royal Assent on 8 August 1845. Its long title was:

> An Act to facilitate the Inclosure and Improvement of Commons and Lands held in common, the Exchange of Lands, and the Division of intermixed Lands; to provide Remedies for defective or incomplete Executions, and for the Non-execution of the Powers of general and local Inclosure Acts; and to provide for the Revival of such Powers in certain Cases.[25]

This was something of an understatement. The Act was long, detailed, and contained 169 sections. It brought a dramatic increase in the extent of government power, control and consent across the whole spectrum of the enclosure process. Applications for enclosure now had to be

---

23 See s 70 of the Scottish Act.

24 10 & 11 Vic. c.17 (see s 18)

25 8 & 9 Vic. c. 118.

submitted to government commissioners to investigate and report directly to Parliament. Where commissioners recommended enclosure, they prepared a provisional order which, alongside similar orders proposed on other applications, they would submit annually to parliament for approval. The provisional order could include conditions requiring that parts of the land included within the application were allotted for public purposes, either for exercise and recreation or for the labouring poor.[26] Once allotted, these lands were to be held in trust by the local churchwardens or overseers of the poor in the parish where the land was situated.[27] Once enacted, unlike all previous Inclosure Acts which were private acts, such acts were deemed public general acts.[28] The 1845 Act did not affect minerals or minerals' ownership and did not obviously diminish the powers of lords of the manor, but it was a landmark development. Lords had a right to veto a proposed conditional order[29] before it reached Parliament but, if they did not, they probably also had to see part of their land being given away for public purposes. The involvement of government officials at every stage of a prescribed and detailed process meant that earlier opportunities for corruption were reduced.

The lord's right to minerals existing beneath the surface of the land to be enclosed, and for which he was not compensated under the inclosure, remained unaffected. Section 98 provided:

> in every case in which the right to all or any of the mines, minerals, stone, and other substrata under any land inclosed under this Act shall exist as property distinct and separate from the property in the surface, and shall not be compensated upon the inclosure, the right and property in such mines, minerals, stone, or other substrata, and all rights and easements auxiliary to or connected with the exercise or enjoyment of the right and

---

26 Sections 30 and 31.

27 Section 73.

28 Section 32.

29 Section 29.

> property in such mines, minerals, stone, or other substrata, shall be in nowise affected by the inclosure; and in case any mines, minerals, stone, or other substrata under any land inclosed under this Act, or the right of searching for or getting the same, shall have been leased or agreed to be leased to any person as property distinct and separate from the property in the surface, with or without powers over the surface of the land auxiliary to the purposes of such lease, the rights of the lessee or tenant under such lease or agreement shall be in nowise affected by the inclosure.

Although the statutory mineral reservations formula appears to have been broader in the Inclosure Act 1845 then it was in the Railway Clauses Consolidation Act passed earlier the same year, there appears to be no reported instance of any court considering the difference between the two.

Much of the Act was repealed in 1991 and 1998.[30]

The Copyhold Act 1852[31]

The 1852 Act went further than the 1841 Act by providing at section 1 that either the lord or the tenant could compel enfranchisement of copyhold lands in the manner prescribed by the Act.

Section 7 provided that valuers appointed by the Copyhold Commissioners were to determine the value of the manorial rights and incidents of tenure of the land to be enfranchised and the value of the compensation to be received by the lord for the enfranchisement. Section 16 of the Act provided that in making any valuation under the Act

---

30 See https://www.legislation.gov.uk/ukpga/Vict/8-9/118/contents for the timeline of repeals and what remains.

31 15 & 16 Vict. c.51

> … the valuers shall take into account the facilities for improvement, customs of the manor, fines, heriots, reliefs, quit-rents, chief rents, escheats, forfeitures, and all other incidents whatever of copyhold or customary tenure, and all other circumstances affecting or relating to the land which shall be included in such enfranchisement.

Section 48 provided:

> No enfranchisement under this Act shall extend to or affect the estate or rights of any lord or tenant in or to any mines, minerals, limestone, lime, clay, stone, gravel, pits, or quarries within or under the lands enfranchised, or within or under any other lands, or any rights of entry, rights of way and search, whether easements of any lord or tenant in, upon, through, over, or under any lands, or any powers which in respect of property in the soil might but for such enfranchisement have been exercised for the purpose of enabling said lord or tenant, their or his agents, workmen, or assigns, more effectually to search for, win, and work any mines, minerals, pits, or quarries, or to remove and carry away any minerals, limestone, lime, stones, clay, gravel, or other substances had or gotten therefrom, or the rights, franchises, royalties, or privileges of any lord in respect of any fairs, markets, right of chase or warren, piscaries, or other rights of hunting, shooting, fishing, fowling, or otherwise taking game, fish, or fowl, unless with the express consent in writing of such lord or tenant …

Both the 1841 and 1852 Acts[32] were consolidated in the Copyhold Act 1894.[33] The effect of section 48 was, unless the lord and tenant agreed otherwise, to leave the mines and minerals and mining rights exactly where they were, and with the same title as existed immediately before the enfranchisement took effect, whether in the lord or in the tenant.

---

32 Together with the Copyhold Acts of 1858 (21 & 22 Vict. c.94) and 1887 (50 & 51 Vict. c. 73), which amended the 1851 Act.

33 57 & 58 Vict. c. 46.

These words from section 48 of the 1852 Act were incorporated (with very minor and insubstantive amendments) in the 1894 Act[34] and then into the LPA 1922.[35] The 1894 and 1922 Acts each contained the same proviso to them, which followed immediately afterwards and enabled the enfranchised landowner to use the surface of the land in a way giving him practical enjoyment of his property while giving the owner of the minerals every reasonable profit from them.[36]

Rolla Rouse wrote, in his commentary for practitioners on section 16 of the 1852 Act: 'On the part of lords of manors generally, it will be advisable not to include rights in mines, minerals, etc, which, under section 48 are not to be included without consent, unless a fixed sum is agreed on as the compensation in respect of such rights, as it may be imprudent to trust to the allowance of valuers in respect of such rights.'[37]

The Inclosure Act 1857[38]

Through section 12 of this Act, Parliament conferred a significant measure of protection on village greens and lands allotted under the Inclosure Act 1845 for recreation and exercise. Any act which injured such greens and lands or interrupted their use and enjoyment as a place for exercise and recreation was hitherto unlawful but now became a criminal offence. The section remains in force today. It applies not only to lands allotted under the 1845 Act but also to further allotments made on enclosures and approved by Parliament under the Commons Act 1876.

---

34 At s 23(1).

35 At Sch 12, para 5.

36 See below the text on the Copyhold Act 1894 and the LPA 1922.

37 *The Copyhold Enfranchisement Manual* (2nd edn, 1857), p.231.

38 (1857) c.31 (Royal Assent: 10 August 1857).

And whereas it is expedient to provide summary means of preventing nuisances in town greens and village greens, and on land allotted and awarded upon any inclosure under the said Acts as a place for exercise and recreation: If any person wilfully cause any injury or damage to any fence of any such town or village green or land, or wilfully and without lawful authority lead or drive any cattle or animal thereon, or wilfully lay any manure, soil, ashes, or rubbish, or other matter or thing thereon, or do any other act whatsoever to the injury of such town or village green or land, or to the interruption of the use or enjoyment thereof as a place for exercise and recreation, such person shall for every such offence, upon a summary conviction thereof before two justices, upon the information of any churchwarden or overseer of the parish in which such town or village green or land is situate, or of the person in whom the soil of such town or village green or land may be vested, forfeit and pay, in any of the cases aforesaid, and for each and every such offence, over and above the damages occasioned thereby, any sum not exceeding [level 1 on the standard scale][39]; and it shall be lawful for any such churchwarden or overseer or other person as aforesaid to sell and dispose of any such manure, soil, ashes, and rubbish, or other matter or thing as aforesaid; and the proceeds arising from the sale thereof, and every such penalty as aforesaid, shall, as regards any such town, or village green not awarded under the said Acts or any of them to be used as a place for exercise and recreation, be applied in aid of the rates for the repair of the public highways in the parish, and shall, as regards the land so awarded, be applied by the persons or person in whom the soil thereof may be vested in the due maintenance of such land as a place for exercise and recreation; and if any manure, soil, ashes, or rubbish be not of sufficient value to defray the expense of removing the same, the person who laid or deposited such manure, soil, ashes, or rubbish shall repay to such churchwarden or overseer or other person as aforesaid the

39 Words substituted by the Criminal Justice Act 1982 (c.4), ss.38 and 46.

> money necessarily expended in the removal thereof; and every such penalty as aforesaid shall be recovered in manner provided by the Summary Jurisdiction Act 1848; and the amount of damage occasioned by any such offence as aforesaid shall, in case of dispute, be determined by the justices by whom the offender is convicted; and the payment of the amount of such damage, and the repayments of the money necessarily expended in the removal of any manure, soil, ashes, or rubbish, shall be enforced in like manner as any such penalty.

The Commons Act 1876[40]

The measure introduced by Parliament in section 12 of the Inclosure Act 1857 was a sign of things to come. The progress of urbanisation and democratisation in 19th century Britain had produced, by the 1860s, an awareness that open lands – whether fields or commons – were an important recreational resource that should be available to everyone. Whereas earlier Inclosure Acts had focussed on the improvement of land management for increased agricultural production in favour of a landowning class, acts passed from the 1860s included a requirement for 'public benefit' within the arrangements set out in the provisional order. This was a development of the public purposes concept which had first appeared in the General Inclosure Act 1845. It became an important factor in the deliberations of those government officials who examined enclosure applications and made recommendations to parliament. To signal this change of approach, Parliament decided that titles for enclosure statutes should drop the word 'inclosure' and replace it with 'commons'.

The most important of the late 19th century commons acts was the Commons Act 1876, whose long title was an 'Act for facilitating the regulation and improvement of Commons, and for amending the Acts

40 39 & 40 Vict. (1876) c.56 (Royal Assent: 11 August 1876).

relating to the Inclosure of Commons.'[41] The priority which 'regulation' was given over 'improvement' in the title was reflected in the content of the Act. The preamble went further in terms of narrowing the circumstances in which future enclosures were to be approved: 'inclosure on severalty as opposed to regulation of commons should not be herein-after made unless it can be proved to the satisfaction of the said Commissioners and of Parliament that such inclosure will be of benefit to the neighbourhood as well as to private interests, and to those who are legally interested in any such commons'. If the Commissioners approved an inclosure application, section 7 of the Act spelt out provisions for the benefit of a neighbourhood applicable alike to orders for regulation and orders for inclosure.

> In any provisional order in relation to a common, the Inclosure Commissioners shall, in considering the expediency of the application, take into consideration the question whether such application will be for the benefit of the neighbourhood, and shall, with a view to such benefit, insert in any such order such of the following terms and conditions (in this Act referred to as statutory provisions for the benefit of the neighbourhood) as are applicable to the case; that is to say,
>
> (1) That free access is to be secured to any particular points of view; and
>
> (2) That particular trees or objects of historical interest are to be preserved; and
>
> (3) That there is to be reserved, where a recreation ground is not set out, a privilege of playing games or of enjoying other species of recreation at such times and in such manner and on such parts of the common as may be thought suitable, care being taken to cause the least

41 39 and 40 Vict. c.56.

possible injury to the persons interested in the common; and

(4) That carriage roads, bridle paths, and footpaths over such common are to be set out in such directions as may appear most commodious; and

(5) That any other specified thing is to be done which may be thought equitable and expedient, regard being had to the benefit of the neighbourhood.

Once any or all of the section 7 conditions had been inserted into a provisional order and the Commissioners' recommendations had been enacted by Parliament, the conditions could be recorded in the Award. Commons which were regulated under the 1876 Act were given an additional measure of protection by providing in section 36 that they were not to be enclosed without the sanction of Parliament.[42]

> Where an Act of Parliament has been passed confirming a provisional order under this Act for the regulation of a common, then, subject to and without prejudice to the provisions of that order, such common shall not, nor shall any part thereof, be inclosed without the sanction of Parliament subsequently obtained.

In *Lewis v Mid-Glamorgan County Council* the House of Lords considered sections 7 and 36 when addressing the question of whether a local Act of 1968 had extinguished public rights of access under a Provisional Order Confirmation Act of 1919.[43] Lord Browne-Wilkinson said:

[42] See DEFRA publication 'Commons which have been the subject of inclosure under the Commons Act 1876' on https://www.gov.uk/guidance/managing-common-land (accessed 5 October 2022).

[43] [1995] 1 All ER 760.

> So elaborate is the machinery laid down by the 1876 Act that very few provisional orders have been made under it. … Your lordships are therefore concerned with a very special form of public right. It was created by statute [The (Coity Wallia) Provisional Order Confirmation Act 1919] pursuant to a statutory procedure introduced by the 1876 Act for the specific purpose of ensuring that only inclosure schemes 'for the benefit of the neighbourhood' were to be sanctioned. The 1876 Act expressly provided for the inclusion of rights for the public at large…. In my judgment, a public right of access created for the specific purpose of ensuring access to an open space for the benefit of the public of the neighbourhood is not to be extinguished save by clear words or inescapable implication.'[44]

Section 7 remains in force and is of continuing importance even though section 36 was repealed by the Commons Act 2006.[45] Where a statute is repealed, rights or privileges that were granted pursuant to it will not be affected unless a contrary intention appears in a statute extinguishing those rights and privileges.[46] Lords of the manor who own commons enclosed under the 1876 Act and third parties proposing to carry out activities on the common must pay careful regard to this because they will need to take account not only of commoners rights but public rights of access as well. There may be a question whether this is a separate requirement from that raised by section 38(5)(b)(i) of the Commons Act 2006 prohibiting works on commons regulated by an Act made under the 1876 Act without consent of the appropriate national authority.[47] They will also need to take account of potential criminal liability under section 12 of the Inclosure Act 1857.

---

44 At 778 (Lords Griffiths and Ackner agreeing).

45 Sch 6, Part 2.

46 Interpretation Act 1978, sections 16(1)(b) and (c).

47 The appropriate national authority is defined as the Secretary of State in England and as Welsh Ministers in Wales: see s 61(1) Commons Act 2006.

The Copyhold Act 1894

Previous copyhold acts were consolidated in the Copyhold Act 1894.[48]

Sections 22 and 23 of the 1894 Act dealt respectively with rights of common and with exceptions for mines and mineral rights. Section 22 repeated the provisions as to commonable rights in section 81 of the Copyhold Act 1841 and section 45 of the Copyhold Act 1852. It expressly preserved a former copyholder's right of common over the lord's waste. The second part of the sentence, following the comma, preserved the same right which a former copyholder may have had over waste other than that of the particular manor where he had been a tenant.

> 22. An enfranchisement under this Act shall not deprive a tenant of any commonable right to which he is entitled in respect of the land enfranchised, but where any such right exists in respect of any land at the date of the enfranchisement thereof it shall continue attached to the land notwithstanding the land has become freehold.

The wording of section 23(1) as far as the proviso repeated the similar provisions of section 48 of the Copyhold Act 1852; while the proviso re-enacted the provisions of section 14 of the Copyhold Act 1858. Whereas section 48 of the 1852 Act excepted minerals from the statutory enfranchisement process, section 14 of the 1858 Act ensured that owners of enfranchised lands were able to use the soil for purposes connected with the enjoyment of surface.

> 23(1) An enfranchisement under this Act shall not without the express consent in writing of the lord or tenant respectively affect the estate or right of the lord or tenant in or to any mines, minerals, limestone, lime, clay, stone, gravel, pits, or quarries whether in or under the land enfranchised or not, or any right

48 Together with the Copyhold Acts of 1858 (21 & 22 Vict. c.94) and 1887 (50 & 51 Vict. c. 73), which amended the 1851 Act.

> of entry, right of way and search, or other easement of the lord or tenant in, on, through, over, or under any land, or any powers which in respect of property in the soil might but for the enfranchisement have been exercised for the purpose of enabling the lord or tenant, their or his agents, workmen, or assigns, more effectually to search for, win, and work any mines, minerals, pits, or quarries, or to remove and carry away any minerals, limestone, lime, stones, clay, gravel, or other substances had or gotten therefrom, or the rights, franchises, royalties, or privileges of the lord in respect of any fairs, markets, rights of chase or warren, piscaries, or other rights of hunting, shooting, fishing, fowling, or otherwise taking game, fish, or fowl.
>
> Provided that the owner of the land so enfranchised shall, notwithstanding any reservation of mines or minerals in this Act or in the instrument of enfranchisement, but without prejudice to the rights to any mines or minerals, or the right to work or, carry away the same, have full power to disturb or remove the soil so far as is necessary or convenient for the purpose, of making roads or drains or erecting buildings or obtaining water on the land.

As noted above, in the 1858 edition of his *Copyhold Enfranchisement Manual*, Rolla Rouse had advised that the safest course for lords was to leave out minerals from the enfranchisement document because of the difficulties attendant on valuing them. Tenants, it seems, were equally reluctant to address minerals in the enfranchisement agreement because their inclusion within the freehold title to be conveyed would increase its cost when there was no certainty that the minerals valuation element of the cost would be correct. However, most tenants wanted to build or to maintain existing buildings upon the land, and where the lord had reserved mineral rights upon enfranchisement it was necessary to allow the tenant some flexibility in relation to using or disturbing sub-surface minerals so that he could build on and enjoy the surface free of any potential intervention or complaint by the lord. This flexibility was safeguarded by the proviso, which granted the tenant limited rights in relation to the minerals while leaving the ownership of them and the right to work and carry them away in the lord. The commentary in the 1903 edition of Archibald Brown's *Law and Practice on Enfranchisement and Commutations* explained the proviso in this way:[49]

> This right to 'disturb or remove the soil' extends, of course, to disturbing or removing the sand or gravel, or the stone, lime, or clay, – wherever these are (as usually they are) portions of the 'soil'; but the right to 'disturb and remove' does not extend to anything beyond the mere disturbing and removal; e.g., it does not extend to authorise the tenant to 'use' the sand and gravel, or the stone, lime, or clay for the specified purposes, or for any of them; that is to say, he cannot use the dislocated materials for making or ballasting roads, or for constructing buildings or the concrete foundations thereof, or for constructing drains or sewers, or for constructing aqueducts or wells. But he may disturb and remove the soil, 'so far as is *necessary* or convenient', for the purpose of sinking a well on the enfranchised tenement, or leading water by aqueduct constructed thereon, or collecting water in a reservoir dug therein; or for the purpose of constructing a drain or sewer; or for the purpose of getting at a good foundation for any building to be erected; or for the purpose of making a road in a proper or convenient direction, and with proper or convenient levels, – building his well or aqueduct, or reservoir, or his drain or sewer, or his house, with materials acquired, by purchase or otherwise, elsewhere; or else, (but only by special agreement with the lord in that behalf first entered into) with the materials dislocated from the enfranchised tenement.

The issues addressed in some detail by the proviso to section 23(1) of the 1894 Act, together with its previous and subsequent enactments at section 14 of the 1858 Act and in the proviso to paragraph 5 of Schedule 12 of the LPA 1922, formed the substance of what Falk J in *Wynne-Finch* described as 'important issues of practicality' when construing

49 See pp.226-27 of Brown's 3rd edition, published by Butterworths.

minerals reservations in the Arwystli Inclosure Act 1816 and in grants of 1919. For both the judge and the Court of Appeal these issues were of considerable significance in construing the reservations, although there is no reference in either the judgment at first instance or on appeal to the existence and subsequent history of section 14 of the 1858 Copyhold Act.[50]

Robert Forster MacSwinney, extracts from the 1907 and 1912 editions of *The Law of Mines, Quarries and Minerals*

Robert Forster MacSwinney was a distinguished Chancery barrister who between the 1880s and 1920s appeared in many reported cases in the Chancery Division, Court of Appeal and House of Lords. He specialised in property and mining law. Although he never took silk, he was the energetic and well-regarded author of a leading practitioner text, often cited in court, *The Law of Mines, Quarries and Minerals*. Not surprisingly, he regarded the legal definition of minerals as the foundation of his subject, and followed with attention and concern the progress of the courts' treatment of the definition as it evolved after 1872 from the rule in *Hext v Gill*. The extracts below come from the preface of the 1907 (third) edition of his book, where he highlighted what he regarded as the then uncertainty about the definition, and from the text of the 1912 (fourth) edition which shows that he believed that the uncertainty, at least in relation to the definition of minerals as they appeared in manorial minerals reservations, had been resolved. In the years between the two editions, the House of Lords had decided *Budhill* and other cases which MacSwinney believed had left unquestioned the correctness of the decisions in *Rosse v Wainman* and *Micklethwait v Winter* on which Mellish LJ had relied to formulate the rule in *Hext v Gill*.

> The previous position [set out in the preface of the 1897 edition] is worth recalling. In *Hext v Gill* Mellish LJ stated that,

50 See first instance judgment of Falk J at [122] to [125] and the Court of Appeal judgment at [45].

prima facie, a reservation of 'minerals' includes 'every substance which can be got from underneath the surface of the earth for the purpose of profit'. In the same case James LJ suggested, that the question ought to be one of fact to be determined according to the 'the vernacular' of the classes interested at the days of the instrument. In *Glasgow v Farie* (in the House of Lords) Lords Halsbury and Macnaghten objected to the definition of Mellish LJ; on the ground of the uncertainty arising from the element of profit; and Lord Halsbury expressed a preference for the view of James LJ. In *Jersey v Neath Poor Law Union* the Court of Appeal expressed the view, that, when Mellish LJ referred to 'profit', he meant a substance which had an 'independent use and value'; and, with this reading of his definition, they stated, that it stood undisturbed. Bowen LJ went even further; suggesting, that in *Glasgow v Farie* Lord Halsbury might not have been open 'perfectly reported'. Subsequently in the Irish Court of Appeal Lord Ashbourne expressed approval of the definition.

In this state of the previous authorities judges of first instance held themselves, in recent cases, bound by the definition. But, in the still more recent case of *Todd Birleston & Co v North East Railway Company* (in the Court of Appeal) Lord Halsbury again found his opportunity, and used it; and not without emphasis. He stated, that, in his opinion, the House of Lords did not adopt the definition: he repeated his opinion that it was wrong; and he repudiated the innuendo in the suggestion that he had been misreported.

It is difficult to see how the amendment suggested by the Court of Appeal meets the objection of Lords Halsbury and Macnaghten; and meanwhile no further definition has been attempted. It is hardly too much to say, that, in the result, it is now impossible to tell for certain what the word 'mineral, in its legal sense; the very foundation of the subject of this treatise; really means.[51]

In *Rosse v Wainman*, an Inclosure Act of 1815 reserved to the lords 'all mines and minerals' in the large terms usual in such cases; and gave to the lords full powers of working 'the said mines and minerals, and carrying away the lead or, lead, coals, ironstone, and fossils to be gotten there out;' provided that the lords should keep the first stratum of earth 'separate and not mix' it 'with the lower strata'. It was held, that, notwithstanding the use of the word lead ore and the subsequent words, the lord was entitled to stone common in the district, lying near the surface, and worked by quarrying from one of the allotments. *Micklethwaite v Winter* was a similar decision under an Inclosure Act of 1760. It has been already seen that the nature of the transaction has frequently made it necessary to read the word minerals in a restricted sense. In *Rosse v Wainman* and *Micklethwaite v Winter* similar ground was relied on for reading it in an enlarged sense. A reservation to a lord in an Inclosure Act is construed more liberally than a similar reservation in an ordinary grant. There is nothing in *North British Railway Co. v Budhill & Co.* which throws doubt on these cases.[52]

The Law of Property Act 1922

Part V of the LPA 1922 abolished copyhold and customary tenure after 31 December 1925, and Part VI provided for the compensation payable upon the extinguishment of the manorial incidents affecting the

[51] Robert Forster MacSwinney, *The Law of Mines, Quarries and Minerals* (Third edn, 1907), pp.v-vi.

[52] MacSwinney (Fourth edn, 1912), p28. In support of the last sentence, MacSwinney's footnote refers to *Budhill* [1910] AC 116 at 133-134 (Lord Gorell) and 138 (Lord Shaw).

copyhold and customary lands enfranchised by the Act. Section 202 of the LPA 1925 was in these terms:

> For giving effect to this Act, the enfranchisement of copyhold land, and the conversion into long terms of perpetually renewable leaseholds, and of leases for lives and of leases for years terminable with life or lives or on marriage, effected by the Law of Property Act, 1922, as amended by any subsequent enactment, shall be deemed to have been effected immediately before the commencement of this Act.

The LPA 1922 contains the details of how compulsory statutory enfranchisement was carried out. Although most of the Act is now repealed, some passages in it remain important despite repeal. Section 189 identified particular types of copyhold land, not known to contemporaries as copyhold, but which were treated by the legislature as such.[53]

> In this Act, and in particular in Part V, unless the context otherwise requires,—
>
> "Copyhold land" includes—
>
> (a) Land commonly known as customary land or customary freehold land where the freehold is in the lord and not in the customary tenant: and
>
> (b) Land of copyhold tenure held for life or lives or for years, whether or not determinable with life, where the tenant has by custom a perpetual right of renewal, subject or not to the fulfilment of any conditions;
>
> (c) Land held in free tenure for life or lives or for years, whether or not determinable with life, (but subject to

53 Section 189 was repealed by Statute Law (Repeals) Act 1969 (c. 52), Sch. Pt. III.

custom) where the tenant has by custom a perpetual right of renewal, subject or not to the fulfilment of any conditions;

"Copyholder in fee" means the person who is admitted in respect of the inheritance;

"Tenant" means the person in whom the enfranchised land is vested by virtue of this Act, and includes the persons deriving title under him…

The Twelfth Schedule to the Act was concerned with the effect of enfranchisement on rights of common, the lord's rights to mines and minerals and associated matters, and liabilities for certain kinds of works. Paragraphs (4) to (6) of the Schedule show how those rights and liabilities which existed at the date of the LPA 1922's commencement continued after 1925 either as overriding interests or liabilities unaltered from the mid-19th century copyhold legislation.[54] Paragraphs (4) and (5) re-enacted sections 22 and 23(1) of the Copyhold Act 1894,[55] while paragraph (6) provided

> (6) An enfranchisement by virtue of this Act shall not affect any liability subsisting at the commencement of this Act (whether arising by virtue of a court leet regulation or otherwise) for the construction maintenance cleansing or repair of any dykes, ditches, canals, sea or river walls, piles, bridges, levels, ways and other works required for the protection or general benefit of any land within a manor or for abating nuisances therein; and any person interested in enforcing the liability may apply to the court to ascertain or apportion the liability and to charge the same upon or against the land or any interest therein; and the court may make such order as it thinks fit; and the charge when made by the order shall, be deemed to be a land charge within

54 The Twelfth Schedule was repealed by Statute Law (Repeals) Act 1969 (c. 52), Sch. Pt. III

55 See above.

> the meaning of the Land Charges Registration and Searches Act, 1888 [56] (as amended by any subsequent enactment), and may be registered accordingly; and, in addition, the jurisdiction of any court leet, customary or other court, in reference to the matter is hereby transferred to the court.

Anyone seeking to acquire a lordship today should keep the potential liability under paragraph (6) in mind.

The Law of Property Act 1925

Conveyancing of manors

The LPA 1925 contained at s 62(3) a provision dealing with general words implied in conveyances as they applied to manors. Save for its last two lines (which were new), s 62(3) repeated s 6(3) of the Conveyancing Act 1881.[57]

> A conveyance of a manor shall be deemed to include and shall by virtue of this Act operate to convey, with the manor, all pastures, feedings, wastes, warrens, commons, mines, minerals, quarries, furzes, trees, woods, underwoods, coppices, and the ground and soil thereof, fishings, fisheries, fowlings, courts leet, courts baron, and other courts, view of frankpledge and all that to view of frankpledge doth belong, mills, mulctures, customs, tolls, duties, reliefs, heriots, fines, sums of money, amerciaments, waifs, estrays, chief-rents, quitrents, rentscharge, rents seck, rents of assize, fee farm rents, services, royalties jurisdictions, franchises, liberties, privileges, easements, profits, advantages, rights, emoluments, and hereditaments whatsoever, to the manor appertaining or reputed to appertain, or, at the

---

56 51 & 52 Vict. c. 51.

57 1881 c.41

time of conveyance, demised, occupied, or enjoyed with the same, or reputed or known as part, parcel, or member thereof.

For the purposes of this subsection the right to compensation for manorial incidents on the extinguishment thereof shall be deemed to be a right appertaining to the manor.

Definition

The general definitions section at s 205(1)(ix) defined land so as to include a 'manor', and manor itself so as to include 'a lordship, and reputed manor or lordship'.

In this Act unless the context otherwise requires, the following expressions have the meanings hereby assigned to them respectively, that is to say:—

"Land" includes land of any tenure, and mines and minerals, whether or not held apart from the surface, buildings or parts of buildings (whether the division is horizontal, vertical or made in any other way) and other corporeal hereditaments; also a manor, an advowson, and a rent and other incorporeal hereditaments, and an easement, right, privilege, or benefit in, over, or derived from land; [but not an undivided share in land;] and "mines and minerals" include any strata or seam of minerals or substances in or under any land, and powers of working and getting the same [but not an undivided share thereof]; and "manor" includes a lordship, and reputed manor or lordship; and "hereditament" means any real property which on an intestacy occurring before the commencement of this Act might have devolved upon an heir;[58]

[58] The words in square brackets were repealed on 1 January 1997 by the Trusts of Land and Appointment of Trustees Act 1996 c. 47, s. 25(2), Sch.4.

Commons and waste lands

Section 193 dealt with rights of the public over commons and waste lands. Since 1925 it has been subject to amendment, and subsection 2 has been repealed.[59]

Rights of the public over commons and waste lands.

(1) Members of the public shall, subject as hereinafter provided, have rights of access for air and exercise to any land which is a metropolitan common within the meaning of the Metropolitan Commons Acts, 1866 to 1898, or manorial waste, or a common, which is wholly or partly situated within [an area which immediately before 1st April 1974 was][60] a borough or urban district, and to any land which at the commencement of this Act is subject to rights of common and to which this section may from time to time be applied in manner hereinafter provided:

Provided that—

(a) such rights of access shall be subject to any Act, scheme, or provisional order for the regulation of the land, and to any byelaw, regulation or order made thereunder or under any other statutory authority; and

(b) the Minister shall, on the application of any person entitled as lord of the manor or otherwise to the soil of the land, or entitled to any commonable rights affecting the land, impose such limitations on and conditions as to the exercise of the rights of access or as to the extent of the land to be affected as, in the opinion of the Minister, are necessary or desirable for

59 See chapter 4 above for discussion of ss. 193 and 194 as they affected lords.

60 Words in square brackets inserted by Local Government Act 1972 (c. 70), s. 189(4).

preventing any estate, right or interest of a profitable or beneficial nature in, over, or affecting the land from being injuriously affected, [for conserving flora, fauna or geological or physiographical features of the land,][61] or for protecting any object of historical interest and, where any such limitations or conditions are so imposed, the rights of access shall be subject thereto; and

(c) such rights of access shall not include any right to draw or drive upon the land a carriage, cart, caravan, truck, or other vehicle, or to camp or light any fire thereon; and

(d) the rights of access shall cease to apply—

(i) to any land over which the commonable rights are extinguished under any statutory provision;

(ii) to any land over which the commonable rights are otherwise extinguished if the council of the county [county borough][62] [or metropolitan district][63]. . . in which the land is situated by resolution assent to its exclusion from the operation of this section, and the resolution is approved by the Minister.

---

61 Words in square brackets at s. 193(1) in para. (b) of the proviso inserted (1.4.2001 for E. and 1.5.2001 for W.) by 2000 c. 37, s. 46(3), Sch. 4 para. 1 (with s. 43); S.I. 2001/114, art. 2(2)(b)(j); S.I. 2001/1410, art. 2(b)(j).

62 Words in s. 193(1)(d)(ii) inserted (1.4.1996) by 1994 c. 19, s. 66(6), Sch. 16 para. 7(1) (with s. 54(7), Sch. 17 paras. 22, 23(2)); S.I. 1996/396, art. 4, Sch. 2

63 Words inserted by Local Government Act 1985 (c. 51, SIF 81:1), s. 16, Sch. 8 para. 10(5)

[(2) The lord of the manor or other person entitled to the soil of any land subject to rights of common may by deed, revocable or irrevocable, declare that this section shall apply to the land, and upon such deed being deposited with the Minister the land shall, so long as the deed remains operative, be land to which this section applies.][64]

(3) Where limitations or conditions are imposed by the Minister under this section, they shall be published by such person and in such manner as the Minister may direct.

(4) Any person who, without lawful authority, draws or drives upon any land to which this section applies any carriage, cart, caravan, truck, or other vehicle, or camps or lights any fire thereon, or who fails to observe any limitation or condition imposed by the Minister under this section in respect of any such land, shall be liable on summary conviction to a fine not exceeding [£20][65] for each offence.

(5) Nothing in this section shall prejudice or affect the right of any person to get and remove mines or minerals or to let down the surface of the manorial waste or common.

(6) This section does not apply to any common or manorial waste which is for the time being held for Naval, Military or Air Force purposes and in respect of which rights of common have been extinguished or cannot be exercised.

64 Section 193(2) repealed (21.6.2004 for W. and 6.12.2006 to the extent not already in force for W. and otherwise prosp.) and superseded by 2000 c. 37, ss. 46(1)(a), 102, 103, Sch. 16 Pt. I (with s. 43); S.I. 2004/1489, art. 2 (with saving in art. 3); S.I. 2006/3257, art. 2(c)(i) (with saving in art. 4)

65 Figures substituted by Criminal Justice Act 1967 (c. 80), Sch. 3 Pt. I

Section 194 dealt with restrictions on 'inclosure of commons' and has now been repealed in its entirety. Its successor section is section 38 of the Commons Act 2006.

Commons Registration Act 1965 and Commons Act 2006[66]

The Commons Registration Act received Royal Assent on 5 August 1965 but was not wholly in force until 1 January 1970. Its long title was 'an act to provide for the registration of common land and of town or village greens; to amend the law as to prescriptive claims to rights of common; and for purposes connected therewith.' Unfortunately, registration of common land and amendment to claims to rights of common proved too complex a challenge for those responsible for framing the Act, which received significant criticism in the courts for its poor drafting and, notably, judicial amendment to one of its key provisions by the House of Lords in *Hampshire County Council v Milburn* in 1990. The Act was meant to be superseded by the Commons Act 2006. Although the 1965 Act is prospectively repealed by the 2006 Act, the problems of implementing the 2006 Act have led to the situation where the 1965 Act has only been repealed in its entirety in nine areas of England, known as 'pioneer areas';[67] whereas in the rest of England, and across Wales, parts of it remain in force. The current state of the application and implementation of the 1965 and 2006 Acts is one of great complexity.[68]

---

[66] See above for discussion of the Act at chapter 4.

[67] Kent County Council, Devon County Council, Cornwall Council, County of Herefordshire District Council, Hertfordshire County Council, Lancashire County Council, Blackburn with Darwen Borough council, and (from 2014) Cumbria County Council, and North Yorkshire County Council.

[68] For an authoritative account of the application of the 1965 and 2006 Acts see *Gadsden & Cousins on Commons and Greens* (3rd edn, 2020), pp.89-90, 697-700.

The interpretation provision at section 22(1) of the 1965 Act contained this definition of 'common land':

> In this Act, unless the context otherwise requires, "common land" means—
>
> (a) land subject to rights of common (as defined in this Act) whether those rights are exercisable at all times or only during limited periods;
>
> (b) waste land of a manor not subject to rights of common…

The effect of section 22(1)(b) was to make registrable as common any land which was waste land of a manor but had never before been subject to rights of common. But the Act, on its face, did not apply to land that was not waste land of a manor; and in 1990, faced with a landowner lord who had separated his ownership of the lordship title from his ownership of manorial waste, the House of Lords held in *Milburn* that section 22(1)(b) was to be read as if it applied to land that was of manorial origin or was formerly waste land of a manor. This wider construction of section 22(1)(b) occurred long after many applications for registering waste as common had been given provisional registration but were then rejected and were out of time to be appealed. So in the Commons Act 2006 Parliament included provisions designed to allow registration of waste land of a manor where it had not been registered as common land. These provisions appear at paragraph 4 of Schedule 2.

> (1) If a commons registration authority is satisfied that any land not registered as common land or as a town or village green is land to which this paragraph applies, the authority shall, subject to this paragraph, register the land as common land in its register of common land.
>
> (2) This paragraph applies to land which at the time of the application under sub-paragraph (1) is waste land of a manor and where, before the commencement of this paragraph—

(a) the land was provisionally registered as common land under section 4 of the 1965 Act;

(b) an objection was made in relation to the provisional registration; and

(c) the provisional registration was cancelled in the circumstances specified in sub-paragraph (3), (4) or (5).

(3) The circumstances in this sub-paragraph are that—

(a) the provisional registration was referred to a Commons Commissioner under section 5 of the 1965 Act;

(b) the Commissioner determined that, although the land had been waste land of a manor at some earlier time, it was not such land at the time of the determination because it had ceased to be connected with the manor; and

(c) for that reason only the Commissioner refused to confirm the provisional registration.

(4) The circumstances in this sub-paragraph are that—

(a) the provisional registration was referred to a Commons Commissioner under section 5 of the 1965 Act;

(b) the Commissioner determined that the land was not subject to rights of common and for that reason refused to confirm the provisional registration; and

(c) the Commissioner did not consider whether the land was waste land of a manor.

(5) The circumstances in this sub-paragraph are that the person on whose application the provisional registration was made requested or agreed to its cancellation (whether before or after its referral to a Commons Commissioner).

(6) A commons registration authority may only register land under sub-paragraph (1) acting on—

(a) the application of any person made before such date as regulations may specify; or

(b) a proposal made and published by the authority before such date as regulations may specify.

FURTHER READING

The leading work on manorial law is Christopher Jessel's *The Law of the Manor* (3rd edn, 2024). This is a comprehensive and detailed practitioner's text by a solicitor with vast experience of all those aspects of manorial law conducted over many years at Farrer & Co. A concise and extremely valuable analysis of manorial law by Professor Sir John Baker KC appears in the Custom and Usage title in volume 32 of *Halsbury's Laws of England* (2023). On particular aspects of manorial law there are *Gadsden & Cousins on Commons and Greens* (3rd edn, 2020) and Pease, Chitty and Cousins, *Law of Markets and Fairs* (7th edn, 2020). Dated but still useful as an introduction to general principles is *Manorial Law* by A.W. and C. Barsby (1996). For issues surrounding the registration of minerals and manorial minerals, see James Maxwell, "Underground Overground – Minerals and Profits", Blundell Lectures Paper given on 18 June 2018. There are two nineteenth century works which are important where it is necessary to identify the broader framework of property and manorial law in which a judgment of the period is to be understood. They are *Watkins on Copyholds* (4th edn, 1825), edited by Thomas Coventry; and *Scriven's Law of Copyhold and Manors* (7th edn, 1896), edited by Archibald Brown. For a review of the impact of the 1922-1925 legislation see T. Cyprian Williams, "The Fundamental Principles of the Present Law of Ownership of Land" (1931) 75 *Solicitors' Journal* 843; and Edward Nugee QC "The Feudal System and the Land Registration Acts" (2008) 124 *Law Quarterly Review* 586 for a similar review on the impact of the Land Registration Act 2002.

INDEX

MORE BOOKS BY LAW BRIEF PUBLISHING

A selection of our other titles available now:-

'A Practical Guide to Probation Breaches and Other Applications' by Mark Thomas
'A Practical Guide to Remarriage and Divorce' by Cordelia Williams & Claire Howard
'A Practical Guide to Privacy, Transparency, Reporting Restrictions and Closed Proceedings in the Court of Protection' by Laura Mannering
'Beaumont on Barristers – A Guide to Defending Disciplinary Proceedings (Second Edition)' by Marc Beaumont
'A Practical Guide to Payments for Environmental Services' by Ben Sharples
'A Practical Guide to the Law of Pregnancy and Maternity at Work' by Rebecca Thomas
'A Practical Guide to Redundancy – Second Edition' by Philip Hyland & Collette Moore
'A Practical Guide to International Issues for Scottish Family Lawyers' by Susie Mountain, Donna McKay, Ken MacDonald
'A Practical Guide to the Law on Deprivation of Liberty' by Ben Troke
'A Practical Guide to Rights over Airspace and Subsoil – Second Edition' by Daniel Gatty
'A Practical Guide to the Law in Relation to Inquests' by Ramya Nagesh
'A Practical Guide to the Construction and Rectification of Wills and Trust Instruments (Second Edition)' by Edward Hewitt
'A Practical Guide to Data Protection in Social Housing' by Clare Paterson
'A Practical Guide to Spousal Maintenance – Second Edition' by Liz Cowell
'A Practical Guide to International Parental Child Abduction Law (England and Wales)' by Dr Onyója Momoh
'A Practical Guide to Deprivation of British Citizenship' by Sean Ell
'A Practical Guide to Commercial Property Service Charges' by Rachel Garton
'A Practical Guide to Clinical Negligence – Third Edition' by Geoffrey Simpson-Scott (Geoff)

'A Practical Guide to the Rights of Grandparents in Children Proceedings – Second Edition' by Stuart Barlow
'The Electronic Communications Code: A Practical Guide – Second Edition' by Kerry Bretherton KC, James Castle, Mark Loveday
'A Practical Guide to the Independent School Standards – September 2023 Edition' by Sarah McKimm
'A Practical Guide to Estate Administration and Crypto Assets' by Richard Marshall
'A Practical Guide to Parental Alienation in Private and Public Law Children Cases' by Sam King QC & Frankie Shama
'Contested Heritage – Removing Art from Land and Historic Buildings' by Richard Harwood QC, Catherine Dobson, David Sawtell
'The Limits of Separate Legal Personality: When Those Running a Company Can Be Held Personally Liable for Losses Caused to Third Parties Outside of the Company' by Dr Mike Wilkinson
'A Practical Guide to Transgender Law' by Robin Moira White & Nicola Newbegin
'A Practical Guide to 'Stranded Spouses' in Family Law' by Mani Singh Basi
'A Practical Guide to Residential Freehold Conveyancing' by Lorraine Richardson
'A Practical Guide to Pensions on Divorce for Lawyers' by Bryan Scant
'A Practical Guide to Challenging Sham Marriage Allegations in Immigration Law' by Priya Solanki
'A Practical Guide to Digital Communications Evidence in Criminal Law' by Sam Willis
'A Practical Guide to Legal Rights in Scotland' by Sarah-Jane Macdonald
'A Practical Guide to New Build Conveyancing' by Paul Sams & Rebecca East
'A Practical Guide to Inherited Wealth on Divorce' by Hayley Trim
'A Practical Guide to Practice Direction 12J and Domestic Abuse in Private Law Children Proceedings' by Rebecca Cross & Malvika Jaganmohan
'A Practical Guide to Confiscation and Restraint' by Narita Bahra QC, John Carl Townsend, David Winch
'A Practical Guide to the Law of Forests in Scotland' by Philip Buchan
'A Practical Guide to Health and Medical Cases in Immigration Law' by Rebecca Chapman & Miranda Butler
'A Practical Guide to Bad Character Evidence for Criminal Practitioners by Aparna Rao

'A Practical Guide to Extradition Law post-Brexit' by Myles Grandison et al
'A Practical Guide to Hoarding and Mental Health for Housing Lawyers' by Rachel Coyle
'Stephens on Contractual Indemnities' by Richard Stephens
'A Practical Guide to the EU Succession Regulation' by Richard Frimston
'A Practical Guide to Solicitor and Client Costs – Second Edition' by Robin Dunne
'Constructive Dismissal – Practice Pointers and Principles' by Benjimin Burgher
'A Practical Guide to Religion and Belief Discrimination Claims in the Workplace' by Kashif Ali
'A Practical Guide to the Law of Medical Treatment Decisions' by Ben Troke
'Fundamental Dishonesty and QOCS in Personal Injury Proceedings: Law and Practice' by Jake Rowley
'A Practical Guide to the Law in Relation to School Exclusions' by Charlotte Hadfield & Alice de Coverley
'A Practical Guide to Divorce for the Silver Separators' by Karin Walker
'The Right to be Forgotten – The Law and Practical Issues' by Melissa Stock
'A Practical Guide to Planning Law and Rights of Way in National Parks, the Broads and AONBs' by James Maurici QC, James Neill et al
'A Practical Guide to Election Law' by Tom Tabori
'A Practical Guide to the Law in Relation to Surrogacy' by Andrew Powell
'A Practical Guide to Claims Arising from Fatal Accidents – Second Edition' by James Patience
'A Practical Guide to Asbestos Claims' by Jonathan Owen & Gareth McAloon
'A Practical Guide to Stamp Duty Land Tax in England and Northern Ireland' by Suzanne O'Hara
'A Practical Guide to the Law of Farming Partnerships' by Philip Whitcomb
'A Practical Guide to the Law of Unlawful Eviction and Harassment – Second Edition' by Stephanie Lovegrove
'A Practical Guide to Costs in Personal Injury Claims – Second Edition' by Matthew Hoe
'A Practical Guide to the General Data Protection Regulation (GDPR) – Second Edition' by Keith Markham
'A Practical Guide to Working with Litigants in Person and McKenzie Friends in Family Cases' by Stuart Barlow

'Protecting Unregistered Brands: A Practical Guide to the Law of Passing Off' by Lorna Brazell
'A Practical Guide to Secondary Liability and Joint Enterprise Post-Jogee' by Joanne Cecil & James Mehigan
'A Practical Guide to the Pre-Action RTA Claims Protocol for Personal Injury Lawyers' by Antonia Ford
'A Practical Guide to Neighbour Disputes and the Law' by Alexander Walsh
'A Practical Guide to Coercive Control for Legal Practitioners and Victims' by Rachel Horman
'A Practical Guide to the Law of Driverless Cars – Second Edition'
by Alex Glassbrook, Emma Northey & Scarlett Milligan
'A Practical Guide to TOLATA Claims' by Greg Williams
'A Practical Guide to Elderly Law – Second Edition' by Justin Patten
'A Practical Guide to Responding to Housing Disrepair and Unfitness Claims' by Iain Wightwick
'A Practical Guide to the Law of Bullying and Harassment in the Workplace' by Philip Hyland
'How to Be a Freelance Solicitor: A Practical Guide to the SRA-Regulated Freelance Solicitor Model' by Paul Bennett
'A Practical Guide to Prison Injury Claims' by Malcolm Johnson
'A Practical Guide to Advising Clients at the Police Station' by Colin Stephen McKeown-Beaumont
'A Practical Guide to Antisocial Behaviour Injunctions – Second Edition' by Iain Wightwick
'Practical Mediation: A Guide for Mediators, Advocates, Advisers, Lawyers, and Students in Civil, Commercial, Business, Property, Workplace, and Employment Cases' by Jonathan Dingle with John Sephton
'The Mini-Pupillage Workbook' by David Boyle
'A Practical Guide to Crofting Law' by Brian Inkster
'A Practical Guide to the Law of Domain Names and Cybersquatting' by Andrew Clemson
'A Practical Guide to the Law of Gender Pay Gap Reporting' by Harini Iyengar
'NHS Whistleblowing and the Law' by Joseph England
'Employment Law and the Gig Economy' by Nigel Mackay & Annie Powell
'A Practical Guide to Noise Induced Hearing Loss (NIHL) Claims' by Andrew Mckie, Ian Skeate, Gareth McAloon

www.ingramcontent.com/pod-product-compliance
Ingram Content Group UK Ltd.
Pitfield, Milton Keynes, MK11 3LW, UK
UKHW020133290926
15471UKWH00003B/452

9 781913 715434